THE
RENDEZVOUS

A Case Study of an After-Hours Club

Julian B. Roebuck
and
Wolfgang Frese

THE FREE PRESS
A Division of Macmillan Publishing Co., Inc.
NEW YORK
Collier Macmillan Publishers
LONDON

The Free Press
A Division of Macmillan Publishing Co., Inc.
866 Third Avenue, New York, N.Y. 10022

Collier Macmillan Canada, Ltd.

Library of Congress Catalog Card Number: 75–11289

Printed in the United States of America

printing number
1 2 3 4 5 6 7 8 9 10

Library of Congress Cataloging in Publication Data

Roebuck, Julian B
    The Rendezvous : a case study of an after-hours club.

    Bibliography: p.
    Includes index.
    1. Hotels, taverns, etc.--Social aspects--Case
studies. 2. Music-halls (Variety-theaters, cabarets,
etc.)--Case studies. 3. Deviant behavior--Case studies.
4. United States--Moral conditions--Case studies.
I. Frese, Wolfgang, joint author. II. Title.
HV5201.S6R63   301.5'7   75-11289
ISBN 0-02-926660-2

To Our Children
Marybeth, Lance, Julian, and
Mary Elizabeth Roebuck and
Erich and Robert Frese

CONTENTS

PREFACE

THIS BOOK PRESENTS a case study of one after-hours club—the Rendezvous. There an assortment of deviant and nondeviant types congregate to socialize, cavort, negotiate, and entertain one another after the legal closing hours of public drinking establishments. Unlike most studies of deviants in "the open" where the focus is on individual deviants and deviancy in a closed subculture, we center on the intersection and confluence of deviants and straights and their behaviors in an odd-time, playtime setting. Our research encompasses the deviant and nondeviant behaviors of several types of actors comprising a client system within an organizational setting—a setting which, in addition to facilitating illegal behaviors, supports deviant behavior for "straights" and nondeviant behavior for deviants.

In this analysis of a previously unresearched behavior setting, we address ourselves to the following basic sociological questions: What is an after-hours club? What does it look like? How is such a place possible? What goes on in such a setting? Who goes there? When? To do what with whom? Where in the setting? What are the consequences of these goings-on? These queries are answered within a behavior setting–symbolic interactionism frame of reference. The methodological strategy involves the triangulation of multiple data sources: member participation, participant observation, key informants, indepth interviews, and secondary sources (criminal records). The combination of the theoretical frame and methodology as employed in this project is unique. Our purpose was double-barreled —the reconstruction of the Rendezvous setting in terms of the actors' perceptions and definitions and the examination of a deviant organization. As Albert J. Reiss has pointed out with regard to deviant behavior, the action lies not only in a return to actors but also to their organization.

This work offers students of deviant behavior and criminology a look at a number of deviant and criminal life styles in process as well as biographical notes on the actors involved. Sociologists, ethnographers, social psychologists, and anthropologists interested in leisure and recreation, occupations, and formal organizations should find this book germane to their research. Hopefully, students of sociological theory and qualitative methodology will benefit from our novel approach to the study of sociability and play in a deviant setting.

To men and women seeking a change of pace in nightlife entertainment this investigation could prove suggestive. Nightlife industry employees and others who frequent such places as the Rendezvous will probably enjoy reading about their counterparts at work or play. As critics, with this reference at hand, these "night people" could compare the after-hours club's scene as they "know it" with our reconstruction and interpretation of the Rendezvous setting, one of a genre. Our research indicates that after-hours clubs throughout the country have many common elements.

We acknowledge the help and encouragement of the Rendezvous management, without which this study would not have been possible. We are also heavily indebted to several sets of Rendezvous actors, in particular our key informants and the patron and employee interviewees. Charles E. Smith of The Free Press made important contributions to this publication by supporting our initial ideas and research materials and by criticizing and editing the composition at various stages. He was indeed patient and understanding.

The original Free Press reader, who remains unidentified, gave us crucial suggestions for a necessary revision of the original prospectus. Robert Harrington and his colleagues aided immeasurably with editorial assistance in the final stages of the manuscript. Thanks are also extended to our typists Molly Puhr and Linda Doss, who endured several rewrites. Bob Quan, our graduate assistant, deserves mention for his clerical assistance. Finally, we extend our appreciation to Dee W. Harper, a former colleague, for his critical comments during the early phase of this study.

JULIAN B. ROEBUCK
WOLFGANG FRESE

Chapter 1

THE PROBLEM OF THE STUDY

Introduction

THIS IS A CASE STUDY of one after-hours club, the Rendezvous Club (a pseudonym), an illegal, unserious behavior setting, situated in a northeastern American city of over two million people, which caters to a potpourri of patron types. It is illegal in that alcoholic beverages by the drink are sold on the premises during illegal hours in conjunction with the unlicensed provision of other goods and services. The proprietor has no license to sell alcoholic beverages, to prepare and dispense food, or to provide cabaret entertainment at any time. Though not an incorporated, private club and though no formal requisites of club membership are required for entrance, there is a set of ritual behaviors associated with admission. The management provides for a degree of exclusivity by screening patrons by means of the speakeasy routine. Veiled from outsiders, this unmarked bar and nightspot setting is not identifiable by any outside signs, and so far as the law is concerned it is nonexistent. Patrons, most of whom are regulars, are afforded alcoholic beverages by the drink, good food, live music, a dance floor, and comfortable surroundings in which to play and socialize at odd-time hours.

Our observations at the Rendezvous as member participants prior to the study suggested that the club afforded people of varying degrees of respectability a chance to relax and play while most

regular people are asleep. The setting appeared to be an *intersection of the straight and deviant worlds,* i.e., a setting belying a
common view that the straight world and its actors are separated
spatially and temporally from the deviant world and its actors.
For example, we noted intermingling and intimate social encounters among career criminals and straights. Actors on the scene
turned night into day and created their own social world. How
they regulated their lives according to the assumptions of this
special world became our important area of study. In our preliminary approach we viewed the Rendezvous as a behavior setting
that supported nondeviant behavior for those thought to be
deviant, and deviant behavior for those thought to be straight—*a
regular place for irregular people.*

Equipped with these preliminary insights as member participants of the Rendezvous and with the cooperation and encouragement of the owner-manager, we decided to make an in-depth study
of the club. Because a review of the literature disclosed no studies
on after-hours clubs, and because the studies on public bars did
not provide us with a theoretical model, we decided to address
ourselves to the following sociological questions within a behavior
setting framework: What is an after-hours club? How is such a
place possible? What goes on in such a setting? What are the
consequences of these goings-on? Who goes there? When? To do
what with whom? Where in the setting? For comparative and
analogous purposes, the literature on kindred, unserious settings
(e.g., public bars and parties) was reviewed with the hope that
such an examination would disclose some important features in
common with the Rendezvous setting. The nature of the setting
required that certain names, dates, events, and minor descriptive
details pertaining to the club either be changed, modified, camouflaged, or left out altogether in order to protect the management
and its employees and patrons. We feel these minor alterations do
no damage to the main thrust of the study.

To answer the preceding sociological questions, the behavior
setting framework was utilized in conjunction with an interaction
approach.[1] The Rendezvous was viewed as one behavior setting

---

[1] Man in his daily round interacts with others in a variety of conventional
behavior settings, e.g., playgrounds, schools, churches, work sites, doctors'
offices, bars, clubs, lodges. Associated with these space-time configurations
(including bounded areas and physical objects) are accepted patterns of behavior befitting the setting. These standing patterns of behavior associated

(our unit of study) chosen by some actors in their daily rounds. It was reasoned that the behavior setting approach would enable us to ascertain the more permanent structural features of the Rendezvous, i.e., its physical, space-time configuration in relationship to the accepted patterns of behavior benefitting the setting. In short, what the setting looked like and what consistently took place when and where in relation to the physical milieu. The interaction perspective was incorporated to determine the meanings and motivations underlying the actors' behavior patterns and conduct, and how the actors through their behavior communicated these shared meanings to one another. We were interested in reconstructing (drawing a picture of) the Rendezvous scene from the viewpoints, interpretations, and reactions of the actors— and in determining how the actors presented the scene to one another.

The nature of the Rendezvous setting and our theoretical approach led us to use two major data collection techniques: participant observation and open-ended, topical interviews with a number of Rendezvous patrons and employees outside the setting. Participant observation involved direct participation in the social world of the Rendezvous scene as acceptable bona fide patrons. Thus the researchers experienced the life style of the actors, shared their club problems and satisfactions, and confronted their club problematic situations. In short, by sharing club experiences as insiders the observers were able to study the actors in their natural, playtime habitat without contaminating the scene by disrupting the setting as outsiders. Because the participant observa-

---

with the nonbehavioral factors of milieu and time define for the actor what activities take place as a matter of course and the conduct for which he will be held accountable. There is usually a goodness of fit between the physical milieu and the expected patterns of behavior therein. For example, swimming parties afford a swimming pool to swim in along with other physical accouterments for actors who are properly equipped in attire, interest, and the ability to swim. Churches provide benches for worshippers and a stage, scenery, and props (e.g., pulpit, altar, religious objets d'art, tapestries, choirs, and so on) as well as prescribed patterns of action related to the physical milieu components. Actors, depending upon their interests at hand (goals or purposes) and their biographies (who they are in terms of age, affluence, position in life, self-concept, world view, and the like) have access to a wide range of behavior settings in their everyday lives. Some settings are formal and serious (schools), informal and unserious (parties), public (trials), private (secret societies), voluntary (churches), involuntary (jails), exclusive (lodge meetings), inclusive (football games), permanent (the family), and transitory (cocktail party).

tion part of the research was done secretly (i.e., only the management and a few key informants knew about it), we were able to obtain answers to basic questions about the setting and the interaction occurring within it by avoiding the gap that usually exists between the identity of known researchers and that of group members—a gap that blocks access to certain uncommon knowledge held by accepted members of cultural groups.[2]

Among other things, the interviews enabled us to gather biographical data on Rendezvous actors (e.g., age, education, marital status, occupation, residence, and so on), ascertain their views and reflections on the club scene while removed from the setting (e.g., Why do you go there? What do you do there with whom?), ascertain the life style of the actors without the club, observe the actors in another social context (i.e., in their homes). Combining these two methods we hoped would help us to present as accurate a picture of the Rendezvous setting as possible—one that actors on the scene would recognize and better understand and one that outsiders including sociologists could comprehend.

The major parts of the study are devoted to (1) what the Rendezvous looks like, how it is possible, the primary courses of behavior routinely taking place, and the relationship between the behavior and the physical milieu; (2) a typology of club actors including both patrons and employees; and (3) a comparison of the behavior patterns found in the Rendezvous with those found in kindred, voluntary, time-out, unserious settings—particularly sociability and play behavior.

After-Hours Clubs: An Overview

Because there was no research literature available on after-hours clubs, we were faced with the problem of developing our own definition of an after-hours club. Occasionally one does note allusions to such settings in the press in connection with police raids and/or arrests at illegal bar establishments where liquor is being dispensed by the drink during illegal drinking hours. Other illegal

[2] For a discussion on the merits of covert participation see James M. Henslin, "Studying Deviance in Four Settings: Research Experiences with Cabbies, Suicides, Drug Users, and Abortioners," in *Research on Deviance*, ed. Jack D. Douglas (New York: Random House, 1972), pp. 35–71.

activities are frequently reported in conjunction with the illegal sale of alcoholic drinks: Proprietors operate without a restaurant or cabaret license; prostitution goes on; criminals congregate to transact business; strip acts and pornographic shows or exhibitions occur; drugs are used, dispensed, or purchased. Scattered throughout the popular literature on crime and criminals and in the biographies and autobiographies of criminals, brief mention is made of after-hours clubs in a cursory fashion as places of assignation and pleasure.[3] Our foreknowledge of after-hours clubs was based primarily on personal experiences and observations in such settings.

Personal observations in several after-hours clubs throughout the country suggest that such establishments are found in all big cities in all regions of the United States. Verbal reports received from entertainers, public bar owners, after-hours club owners and employees, regular habitués of after-hours clubs, newspaper clippings, and criminal biographies suggest that these "play pens" provide recreational havens for an assortment of people who work during odd-time hours. For example, a number of entertainers, musicians, and bar employees told us that after serving or performing for a group of squares from nine until two, they must have some after-hours place to go for relaxation after work hours. A number of respectable, middle-class people (including policemen) who work outside the bar and nightlife industry tell us that after-hours clubs are "bad places" frequented by deviants, i.e., criminals, gamblers, prostitutes, homosexuals, drug addicts, strippers, and low-class musicians and entertainers. At best in their voiced opinions these clubs appeal to the hell-raising, thrill-seeking marginals of the middle and upper classes who occasionally go slumming. By their standards, after-hours clubs are unconventional, deviant places that exist outside the law and cater to deviants, criminals, and other disreputable persons.[4]

[3] See for example Gus Tyler, *Organized Crime in America* (Ann Arbor: University of Michigan Press, 1962); Fred J. Cook, *The Secret Rulers: Criminal Syndicates and How They Control the U.S. Underworld* (New York: Duell, Sloan, Sloan and Pearce, 1966); Peter Maas, *The Valachi Papers* (New York: G. P. Putnam's, 1968); John Kobler, *Capone: The Life and World of Al Capone* (New York: G. P. Putnam's, 1971); and especially Vincent Teresa with Thomas C. Renner, *My Life in the Mafia* (New York: Doubleday, 1973), Ch. 11, "Entertainers and the Mob," pp. 113–24.

[4] For a definition of deviant places see John Lofland and Lyn H. Lofland, *Deviance and Identity* (Englewood Cliffs, N.J.: Prentice-Hall, 1969), pp. 168–72.

The moral order prevailing in all public bars is questionable by respectable middle-class Americans in terms of who patronizes them (deviants) and what is thought to go on in them (lewd, lascivious, bawdy, drunken, and illegal behavior among strangers).[5] From what we can gather, respectable middle-class Americans hold after-hours clubs in lower esteem than public bars. They regard them as dives for all sorts of illicit and criminal behavior.

Before, during, and after studying the Rendezvous (from 1960 through 1974), the authors visited as patrons over fifty after-hours clubs located in the northeastern, midwestern, far western, southwestern, and southeastern United States. Over this time period many hours were spent in various clubs as observers and patrons. Information on after-hours clubs was also obtained through discussions with several different after-hours club owners, employees, and patrons (representing the various geographical areas designated) on and off the club scene, musicians and entertainers who were working in or who had worked at various locales where after-hours clubs operated, and an assortment of police, city officials, and legitimate night club and bar owners in these geographical regions. Finally, information about after-hours clubs was solicited from a number of students, friends, colleagues, and criminals who were patrons of after-hours clubs.

After attending a number of legal drinking establishments and a number of after-hours clubs, we discovered that the distinction between the two was not always as clean-cut as anticipated. For example, we found that a few public bars remained open and carried on business as usual after legal closing hours, oftentimes with policemen patrolling in the area. In other cases, bartenders and/or the owner would ask all unknown patrons to depart and then lock the doors, turn off the outside lights, and continue business as usual with regular patrons and friends. In a handful of these bars, after the doors were locked, the type of services and activities would also change. Examples encountered include such things as switching from strictly alcohol to alcohol and drugs, sexually risque shows including a number of "stunts" not performed during regular hours, sexual intercourse among patrons in some secluded spots. On the other hand, the clubs designated as after-hours clubs by the owners, employees, patrons and police

---

[5] See Sherri Cavan, *Liquor License: An Ethnography of Bar Behavior* (Chicago: Aldine, 1966), Ch. 2, "The Public Drinking Place: An Overview," pp. 23–48.

operated only during illegal hours, i.e., after legal closing hours. All those we visited restricted patron membership and facilitated this selectivity by the use of screening devices and procedures such as the speakeasy entrance routine, which will be discussed later. These clubs were not identifiable by any outside signs, and none existed within or were connected to other types of business establishments. It is this designated type of after-hours club as represented by the Rendezvous on which this study focuses.

Therefore in this study an after-hours club is defined as an illegal, semisecret drinking establishment where alcoholic beverages are sold and dispensed by the drink during illegal closing hours. Such clubs, according to our definition, are operated by proprietors without municipal or state licenses to sell alcoholic drinks or provide other forms of entertainment or services usually associated with drinking establishments, e.g., food and music. Fixed in time and place as independent physical structures, after-hours clubs are viewed as entities separate from legal drinking places and legal private clubs. Drinking after hours occurs legally and illegally in all kinds of settings. For example, as mentioned above, some legal proprietors occasionally permit bar regulars and friends the privilege of drinking in their establishments after closing hours. Country clubs and private clubs are another case in point. This study is not concerned with these settings.

On the basis of data received from informants and our own observations in after-hours clubs, we arrived at certain tentative descriptive impressions about after-hours clubs in general. They seem to be more frequently found in cities of over 250,000 than in smaller towns and cities. Apparently these clubs require a substantial population base for patrons. After-hours clubs found in smaller cities and resort areas are usually based on gambling or prostitution activities. After-hours clubs operate more frequently in cities with abundant legitimate bars, restaurants, night clubs, and nightlife entertainment spots than in cities deficient in such establishments. This is so in part because after-hours clubs' patrons appear to be heavily drawn from people who work in the legitimate nightlife industry[6]—working at odd-time hours—and therefore needing odd-time play hours and places to play. Furthermore, those cities that strictly enforce the closing hours for legal drinking establishments seem to afford a larger number of clubs than those cities that allow legal bars to remain open after legal

[6] Particularly Sunday through Thursday nights.

hours. The same holds true where police will not tolerate "private" parties in bars after legal closing hours.[7] After-hours clubs seem to be more prevalent in cities that impose early closing hours and Sunday blue laws on legal drinking establishments than in cities without such restrictions. Cities where arrangements can be made to reduce and control club visibility (with police cooperation) are more likely to afford after-hours clubs than cities without these restrictions. It is our further observation that where one finds a heterogeneity of life styles and compartmentalized work, social, and familial activities one is likely to find after-hours clubs (usually in larger cities).

Though after-hours clubs seem to appeal to a variety of patrons with different life styles, all provide for illegal liquor by the drink on the premises. Some illegally provide for additional commodities, e.g., entertainment, food, music—or something else that patrons cannot find in legal establishments in terms of place, time, service, or commodity. It is our impression that the overwhelming number of after-hours clubs provide booze, some type of entertainment, food, and a place for sociability. These unserious settings appear to cater primarily to the odd-time recreational needs of a group of patrons employed at odd hours.

History of the Rendezvous

The Rendezvous was opened in 1959 under the aegis of the present owner-manager, our most important key informant. It has been in continuous operation employing the current program format with the exception of a few brief periods (one to three months) of cessation following mock police raids prearranged by the proprietor and cooperating police. Raids have been staged at intermittent intervals (every two or three years) to pacify some few vociferous, disgruntled community informers who blew the whistle on the club and a few "honest" police who reacted to the wider community's heat about the club's existence. Prior to each ingression, the aforewarned management dismantled and rolled out the expensive appointments (bar and bar furnishings, tables, chairs, rugs, wall adornments) and replaced them with cheaper

---

[7] We suspect that police payoffs by illegal after-hours clubs in some cities lead to stricter enforcement of closing hours for legitimate places.

models and bric-a-brac. Three or four weeks following the simulated intrusions upon an empty house, which resulted only in some crushed junk furniture and a temporary entrance door padlock, the original furnishings were returned and business as usual was resumed without fanfare. As the owner explained to the researchers in private discussions:

When you feel a little heat that you can't cool off or pay off, you close for a while. That way you satisfy a lot of people—and you keep the police from looking too bad. All you have to do is put the word out so some clown won't be here for the bust. Then you roll out the good stuff, and roll in a bunch of junky props. Cool it for awhile, and then move back in. Sure it's a goddamned nuisance, but that's the easiest way.

The club provides what all other after-hours clubs afford: alcoholic drinks on the premises after the legal closing hours of legitimate bars. Legitimate bars in the city of this club's operation close at 2 A.M. The Rendezvous opens at 1 A.M. and closes at 7 A.M., Tuesdays through Sundays. In addition to all kinds of alcoholic beverages served by the drink, the club provides live music, food, cigarettes, cigars, soft drinks, coffee, tea and milk along with the necessary supporting physical accommodations and service personnel. Unlike some other after-hours clubs, no programmed entertainment is provided and certain illegal goods and services are not available, and in fact prohibited: drugs, heavy gambling, in-house prostitution, and the overt sale or direct purchase of stolen property and contraband. The owner has no liquor, restaurant, or cabaret license, nor does he have any kind of legal permission to operate a club during or after closing hours. The Rendezvous is not incorporated as a private club and by legal accounts is nonexistent.

The owner-manager told us that he conceived the club over a period of years (1945–1959) while managing and/or owning several legitimate night clubs. Throughout his career he has been, among other things, a sometime waiter, bartender, bookie, and gambler. Prior to the Rendezvous enterprise, he was already a well-known, well-liked, and respected night club impresario in the entertainment world. Among nightlife devotees, members of the gambling and sporting fraternity, and underworld characters, he was regarded as a well-connected producer who always put on good shows in "fashionable clubs"; a mover who spared no expense

where talent (some nationally known) and stage sets were concerned. Additionally, a player himself (women and gambling), he
had been closely acquainted and associated with many upper
world and underworld high rollers, sports, playboys, party girls,
swingers, and good-time charlies.

In several discussions the owner-manager, in recapitulating the
birth of the Rendezvous, acknowledged the prescient background
that presaged his present role and success as an after-hours club
host and proprietor.

*It's like this, I knew everybody who was somebody in the night-
life and entertainment circuit anyhow—and worked at everything
from a bartender to an emcee. I'm talking now about club owners
and managers and people who operated bars, agents, musicians,
entertainers, and show girls. I knew pretty good too a bunch of
people like bartenders, waiters, waitresses and guys and broads
who work and hang out in the nightlife joints. I had connections
up and down the line. You meet them all in the kind of business
I had been in before hustlers, gamblers, players. Some in and
out of the life. I mean winners and losers, has-beens, and never-
will-be's. I had a good reputation as a guy who played people
straight. I was even good for a touch now and then. I guess the
biggest thing I had going was the fact that everybody knew I
could put on a good show. Now you know we don't have programmed entertainment in here, but that's not the point. People
figure if you can put on a good show in one place, you can do it
at another. The kind of show makes no difference. If you give
them what they want, it's a good show—do you follow?*

The owner's account of his initial production ideas and the
rationale supporting these thoughts about why and how he conceived the Rendezvous follow in a paraphrased form. He reasoned
in the late 1950s that the heyday of legitimate nightclubs with
lavish floor shows was over, that the big bands that played exclusively dance music "had had it," that television had dimmed the
lustre of live entertainers, and that former customers now living
in the suburbs would not fight the traffic and pay the freight for
traditional nightlife entertainment. He knew that jazz clubs,
attracting smaller audiences, had partially filled the vacuum, but
that big-name entertainers were beginning to play to larger audiences outside night clubs (in auditoriums, coliseums, concert halls,
and at jazz festivals)—and that name jazz groups were increasingly

expensive to book in jazz clubs. He figured that the ever increasing number of night clubs (many of them clip joints) that were catering to the masses and providing cheap entertainment and services in overcrowded, uncomfortable places had "turned off" many potential night club patrons. He reasoned further that "well-heeled, good people," the sustaining economic base of any club, were beginning to desire a more intimate format of night life entertainment where they could relax away from a hurly-burly crowd of affluent squares—squares who were now beginning to take over even the better places. By cosmopolitan standards, he knew that his city did not afford plush clubs.

Desiring to remain in business as a viable club owner, wishing to run a plush (relative to other clubs in the city) establishment in keeping with his own life style, and expecting to attract on a continuing basis affluent "good people" as patrons, he decided to switch from hosting a legitimate night club operation to hosting an after-hours club enterprise. In short, he planned a respectable but risque decor, a charismatic host, good jazz with a balance between dancing and listening numbers, a high quality sound system, good food and drink, and a clubby atmosphere that would attract his kind of patron and turn off undesirables. Figuring that he should at least double his yearly club investment, he calculated about an 80 per cent profit per drink and a 60 per cent profit on each serving of food. The club was set up with the thought in mind that the alcoholic drinks would be the major source of profit.

Conjecturing on what he could offer by way of an after-hours club vis-à-vis legitimate clubs in his city, he arrived at several presentations that may be outlined as follows:

1. A convenience club for potential patrons employed at odd-time hours, e.g., nightlife entertainers, promoters, agents, musicians; bar, restaurant, theater, and night club employees
2. A club accommodating revelers who for one reason or another wished to extend playtime beyond public bars' closing time
3. An exclusive club for affluent, worthy, regular patrons with similar or agreeable life styles (as he put it, "You have to put the right people together, and you have to rule out in front or sometimes discard later undesirables")
4. A plush, sexy, and exciting place in terms of physical accouterments, symbols, decor, and atmosphere

5. Good music by professional musicians befitting the patrons
6. A variety of subsettings appealing to a variety of patrons' interests at hand
7. Superior quality of goods and services—drink, food, comfort, and treatment
8. A hideaway or haven for those who wished to meet, socialize, or play away from the public eye in a comfortable, safe arrangement
9. A more balanced heterosexual scene than that found in legitimate clubs—by welcoming and encouraging the attendance of unescorted as well as escorted female patrons.

The owner anticipated little competition from existing after-hours clubs at the time, characterizing them as "frequently busted, low grade, fly-by-night clip joints patronized by low-class people." Several considerations prompted the location of the Rendezvous: low visibility, space, accessibility, convenience, costs, and security. In meeting these requirements, he chose a spacious three-story (one story below street level and open on three sides) brick, detached, three-family dwelling situated in a quiet, lower-middle-class neighborhood three miles from the city's dominant business district. Descending outside steps at street level on the north side of the building afford access to the basement that now houses the club's major theater of action—including a foyer, waiting room, hallway, hat check room, nightspot setting, two booth settings, and a bar setting. The street level or first story is accessible to the nightspot, bar, and booth subsettings by means of two (installed by the owner-operator) elevators (a patron's elevator and a service elevator). It houses the owner's office, secretary's office, the kitchen, male employees' dressing room and toilet, male patrons' lounge, female employees' dressing room and toilet, and a female patrons' lounge. The second story (top floor) serves as storage space. (See physical layout on pages 78 and 92.)

The surrounding area, formerly a white, middle-class residential section, has changed to a racially mixed, residential-commercial configuration. However, no commercial establishments are situated within the block where the club is located. Three-story dwellings (typically occupied by blue-collar workers and renters) very similar in outside physical structure to that housing the club stand on either side of the Rendezvous' street. At the north end of the club's street, one and a half blocks away, there is a major avenue leading to the central city.

Inhabitants of this area are newcomers from other less desirable locations in the city and share no strong sense of place or neighborhood. They live and let live, and in fact are not bothered by the club's functions for several practical reasons. Patrons and most employees come to and leave the Rendezvous quietly on foot, disembarking from cabs or from parked autos left in parking spaces and parking lots on the avenue a short distance away— therefore, no vehicular congestion. Club noise is deadened by the traffic boom on the nearby avenue and by structural conditions (e.g., the main theater of the club's operation is below street level and is now equipped with soundproof walls). Neither Rendezvous employees nor patrons intrude physically or socially into the lives of the local residents, who are indifferent toward an innocuous club that is outside their life style. Each family in the immediate area surrounding the club is happy, however, to receive a gift turkey and a Christmas basket every Christmas from the owner.

The owner reported that the initial property costs were high because of the commercial potential of the land. Moreover, structural modifications necessary to the transformation of a three-family dwelling into an after-hours club were great, e.g., the installation of an elaborate sound system, two elevators, a commercial kitchen, lounges, dressing rooms, and so on. Capital was also necessary for, among other things, stock (booze and bar supplies, cigarettes, cigars, food), kitchen supplies, bar equipment, furniture, employees' uniforms, electrical fixtures, rugs, wall ornaments, payrolls, and other overhead expenses. The following comments reveal the owner's initial thoughts about the club's site, spatial considerations, accessibility, financing, and security:

Well, as I've told you before, I picked a good spot where I didn't think the locals would bother me. As you can see, it's a big place and takes care of our needs. People can come and go by the outside steps from the sidewalk. They can walk from the avenue. So there's no parking or transportation problems. The noise we make doesn't bother outsiders. I saw to that, and we got soundproof walls. It cost a lot of money to get started, but I had some of it. I borrowed some from the bank, the rest from private sources —real private including the interest rates. All my help's straight, and I have a working arrangement with the police. So you see, it wasn't too hard getting started.

Since its beginning in 1959, the club has not lacked for a steady stream of patrons, many of whom are regulars. Individual patrons come and go—some die, some age out of the club, some move out of the city, others discontinue attendance because of poor health, legal problems, or financial reversals. But the same type of patrons (to be discussed in detail later) keep coming to the Rendezvous. The owner explained this institutionalized pattern of attendance and the unlikelihood of competition from other after-hours clubs in this way:

I haven't changed my operation much. We renovate now and then and bring in new furniture and things, but we go on with the same program. It's a winner, the same type of people come in here year after year. I mean regularly. I give them what they want. I'm not afraid of anybody else muscling in on my action. In the first place, this town can't afford another club like mine. There wouldn't be enough customers. Nobody else has my connections.

Commenting on city-wide leisure time and recreational settings throughout the years that might have given him competition, he explained further:

This town never had big time, nightlife entertainment. It's not that kind of town. We have a bunch of small clubs that do all right, and a number of restaurants, hotels, and bars where musicians work. Known entertainers pass through often for a performance here and there. We get a hell of a lot of tourists, and we have a big population that likes jazz. During the sixties, we had a few discotheques and a Playboy Club nearby, but that trade doesn't bother me. Playboy Clubs are for suckers who take their girl friends and wives to square joints. No one gets to the bunnies. I guess that's why these jokers go. They can look at them and don't have to worry about picking them up—or being faced with a real woman who might say yes. Put a dress on them and they look like your well-stacked sister or the nice girl next door. What a drag. Now about discotheques, who the hell in his right mind wants to dance to a record player's turntable? Maybe a bunch of young squirts who think they're being in. My clientele wants to dance to live music. I'll be here when they fold.

Chapter 2

REVIEW OF THE LITERATURE

Public Drinking Establishments

BECAUSE THE FOCUS of this study is one after-hours club, and because literature sources on this kind of drinking place are virtually nonexistent, we reviewed the bar literature in search of common transsituational features obtaining in public drinking establishments—kindred settings to the Rendezvous. We reasoned that such an examination might provide tentative guidelines for the study of our specific setting.

Most voluminous are short, journalistic, "travelog" articles found in travel and popular magazines. Because these brief accounts deal only with a hodgepodge of descriptive vignettes (about club decor, type, quality, and price of foods and drink, entertainment format, popularity and social visibility, and the qualities of individual proprietors) without any central theme of analysis, they are not reviewed here. Reference is made subsequently, when appropriate, to a few of these selections by means of footnotes. We deal here with research studies.

Though there is some overlap in the themes of analysis, the few research studies dealing with drinking establishments focus primarily on one or more of the following topics: (1) public drinking establishment typologies, (2) public drinking establishment patron characteristics, and (3) purposes of public drinking establishments. For heuristic and classificatory purposes we discuss representative studies falling within these frameworks.

PUBLIC DRINKING ESTABLISHMENT TYPOLOGIES

Typological attempts have included several dimensions of study. Clinard and Macrory based their typologies of public drinking places mainly on ecological location, physical structure, patronage, and function.[1] Because these two typologies are very similar, only Clinard's is reviewed here. He describes five types of establishments: skid row taverns, downtown bars and cocktail lounges, drink-and-dine taverns, night clubs and roadhouses, and neighborhood taverns. Skid row taverns are generally located in tenderloin areas near cities' central business districts. Clinard reports that though these latter establishments function primarily as cheap drinking places, they are often sites for gambling and soliciting for prostitution.[2] The downtown bars and cocktail lounges are situated in business and shopping areas and cater mostly to transient white-collar patrons who come there to have a drink and discuss business problems.

Drink-and-dine taverns are found in either the central business district or near the city limits along major highways where most patrons are businessmen who come to transact business deals. The primary drawing card is not the drinks per se but good food and music. Night clubs and roadhouses are generally positioned in the amusement centers of the city or on the main highways just beyond the city limits where they cater mainly to couples out to have a good time on weekends. The chief activities here are dancing, enjoying fine foods, listening to the orchestra, and watching the floor show.[3]

The last type discussed by Clinard, the neighborhood tavern, is the most numerous of all the types and is delineated into four

[1] Marshall B. Clinard, "The Public Drinking House and Society," in *Society, Culture and Drinking Patterns,* ed. David J. Pittman and Charles R. Snyder (New York: John Wiley and Sons, 1962), pp. 270–92. The categories are similar to those used by Macrory. Boyd E. Macrory, "The Tavern and the Community," *Quarterly Journal of Studies on Alcohol,* vol. 13, no. 4 (Dec. 1952): 609–37.

[2] Clinard, *"Public Drinking House,"* p. 276.

[3] *Ibid.,* p. 277.

subtypes (depending on location): rural, village, suburban, and city taverns. All these neighborhood taverns function as places for people to relax and converse—to get away from the monotony of work. Most tavern patrons are local regulars who are well acquainted with one another, the owner, the bartender, and with other employees.

Gottlieb utilized criteria similar to Clinard's to differentiate the cocktail lounge from the neighborhood tavern.[4] The lounge, located in a commercial area, caters to a transient clientele who do not form a cohesive group. It provides a bar, booths, television, and in some cases professional performers. The primary emphasis is placed on serving mixed drinks to a heterogeneous group of patrons during the early afternoon and evening.[5] The tavern, on the other hand, a product of the neighborhood, caters to individuals with similar backgrounds who do things together in an organized fashion in and outside the tavern setting. It becomes the center of a voluntary association enforcing group norms and organizing group action. Taverns are located in residential areas of the city and afford a bar and, in some cases, tables. The principal drinks are draught beer and whiskey. For the amusement of patrons there is usually television and perhaps a game or two (e.g., pin ball, electric bowling) and a joke box. It opens for business early in the morning.[6] Gottlieb also pointed out that there is variation within each type and that there are marginal establishments of both types.

In her book *Liquor License*, Cavan criticized Clinard's and Gottlieb's typologies because much of the behavior they described cuts across all the types they distinguished, as well as a good deal of behavior they do not mention. She claimed that ecological location and characteristics of bar patrons may not be the most important variables for differentiating the uses of public drinking places.[7] She developed a bar typology based on the primary uses to which such settings are routinely put by those who patronize

---

[4] David Gottlieb, "The Neighborhood Tavern and the Cocktail Lounge: A Study of Class Differences," *American Journal of Sociology*, vol. 62, no. 6 (May 1957): 559–62.

[5] *Ibid.*, p. 559.

[6] *Ibid.*

[7] Sherri Cavan, *Liquor License: An Ethnography of Bar Behavior* (Chicago: Aldine, 1966).

them. Cavan arrived at four types: the convenience bar, the nightspot, the marketplace bar, and the home territory bar.

The convenience bar is a place to kill time or rest between courses of activities. This type of bar provides the patron with a minor course of action that may be brief or prolonged in duration, unplanned or routine. Whatever the course of action, it is only an adjunct to the daily round of activity. Cavan describes the typical patron behavior there: "Either single or in the company of others, they enter, order, and, once the drink is consumed, typically leave."[8] Convenience bars are also used by revelers who wish to extend the activities of a night out beyond that time which was originally planned. They choose the bar because it happens to be conveniently located (inadvertently) near the initial and primary site of entertainment (a theater, ball park, restaurant, coliseum, pool hall, somebody's house). Patrons may also drop by these establishments en route home after work to unwind from their daily routine. The point is that the convenience bar happens to be nearby some other activity center in the daily round; it is not chosen as a primary theater of action.

The nightspot provides programmed entertainment, a course of activity that is in some fashion scripted, rehearsed, and presented. Patrons attend the nightspot setting, usually on a couple basis, to see the show. The physical arrangements of tables and chairs, bar, and central stage of action do not afford a milling area. This lack of a milling area and certain ground rules (e.g., no table hopping) are geared for a controlled audience and a performance situation. Interaction among those unacquainted and those not attending the performance together is at the minimum.[9]

The marketplace bar is used primarily as a center for the exchange or trading of various goods and services such as sex, narcotics, gambling, and stolen merchandise. Usually the dealers are not connected with the running of the bar. Like marketplaces in general, the bar itself is in most instances merely the physical setting where varied kinds of transactions may transpire—some legal and some illegal. These establishments serve not only as service arenas for prostitution and "B" girls and their customers but for men and women on the prowl who are looking for non-commercial pickups. Finally, marketplace bars provide a locale where strangers with many different interests at hand may interact

8 *Ibid.*, p. 145.
9 *Ibid.*, pp. 156–57.

and dally around with one another without commitment beyond the here-and-now—and without worry about future consequences associated with their actions within the setting.

The fourth type, home territory bars, are conceived of and used as if they were not public places at all but rather as though they were the private retreat for some special group.[10] Patrons (referred to as habitués) who attend on a frequent and recurring basis share one or more characteristics of a common social identity, e.g., occupational group (newspapermen, writers, artists, entertainers, seamen, hard hats, fighters); criminals (pimps and prostitutes); ethnic groups (blacks, Italians, Irishmen, Mexican Americans); marital status (singles bars); sex (strictly male bars, homosexual bars); social class (skid row bars, plush cocktail lounges). Frequently patrons of home territory bars vary in their daily rounds from other bar patrons whose daily routine and occupations are more conventionally timed or spaced. The more homogeneous the collectivity of patrons (i.e., the more characteristics and social identities they share) the less open the bar is to outsiders. The restriction of patron collectivities varies from bar to bar, and some bars are much more exclusionary than others. Guest members (outsiders usually in the company of regulars) and neutral persons (those whose presence is tolerated) are limited in terms of the privileges and behavior patterns open to habitués (e.g., check cashing, tab running, singing, dancing, use of the telephone, acceptance for sociability). Many patrons act as though the bar "belongs to them." They make and receive telephone calls, receive and leave messages with the bartender, mail and receive mail, receive and deposit money, borrow money, and the like.[11]

In home territory bars the management accepts and supports certain kinds of patron collectivities and helps its patrons exclude outsiders, e.g., by extending poor service to those not wanted, making derogatory remarks about undesirables, eighty-sixing strangers (cutting them off from drinks) without legal justification. Moreover, habitués ostracize outsiders in a number of ways. They stare at them as though they were nonpersons, sound them out with insulting remarks, preclude them from conversation and other sociable behaviors, and josh them verbally and physically. By design some home territory bars are camouflaged and hard to

---

[10] *Ibid.*, p. 205.

[11] These findings of Cavan are corroborated by us in our observation of several home territory bars.

find; some are even unmarked. In this type of bar patrons often stake out proprietary claims on particular seats at the bar or tables and defend these self-appropriated territories from outsiders.[12]

Cavan notes a common denominator of all types of bars: all of them are of questionable moral order. She documents the fact that both the legal statutes governing such settings and the historical characterizations of what goes on in them define these places as "marginal if not disrespectable." Bars are risky places where all sorts of untoward, illegal, rowdy, lascivious behavior is likely to occur among intoxicated people. Therefore all sorts of legal proscriptions and prescriptions are attached to the proprietors, employees, and patrons in these settings. Age limitation, license limitation, time and space limitation, beverage and food limitation, and behavioral limitation are examples.[13]

Though bar typologies demonstrate that bar settings are not all alike, they indicate that there are some transsituational features. All furnish alcoholic beverages by the drink in licensed, public places; all are unserious configurations; all are of a questionable moral order. On the other hand, these studies show that bars are markedly differentiated in terms of location and function.

PUBLIC DRINKING ESTABLISHMENT PATRON CHARACTERISTICS

Although we were unable to locate any studies on after-hours club patrons, there have been a few studies on tavern patrons. Macrory's rather extensive study of taverns and the community included, in addition to a tavern typology, the attitudes of community members toward taverns.[14] While analyzing the characteristics of both tavern patrons and nonpatrons in Dane County, Wisconsin, he found that 62 per cent of the people patronized taverns—75 per cent of the men and 40 per cent of the women. He also found that over 80 per cent of his 1,441 questionnaire respondents were in agreement with statements that would place the tavern in a position diametrically opposed to some of the most important values in contemporary American life, e.g., children

12 *Ibid.*, pp. 205–6.
13 *Ibid.*, pp. 23–45.
14 Macrory, "Tavern and the Community."

and the home. Moreover, about four-fifths of his respondents believed that the tavern provides contacts and associations that lead to crime and attribute to the tavern much drunkenness and disorderly conduct.[15] Macrory's findings revealed that his respondents were actually ambivalent toward taverns. A large proportion of his respondents agreed that the tavern is related to forms of social disorganization, and yet over three-fifths of all respondents patronized taverns either regularly (35 per cent) or irregularly (27 per cent).[16]

As might be expected, Macrory found that as a group tavern patrons were more favorably disposed toward taverns than non-patrons.[17] Among tavern patrons, women were more tolerant toward taverns than men, and urban males had more favorable attitudes toward taverns than did small town and farm males. There was little consensus on whether or not the tavern:

1. contributes much toward making life more enjoyable
2. encourages drinking in moderation
3. is as important as the church to many members of the community
4. helps people who are bored with life
5. is responsible for much sexual promiscuity
6. does more good than harm in the community
7. is a place where meeting friends rather than drinking is the most important of all tavern functions.[18]

Macrory assigned ideal type characteristics to patrons with the most favorable and the least favorable attitudes toward taverns. The professional-proprietor group, Catholics, infrequent or non-churchgoers, those with college education, the youngest and the unmarried were more tolerant toward the tavern than were farmers, Lutherans, regular church attenders, the less educated, the oldest, and the married fathers with all children 20 years of age or over.[19]

Twelve years later, in 1962, Clark conducted an extensive study of tavern patrons in San Francisco using basically the same

[15] *Ibid.*, p. 622.
[16] *Ibid.*
[17] *Ibid.*
[18] *Ibid.*, p. 617.
[19] *Ibid.*, p. 618.

methodology used by Macrory in Wisconsin.[20] The results of this study yielded some additional findings and some small differences from the Macrory study—the latter are probably owing to regional differences such as ethnic composition and degree of urbanization; time differences; and the like. Clark found that of the 1,268 persons in his San Francisco adult sample, nearly half patronized taverns—64 per cent of the male and 45 per cent of the female respondents.

Clark examined to what extent drinkers and abstainers avoid or frequent taverns and found that 46 per cent of the drinkers did not patronize taverns, whereas 7 per cent of the abstainers did. Dividing his respondents into white-collar and blue-collar occupations, he found little difference between the two groups with respect to tavern patronage and concluded that taverns draw patrons from all strata of society.[21] Other findings showed that family income and education are positively related to tavern patronage; that age is inversely related to the patronage of taverns; and that a greater proportion of single and divorced people patronize taverns than is true for married and widowed people. In general these findings were similar to those of Macrory's earlier study.

In a case study of a cocktail lounge utilized primarily by older married men and younger single women for pickup purposes in a California city of 150,000 residents, Roebuck and Spray studied the characteristics of the patrons.[22] They found that the male patrons' occupations were primarily in the professional, managerial, official, or proprietary category. Incomes of the male patrons were all substantial—two-thirds of the men had annual incomes exceeding $10,000 with the remainder earning between $8,500 and $10,000. The women all earned less than $9,000 and were primarily employed as secretaries, clerks, cocktail hostesses, professionals, and college students. As to education, all male patrons had at least a high school education with over half having graduated from college. The women were slightly less educated (20 per cent were college graduates, 40 per cent had attended or were presently at-

[20] Walter Clark, "Demographic Characteristics of Tavern Patrons in San Francisco," *Quarterly Journal of Studies on Alcohol,* vol. 27, no. 2 (June 1966): 316–27.

[21] *Ibid.,* p. 319.

[22] Julian B. Roebuck and S. Lee Spray, "The Cocktail Lounge: A Study of Heterosexual Relations in a Public Organization," *American Journal of Sociology,* vol. 72, no. 4 (Jan. 1967): 388–96.

tending college, 30 per cent had a high school education, and 7 per cent had less than a high school education). Male and female patrons were products of the middle class. The men were mostly middle-aged, whereas the women were all young, under 35. Marital status varied greatly between the sexes—70 per cent of the men were married. None of the women were currently married and living with their husbands.

Regarding religion, church attendance, belief in God, ethnicity, and place of birth the authors found that two-thirds of the men were Catholics, with the remainder being Protestants. All the respondents expressed a belief in God and attended church. None of the patrons were members of ethnic minority groups, despite the fact that the city of the bar site had a high proportion of Mexican Americans (about 40 per cent) and a number of blacks (about 12 per cent). Regarding nativity, twenty-six males and twenty-seven females were born in urban areas outside of California whereas the remaining were California natives.

Roebuck and Spray had the employees of the lounge rate the women patrons on their relative attractiveness. The following distribution resulted: "very sharp" = 30 per cent; "sharp" = 50 per cent; "average" = 20 per cent; "below average" = 0 per cent. The employees also rated the patrons according to their personality stability and found that 80 per cent of both male and female patrons received a stable rating and 20 per cent of each sex received an unstable rating. Only two women patrons received a very unstable rating. This seems to indicate that most of the people who frequented the lounge had "normal" personalities, at least as viewed by the employees. None were found to be alcoholics, drug addicts, delinquents, or criminals. All were products of respectable, conventional home backgrounds where they grew up without childhood or adolescent adjustment problems.[23]

In sum, the foregoing studies indicate that women are more tolerant of public drinking establishments than men; that men patronize public drinking establishments more frequently than women; and that tavern patrons are more favorably disposed toward taverns than nonpatrons. Furthermore, although tavern patrons are drawn from all occupational groups, family income and education are positively related to tavern patronage. Patrons

---

[23] Our impressions from experiences in several types of bars over time indicate that a large number of bar patrons are conventional people mixed in with the unconventional.

of drinking establishments vary in social class and personal characteristics, and they frequent different types of drinking places. Many appear to be conventional people without criminal, delinquent, or deviant backgrounds. Age is inversely related to tavern patronage. Single and divorced people patronize taverns more frequently than the married or widowed. Despite the fact that studies demonstrate that over 60 per cent of the men and about 40 per cent of the women visit taverns or bars, the public seems to be ambivalent toward public drinking establishments.

THE PURPOSE OF PUBLIC DRINKING ESTABLISHMENTS

The literature disclosed that public drinking establishments provide a variety of voluntary, time-out, unserious behavior settings that vary in milieu as well as in the behavior taking place therein. Though patrons of drinking places approach bars with a variety of behavioral expectations over time, *three typical behavioral expectations* were found to be transsituational for all bar patrons: (1) sociability, (2) playing, and (3) drinking. Because most drinking in public bars is an integral part of the sociability routine, we focus here on sociable drinking. Contrary to the "common knowledge" held by many, drinking per se is not the primary interest at hand for most patrons in public drinking establishments.[24] For example, when Macrory asked tavern patrons, "Why do people go to taverns?" he received the following responses: "for social reasons," "relaxation," "entertainment," "mixing with your neighbors," "social reasons mainly: see the gang, play a little cards, shuffleboard, joke, tell stories, meet people."[25] The tavernkeepers gave similar answers when asked why people patronize taverns: "to spend a social hour and relax," "to enjoy a sociable drink with his friends," "get a little relaxation," "a social center," "a place to enjoy oneself," "enjoy visiting and singing," and so on. Other researchers seem to give a similar function to public drinking places as the following quotations illustrate:

[24] See for example, Clinard, "Public Drinking House," p. 279; Clark, "Demographic Characteristics of Tavern Patrons," p. 319; and Cavan, *Liquor License*, p. 42 and pp. 254–55.

[25] Macrory, "Tavern and the Community," pp. 630–36. Although these quotations were taken from Macrory, they are similar to those found in the other articles.

Primarily the saloon is a social center.[26]

Other than drinking there appear to be three chief functions of the tavern: (a) as a meeting place where social relationships with other persons can be established, (b) as a place for recreation such as games, and, (c) as a place to talk over personal problems with the tavernkeeper or others.[27]

. . . the tavern provides space and facilities for entertainment and relaxation. . . . the tavern is an important place for entertainment. . . . the tavern is a public gathering place.[28]

. . . sociability is the most general rule in the public drinking place.[29]

Cavan concluded that bars, among other voluntary unserious behavior settings, serve as places removed from the daily round of everyday life where conventional behavior (behavior that counts) may be temporarily suspended, i.e., given a temporal and spacial status of "time-out." Unserious settings (public drinking places, social parties, vacations, picnics, coffee breaks, beer busts, beach parties, after-hours clubs, resorts, and so on) are characterized by an informality of behavior that clearly differentiates them from the more serious settings of everyday life. In unserious settings sociability and playtime activities are paramount.[30]

In short, bars provide one regular setting for time-out periods that is less constricted than is the case with many other unserious settings. Moreover, by design they are set up to give the impression of an ever-continuing, sociable, playtime atmosphere. Lighting effects give off the impression that it is forever evening time, playtime. However, unserious settings form a part of the larger social order since they are officially controlled temporally and spatially within the context of the wider social order. For example, vacations and parties are scheduled to begin and end within the daily round of more serious behaviors; expressive sexual behavior at an after-hours office cocktail party is not permitted at the office during normal working hours. Furthermore, differentials in social class, ethnicity, occupation, religion, affluence, life style, age,

[26] E. C. Moore, "The Social Value of the Saloon," *American Journal of Sociology*, vol. 3, no. 1 (July 1897): 4.

[27] Clinard, "Public Drinking House," p. 279.

[28] Clark, "Demographic Characteristics of Tavern Patrons," p. 326.

[29] Cavan, *Liquor License*, p. 49.

[30] *Ibid.*, pp. 3–22; 49–66; 234–41.

sex, and marital status among other variables predispose different types of people to seek out different types of unserious settings. Once in these settings their behavior is somewhat constrained to mesh with the ongoing activities and to conform to the reigning ground rules obtaining therein.

Sociability and Play

Because the literature disclosed that sociability and playtime activities were the main behavioral expectations sought in drinking establishments (as well as in many other unserious settings) and because there is a dearth of sociability and play theory related to drinking establishments, sociability and play theory are examined in a wider context and within drinking establishments when possible. We reasoned that such a review would enable us to better understand and analyze sociability and play within the Rendezvous, the drinking establishment under study.

Though the literature does not always make clear-cut distinctions between sociability and play, for review purposes they will be treated separately even though the two are highly interrelated. First we deal with sociability theory and then with play theory.

SOCIABILITY THEORY

For review purposes, we examined the sociability literature (a very limited field of study) within four major categories: (1) classical sociability, (2) contemporary sociability, (3) party sociability, and (4) bar sociability. We briefly analyze key works found in these three areas.

CLASSICAL SOCIABILITY: SIMMEL

In his essay on sociability, a bench mark for many students, Simmel mentioned several attributes of sociability that are recurrent throughout the more recent sociability literature.[31] He noted, among other things, that sociability is autonomous; it exists for its

[31] Georg Simmel, *The Sociology of Georg Simmel*, ed. and trans. Kurt H. Wolff (New York: Free Press, 1965), pp. 40–57.

own sake outside of reality. Pure sociability for Simmel has no objective purpose or aim beyond the success of the moment, the here and now. In his words:

> . . . it is the nature of sociability to free concrete interactions from reality and to erect its airy realm according to the form-laws of these relations, which come to move in themselves and to recognize no purpose extraneous to them.[32]

Participants in sociability settings must divest themselves of attributes external to the setting, such as social status, wealth, fame, and other exceptional capabilities. Actors must also exclude their "inner" selves (i.e., their personal moods, whims, and fate) from the setting.

> It is tactless, because it militates against interaction which monopolizes sociability, to display merely personal moods of depression, excitement, despondency—in brief, the light and the darkness of one's most intimate life.[33]

This suspension of the innermost self also extends to certain external features of behavior, e.g., personal posture, adornment, and dress.

Simmel's principle of sociability states that ". . . each individual should *offer* the maximum of sociable values (of joy, relief, liveliness, etc.) that is compatible with the maximum of values he himself *receives*."[34] This optimization of sociable values for all members in a sociable setting points to the democratic nature of sociability. However, in reality equality or democracy among all actors in a sociability setting is difficult, if not impossible, to achieve. This is true even when all of the participants are from the same social class. Thus Simmel postulated that democracy even among members of the same social class is something that is only played. Furthermore, playing democracy is possible only in an artificial world where material possessions and other differentiating factors are ignored or considered irrelevant for a particular setting at a particular time and place. Through the suspension of their external and inner personal characteristics, actors in a sociability setting become social equals. That is, in sociability settings one does as if all are equal.

---

[32] *Ibid.*, p. 55.
[33] *Ibid.*, p. 46.
[34] *Ibid.*, p. 47.

Simmel found that conversations in sociability settings have a character different from those found in other more serious settings where the conversational content (the topic of discussion) is paramount. In sociability settings the conversation becomes its own purpose. The topic becomes ". . . merely the indispensable medium through which the lively exchange of speech itself unfolds its attraction."[35] Though the stress is on the form or manner in which one converses, the content of sociable conversation is not indifferent—it may be interesting, fascinating, even important. The point is that the content must not become the purpose of the conversation, nor must the conversation pursue an objective result. Since sociable talk is its own legitimate purpose, part of its nature includes the ability to change topics rapidly and with ease. Sociable conversations, like all interaction in sociability settings, require a great deal of tact on the part of the actors because external and intimate personal elements must be screened out. As Simmel states, ". . . the subtlest and best-told stories are those from which the narrator's personality has completely vanished."[36]

Finally, according to Simmel, actors in sociability settings are alloted a great deal of freedom to initiate and terminate encounters at will because sociable interaction is relatively free from the consequences of the real world. Despite its apparent separation from reality, sociability is rooted in and reflects the real world. Sociability in its extreme form loses touch with reality. In Simmel's terms ". . . it ceases to be play and becomes a desultory playing-around with empty forms, a lifeless schematism which is even proud of its lifelessness."[37]

CONTEMPORARY SOCIABILITY

Sociability, a Distinctive Type of Interaction. Perhaps the strongest theme in the more current literature dealing with sociability is that sociable interaction is different from or contrasts with other types of interaction.[38] In her article, "A Formal Analysis of

[35] *Ibid.*, p. 52.
[36] *Ibid.*, p. 53.
[37] *Ibid.*, p. 56.
[38] See for example: Simmel, *Sociology*; Jeanne Watson, "A Formal Analysis of Sociable Interaction," *Sociometry*, vol. 21, no. 4 (Dec. 1958): 269–80;

Sociable Interaction," Watson differentiated sociable interaction from work-oriented interaction and familial interaction on the basis of five criteria:

1. the way in which each type of interaction relates the individual to society
2. the individual needs that each type of interaction fulfills
3. that aspect or part of the self an individual invests in the various types of interaction
4. the style of conversation prevalent in these different types of interaction
5. the subject matter of conversations in the three types of inter-action.[39]

With respect to these five criteria she points out that sociable interaction:

1. provides for the normative integration of the individual with society
2. gives the individual a chance to emphasize his unique personal quality
3. allows the individual to dramatize that part of himself that overlaps with the culture of the group he is in
4. involves a conversational style emphasizing the novelty and entertainment value of topics under discussion
5. provides for conversations that center around nonroutine and special interests of the individuals involved.

Forces Affecting Interaction in Sociability Settings. Watson goes on to identify three types of pressures conducive to giving form to interaction in sociable settings: (1) sociability's historical and social class determinants, (2) its psychological determinants, and (3) its structural properties. In her discussion of historical and class pressures Watson's major point is democratization. Historically sociability is related to leisure time; therefore it is no accident that during feudal times, when the institution of the

David Riesman, Robert J. Potter, and Jeanne Watson, "Sociability, Permissiveness, and Equality: A Preliminary Formulation," *Psychiatry*, vol. 23, no. 4 (Nov. 1966): 323–40; David Riesman, Robert J. Potter, and Jeanne Watson, "The Vanishing Host," *Human Organization*, vol. 19, no. 1 (Spring 1960): 17–27.

[39] Watson, "Formal Analysis."

leisure class reached its highest development,[40] sociability also reached its purest form.[41] Since the "golden age" of sociability (the *Ancien Regime* especially before the French Revolution), both leisure time and sociability have been increasingly extended into the middle and even lower classes in industrializing countries.[42] As a result, as Watson and Riesman *et. al.* have pointed out, there have been some changes in the style of sociability.[43] Watson suggests that this change is due not only to an increased amount of leisure time possessed by the middle class in the United States but also to ". . . a historical change in America from a view of life emphasizing free enterprise and individual initiative to one emphasizing *social and personal security.*"[44]

These changes as well as the change in emphasis upon negative rather than positive aspects of self have affected the style of sociability.[45] Even though middle-class people have more time for sociability, they still lack the time to adequately develop novel and interesting sociable resources. Consequently they often have nothing novel or interesting to talk about, and therefore their conversation tends to deteriorate into routine and reiterative chatter. Additional factors contributing to routine rather than novel and imaginative interaction characteristic of "traditional" sociability include advances in transportation and communication. People nowadays interact with their friends much more frequently than was the case in the past, thereby making it more difficult for them to be novel, entertaining, and dramatic at sociable gatherings. This change in sociability in industrial countries has also received empirical support from Riesman's research on parties.[46]

In discussing sociability from a psychological perspective (i.e., sociability as an anxiety reducing mechanism and as a way to enhance one's self-esteem), Watson postulated that because middle-class people have adopted a nonviolent life style, their aggressive behavioral tendencies must be channeled by and through the use

---

[40] Thorstein B. Veblen, *The Theory of the Leisure Class: An Economic Study of Institutions* (New York: Modern Library, 1899), p. 1.

[41] Simmel, *Sociology*, p. 55.

[42] Watson, "Formal Analysis," pp. 272–74.

[43] *Ibid.* See also Riesman, Potter and Watson; "Sociability, Permissiveness, and Equality," and "The Vanishing Host."

[44] Watson, "Formal Analysis," p. 272.

[45] *Ibid.*, p. 27.

[46] See Riesman, Potter and Watson, "The Vanishing Host" and "Sociability, Permissiveness, and Equality."

of defense mechanisms. Two such mechanisms are projection and scapegoating. By coming together in a group where they project hostility to the environment or some other group, in-group members are able to reduce their aggression by projection. The in-group they form is based on the assumption that all actors in the group love each other. These groups often set up a scapegoat to aggress against; if they do, the sociable conversation revolves around outrageous acts of these outsiders, thereby implicitly affirming the virtues of the individuals present. Watson explains further:

> The price for this, of course, is that one must not compete with the others while in a social setting, must not refer to his own achievements outside the group except in a depreciatory way, and must accept with apparent pleasure whatever topic of conversation is introduced—usually being content with the lowest denominator, so that no one will be excluded.[47]

Because anxiety is also produced by uncertainty in an individual's environment, by unknown, uncontrollable, or ambiguous forces that affect all individuals, one ". . . major function of sociability is to provide acceptable explanations for aspects of the external world which are either puzzling or threatening."[48] Furthermore, these social explanations of reality serve to maximize sociable interaction because sociability often deals with playful fantasizing or the distorting of reality. The last type of anxiety Watson discusses deals with an individual's identity and self-worth. In a sociability setting one is often able to obtain *reassurances from others about one's own reality and importance.*[49]

Finally, Watson examines structural properties that influence interaction in sociability settings. She considers *contrast* one of the major structural properties of sociability; i.e., most sociable occasions provide a contrast to other types of behavior. For example, on the job sociability provides contrast to the segmented, achievement-oriented, productive activities found in work-oriented interaction; whereas in a familial setting sociability provides contrast with the dull, routine activities of daily family life. Some sociability settings such as parties (discussed in the next section) offer a different type of contrast in that they are used to punctuate time sequences, i.e., to note holidays and weekends or to mark

[47] Watson, "Formal Analysis," p. 275.
[48] *Ibid.*
[49] *Ibid.,* p. 276.

rites of passage such as promotions, weddings, and so forth.[50] Another structural property of sociability settings such as parties is the guest list that defines a party as an in-group of people distinguishing themselves from the vast group of outsiders not invited. This tends to give parties, especially small parties, many primary group qualities.

PARTY SOCIABILITY

Sources. Reisman, Potter, and Watson have written two research articles on parties.[51] Using primarily participant observation methodology, they gathered data on 80 parties given by young, middle-class, urban adults. Data collection techniques also included interviewing people about their experiences at parties, and an examination of cross-cultural materials and ethnographies dealing with sociability in various settings and at various points in history.[52]

Changes in Style of Sociability. In "Sociability, Permissiveness, and Equality" Riesman, Potter, and Watson examine problems for sociability created by the growth of equalitarianism in the United States. Sociability is viewed as serving more than just maintenance and repair functions (controlling anomie and affording an interim for working individuals); they see sociability as providing drama to life and intensifying reality—reality both within and outside of the group.[53] Although the linking of the group to larger reality makes sociability more viable, it requires a great deal of work. The authors point out that with a greater adherence to the ethos of spontaneity, permissiveness, and equality people have avoided the big issue, namely, tying sociability into the larger society. Thus without people being fully aware of it, this ethos has put constraints upon sociability (at least middle-class sociability) in the United States today.

Contrary to some, Riesman, Potter, and Watson believe that

50 *Ibid.*, p. 278.

51 Riesman, Potter, and Watson, "Sociability, Permissiveness, and Equality," and "The Vanishing Host."

52 For more details on their methodology see "The Vanishing Host," pp. 17–19.

53 Riesman, Potter and Watson, "Sociability, Permissiveness, and Equality," p. 324.

sociability as an activity pattern is rising rather than declining in the United States. However, unlike sociability among the aristocracy where there is a great deal of agreement on what are acceptable sociable resources, sociability in middle-class America is somewhat more difficult to achieve because (more often than not) there is no known uniform set of sociable resources among partygoers. Consequently a great deal of time at parties is often devoted to prospecting for common hidden resources that will allow the conversation to move quickly away from the familiar to the more novel.

Concentrating on the small invitational party as the prototype of sociability setting, Riesman, Potter, and Watson found three different qualities that people felt made for a "good party": intimacy, festivity, and solidarity. The first two of these were found to be the most difficult to attain. Preoccupied attempts to attain them were noted to be self-defeating, whereas leaving them to chance often meant that they did not develop at all. The authors point out that whereas during the older regimen there was the danger of the overprepared party, today with the stress on spontaneity there is the opposite danger—underpreparation. This increased reliance on spontaneity with a minimal amount of planning and organization results in a wide distribution of leadership functions among party members. At an extreme this decentralization of leadership, this overreliance on spontaneity, can create two problems: (1) spontaneity may not take place at all or (2) once spontaneous festivity does occur it may get out of hand because there is no leadership to control its limits. The researchers point out that in either situation it becomes very easy for a minority of persons to take over a kind of demagogic leadership and disrupt the party for the other guests and in some cases even for themselves.

The ethic of achievement and performance has been relaxed in contemporary society and as a result stress is placed on the equalitarian principle at parties. This distributes equally the responsibility to have fun to all people at a party. This trend places sociability in the sphere of relaxation, where you come as you are and do as you please.[54] Riesman, Potter, and Watson noted that this "come as you are" approach to parties has (1) taken the "front" out of party giving, (2) reduced the threshold of what is expected of people at parties, (3) made it harder for people to refuse invita-

[54] *Ibid.,* p. 330.

tions, and (4) has increased the number of spur-of-the-moment parties. Furthermore, at many parties (especially the bring your own food or liquor parties) the hosting function has been reduced often without an increase in the guesting function. At those parties studied by Riesman, Potter, and Watson where there was a decrease in both the hosting and guesting functions, the solidarity of the group was affirmed by the freedom people felt to take temporary leave, e.g., to fall asleep, read the newspaper, and the like. As a result of the stress on equalitarianism, no one person was permitted to hold the center of attention very long.

This new style of party sociability with its dedication to spontaneity and sincerity frequently imposes rather strict constraints on individuals—i.e., individuals are often required to be just as they have always been stereotyped. The sexy girl is always "forced" to be the dumb blond, the comic to be funny, and so on. Furthermore, because individuals are constrained in the display of their personal achievements at parties, there is the danger that sociability may turn into routine familial type relationships rather than the novelty relationships associated with sociability.

Riesman, Potter, and Watson also point out that sociability affirms a common set of values for people whose working lives are becoming more and more functionally specialized. Thus sociability becomes part of the integrative attempts of people to restore *gemeinschaft* relationships outside their sphere of work. This trend is notable by the fact that small parties have a tendency toward a confluence of values by means of a single activity such as singing songs, playing a game, and so on.

The researchers were most struck by the here-and-now character and the lack of planning they found at the middle-class parties they studied. Parties were rarely considered as experiences to be savored in one's memory nor were they expected to have any future consequences. This stress on the present was accompanied by an inability to transcend the here-and-now by means of vicarious participation with the outside world. The here-and-now character of modern middle-class parties, with their stress on spontaneity and equality, also resulted in many dull and unrewarding affairs. The researchers concluded that unless there is some guidance by leaders sensitive to a party's mood and to things outside the group the party members can partake in vicariously, sociability will remain inadequate. In their words: "An overequalitarian ethos has the same effect on sociability as on the schools; by denying differences of skill and motivation, it compresses all into a limited range of possibility."[55]

In general, Riesman, Potter, and Watson found that older middle-class people have more money but less time to spend on parties than their younger counterparts. Furthermore, sociability for older middle-class people has become more obligatory, more tied in with the other well-established relationships of their work and family. Under such circumstances a successful party is viewed as something one creates and works at, not something that will take place spontaneously. Younger people, on the other hand, feel that success can result only if no effort is put into a party, since any systematic planning and work would be self-defeating—making the party ". . . one more scheduled task instead of a spontaneous escape from routine."[56]

The Changing Role of the Party Host. In their article on "The Vanishing Host" Riesman, Potter, and Watson point out that contemporary American sociability is supposed to be informal, spontaneous, and festive, and therefore a host is not supposed to be ". . . pretentious, or managerial, or overtly preoccupied with being the host."[57] Though they noted that the host has some control over the party both before it starts (by inviting the right combination of people, preparing and arranging the setting, and so on) and once it is underway (by mixing old and new people, helping out trapped victims, and the like), the functions of the host vary with the type of party.

In parties of a heterogeneous nature the host plays an inconspicuous role, but here he does not encounter a uniform pattern of expectations. Instead he is faced with mixed expectations, or in some cases with so great a heterogeneity that no definite pattern of expectations about the party exist. An example of this type of party is a mixer given to bring a large diverse group of single men and women together in order to meet prospective dating partners. At such gatherings, individuals can periodically wander from their friends in search of pickups.

The authors point out that in more heterogeneous parties the stress is more on intimacy and privacy, intimacy in the sense of getting to know another individual well. Such conversation re-

[55] *Ibid.*, p. 340.
[56] Riesman, Potter and Watson, "The Vanishing Host," p. 23.
[57] *Ibid.*, p. 18.

quires a dyad or triad and some privacy. Intimacy and privacy on the other hand tend to make for laissez-faire hosting, and guests tend to be sincere and stress the routine rather than the novel and unusual in the conversations.

Homogeneous parties, however, are characterized by a higher degree of solidarity and a more uniform pattern of expectations, especially those with a history and/or various institutional ties (similar ethnic identification, same place of work, and the like). Although people at such parties are allowed some recognition as individuals, the primary interests are group continuity and solidarity. At this type of party the same people get together frequently and discuss the same kind of topic over and over. Consequently the contribution of the host is minimal and entirely interchangeable with the guests' contribution. He provides the place, cleans up, and on occasion may introduce a stranger to provide special entertainment. In short, the group and its history determine the nature of the party.

With the change in American party ethos to a low pressure, low key, informal style, the host encounters several problems. For example, because the host is supposed to be inconspicuous and nonauthoritarian, and because such parties often have no formal time limits, the guests do not know when to go home; and the host is hesitant to ask everyone to leave simply because he wants to end the party. Therefore many parties drag on, often with people sleeping in and the host feeling an obligation to fix breakfast for them. This relaxation of time limits is attributable to more than a casual attitude toward parties. It is part of the stress on individualism that involves in part the resistance to regimentation as well as to "togetherness." The researchers found time limits to be better defined when there was variation in age and status among party members, when someone in authority announced that the party was over, or when the departure of a high-status person signaled the end of the party.

The host, like the task leader in a work group, performs several management and social engineering functions at a party. Although the host prepares the scene by controlling guest selection, props, decor, liquor flow, and the like, his chief role is conversational manager. Conversation management becomes especially important in heterogeneous groups where the host needs to move the party beyond a superficial level so that the participants can obtain some degree of intimacy. In this endeavor the host might convince guests that their own experiences are good sociable resources of interest to others. This task becomes logistically more difficult as the size of the party increases. Further complications arise because the larger the group, the lower the common denominator and thus the more trite the conversation.

Riesman, Potter, and Watson also found that with an increase in the equalitarianism between the host and guests at contemporary parties, the guests often help perform hosting functions such as helping to mix drinks, encouraging shy guests to partake in activities, helping to clean up, and so on. They found that the equalitarian principle in contemporary parties also applies to the sexes, and as a result the hosting and subhosting activities are equally divided between the sexes. However, too much equality among party members creates a problem, namely a decrease in the likelihood of novelty or surprise. Hosts often avoid this problem by inviting a stranger or a strange couple. As Riesman, Potter, and Watson put it:

. . . a favorite technique among many hostesses is to look for variety by always including one stranger, or strange couple. Under optimal circumstances, a stranger can serve as a catalyst, allowing people who have become too familiar to each other to see each other in novel ways, as it were through the stranger's eyes.[58]

The trio concluded their article on "The Vanishing Host," by pointing out that artfulness, intimacy, and solidarity can be viewed as serving the maintenance processes for the society, the collectivity, and the individual respectively. Unlike Simmel, who argued that interaction stops being sociable when it departs from the artful play with ideas and shifts to more serious collective or personal concerns, these researchers stress that interaction becomes less sociable if restricted to only one of these concerns. Riesman, Potter, and Watson believe that skill in sociability requires the ability to vacilate between society, the collectivity, and the individual all the while demonstrating how they are connected with one another. Thus by focusing on the artfulness of the conversation in order to elicit the unique yet sociably connective attributes of all his guests, the host performs one of his major functions, namely, seeing to it that the guests interweave these three entities in their conversation. This of course may not always be

[58] *Ibid.*, p. 26. Using a stranger to supply a party with an element of the novel and unusual was a fad a few years ago when one could rent a hippie for one's party.

possible because of the particular occasion, composition of the guests, or some other reason. In such cases sociability may be committed to only one of its multiple facets.

BAR SOCIABILITY

Although much of the literature on public drinking establishments emphasizes that the primary purpose of such places is sociability and not drinking per se, only Cavan has made bar sociability and bar behavior a key focus of study.[59] Because of her intensive work in this area and because of the similarities between bar and after-hours club settings, we draw heavily from her work—especially her treatments of bar sociability, bar rituals and ceremonies, and permissible behavior and "normal trouble."

In a study of approximately one hundred bars in San Francisco, Cavan empirically supports many of Simmel's observations on sociability and many of Huizinga's notations on play.[60] She found that public drinking establishments are open regions; all present have the right to engage others, knowns or unknowns, in conversational interaction, while at the same time they themselves must be open to sociability overtures. Because sociability is the most general rule in all bars (regardless of the class of patrons or type of bar) and because all groups or individuals are open to encounters at any time, it is difficult for patrons to sustain any one social encounter without interruption for a long period of time. Sustaining encounters is a problem also because any one patron may terminate an encounter at any time. Cavan found that bar encounters may be terminated in several ways such as terminating eye contact, creating a lull in the conversation, closing in a ceremonial fashion (e.g., "see you around," "see you later,"), or moving away from the encounter site.

In public bar settings Cavan found that all patrons were social equals; little deference was paid to outside status and prior relationships of patrons. She also noted that the form of bar encounters had an effect on the conversational content; their openness and short duration restricted content to casual and general topics such as the weather, sports, music, gossip, and the like. Conversational restrictions were also reinforced by the fact that an individual's external and very personal attributes were also ex-

[59] Cavan, *Liquor License*.
[60] See the section on "Play Theory."

cluded from the setting. In short, Cavan found that bar talk is inconsequential small talk and as a result facilitates interaction between strangers.

Among other things, Cavan analyzed several rituals common to all bar settings—treating by means of gift drinks and round drinking, greetings, and farewells. She also observed that the latitudes of behavior are much greater in bars than in more serious settings. Bar patrons can engage in a number of improper acts without sanction (e.g., quarreling, exhibiting a great deal of affection, belching, falling asleep, stumbling, singing along with the music, exhibiting marked signs of intoxication, and so on).

Cavan also noted that the standing behavior patterns (the primary patterns of behavior expected to take place) in a bar setting may provide some actors with a way to exploit the scene for personal gain.[61] That is, an actor in a bar setting may conform to the expected overt pattern of behavior, or at least closely conform to it while at the same time engaging in covert activities that would be inappropriate if manifested overtly. An example of this is the bar customer who ostensibly engages in sociability at the bar while surreptitiously making a deal to buy stolen property from a fence. Settings vary both in the kinds of improprieties that can be engaged in covertly and in the consequences resulting from the discovery of improper behavior.

SUMMARY OF SOCIABILITY THEORY

The sociability literature indicates that sociability settings, like other unserious settings, afford people a contrast to the daily routines of everyday work and family life. Sociability research points to a change in the style of sociability from the classical European aristocratic style described by Simmel, to the contemporary urban middle-class American sociability described by Riesman, Potter, and Watson. As the latter point out, this change in style is related to general societal trends, especially to the extension of sociability to a rather heterogeneous (in terms of ethnic composition, education, religion, and the like) group of young middle-class adults and to the increasing bureaucratization of all facets of peoples' lives.

[61] Cavan, *Liquor License*, pp. 6–7.

As a result of these and other trends, the style of sociability has changed. Formerly in the salon style:

1. the guest list was restricted to members of the aristocracy (all had relatively homogeneous backgrounds)
2. the party was well planned in advance
3. the individual was allowed to stand out and "shine"
4. the event was often regarded as something to be savored in remembrance
5. the host focused his attention on the artfulness of the conversation, eliciting the unique yet sociably connectable contributions of his guests
6. the guests often had the opportunity to transcend the here-and-now, to partake in the larger world "out there," by means of vicarious participation in the experiences of other guests at the party.

On the other hand, contemporary middle-class sociability is characterized by:

1. greater heterogeneity in the backgrounds of the guests
2. the host doing little in the way of advance planning for the party (since a successful party can only obtain through the absence of effort—through spontaneity)
3. the host having to perform the subsistence duties (because of the lack of servants) in addition to the hosting duties
4. a stress on the equality of all present (as a result, the guests are more sincere and inconspicuous rather than flamboyant or elegant in their presentational strategies)
5. a stress on the present (as a result, a party is not regarded as something to enjoy in memory at some future time)
6. little attempt to link the party (through vicarious participation of personal experiences of various guests) to the world "out there."

The sociability literature indicates not only the above mentioned differences in party style through time, but also a variation in sociability depending on its context.[62]

The only detailed systematic research on sociability in public drinking places has been done by Cavan. She found sociability to be the most general standing behavior pattern in public drinking

[62] Riesman, Potter and Watson, "Sociability, Permissiveness, and Equality," p. 324.

establishments. Furthermore she noted that treating by means of a gift drink or round drinking was the most general of all bar rituals. Gift drinks were used in a variety of ways, including initiating encounters, apologizing for accidents, and the cooling of heated arguments among patrons. Latitudes of behavior in bars were much greater than those allowed in most conventional settings. Some actors, she noted, use accepted ongoing behavior patterns in a setting to exploit that setting for personal gain. Bar behavior reflects a concern for the here-and-now in a playtime, space-time setting removed and apart from the more consequential serious space-time settings found in the daily routines of everyday life.

Play Theory

In our review of play literature we draw heavily from Huizinga's extensive work on play.[63] Huizinga, though recognizing that play defies exact description because it is a primary element of human experience, postulated six formal characteristics of play: freedom, stepping out of reality, space and time circumscriptions, order, permanency, and secrecy.

Freedom

"First and foremost . . . all play is a voluntary activity. . . . Here we have the first main characteristic of play: that it is free, is in fact freedom."[64] This freedom is also noted by others writing about unserious settings; for example, Riezler stated that play ". . . may be the triumph of freedom. . . ."[65] Riesman, Potter, and Watson noted of modern parties that: "Relaxation of the future-orientation and of the traditional structure of host and guests advances . . . spontaneity and freedom of movement."[66]

---

[63] Johan Huizinga, *Homo Ludens: A Study of the Play-Element in Culture* (Boston: Beacon Press, 1950).

[64] *Ibid.*, pp. 7–8.

[65] Kurt Riezler, "Play and Seriousness," *Journal of Philosophy*, vol. 38, no. 19 (Sept. 1941): 517.

[66] Riesman, Potter and Watson, "Sociability, Permissiveness, and Equality," p. 336.

Cavan, dealing with the unserious, playtime bar setting, documented the freedom of verbal expression and movement allotted patrons. Public bars were found to be open regions where those present (open persons), acquainted or unacquainted, had the right to engage others in conversational interaction.[67] She also found greater freedom in the latitudes of permissible behavior in bars than in more serious settings, i.e., the public drinking place is a setting where people can engage in various self-indulgent and otherwise improper acts. For example, she observed a couple in their mid-thirties seated at a bar: "They had been talking softly and holding hands when we got there, but soon he was fondling her breasts and kissing her—all quite openly."[68]

Thus in contrast to serious behavior settings activities in time-out unserious settings are voluntary; the freedom of initiating (or terminating) interaction is high; and a great deal of freedom is allowed in latitudes of behavior.

STEPPING OUT OF REALITY

Huizinga's second characteristic of play is that play is not "ordinary" or "real" life. It is, rather, a stepping out of reality into a temporary sphere of activity with a disposition of its own. When children play they know that it is only for fun; that they are pretending. This "only pretending" quality of play is recognized in the individual's consciousness as inferior to "seriousness." Nevertheless, the consciousness of play as "only pretend," does not prevent it from proceeding with seriousness, absorption, and dura-

[67] Cavan, *Liquor License*, p. 49.

[68] Cavan, *Liquor License*, p. 71. Unserious behavior, even in a serious setting, is permitted greater latitude than serious behavior. Sharon Pepper, R.N., director of a nursing home in New York and a good friend of one of the authors, conveyed to him some interesting events in the nursing home dealing with the sexual behavior (at the age of the patients defined as unserious behavior—having no consequences beyond the here-and-now) of senior citizens. She stated that unless she wore a heavy girdle she would be full of black and blue marks from the pinches she received from the "dirty old men" in the home. She also mentioned another incident that illustrates that among the aged sexual behavior is treated as unserious. When on one occasion a male orderly walked by a couple in the hall, he noticed that one of the male patients had his hand inside a female patient's dress fondling her breasts. When the orderly remarked to the older man, "Now, now, here, here we are not supposed to do this sort of thing, especially not in the hall," the orderly was met with an irate comment from the woman, "You leave him alone! He knows what he is doing!"

tion. In fact one can play very seriously.[69] Play proceeds in a serious fashion when the players shift their attention from "it doesn't matter if you win or lose, it's how you play the game that counts" to the consequences of the events within the game—or to the outcome of the game.[70] Play therefore loses its unserious nature when it is no longer suspended from reality, i.e., it loses its time-out status when the players view its processes or outcome as having consequences for the then-and-there and not just for the here-and-now.[71]

SPACE AND TIME CIRCUMSCRIPTIONS

Huizinga's third characteristic of play is that it is distinctive from ordinary life both as to locality and duration. Play is secluded

---

[69] Huizinga, *Homo Ludens*, p. 8. Also see Riezler, "Play and Seriousness," p. 511.

[70] Cavan, *Liquor License*, p. 9. The "dozens" is a good example of a game where if one player(s) shifts from the here-and-now behavior (or if not aware he is playing a game) as inconsequential and makes it consequential, the results are often grave. In the words of Alfred Hassler in *Diary of a Self-Made Convict* (Chicago: Regnery, 1954), pp. 126–27:

> There is a "game" some of the boys "play" in here called "playing the dozens." I have no idea what the origin of the name can be, but the idea is that the participants try to make each other mad by hurling epithets. The first one to lose his temper loses the game. I listened in on one, and it stood my hair on end. The "players" vie with each other in combining the most obscene and insulting accusations against not only the opponent himself, but anyone for whose reputation he might conceivably have some regard. Mothers, sisters, wives, children all come under the ban, and the players explore possibilities of degraded behavior, generally sexual, of the most revealing nature.
>
> Quite frequently, both players lose their tempers, and actual fights are not unknown. Occasionally, a man will "play the dozens" with someone who has not experienced it before, and in such case the consequence can be serious. One man was knifed not long ago in just such an affair.

Also see John Dollard "The Dozens: Dialect of Insult," *American Imago*, vol. 1, no. 1 (1939): 3–25; R.F.B. Berdie, "Playing the Dozens," *Journal of Abnormal and Social Psychology*, vol. 42 (1947); Thomas Kochman, " 'Rapping' in the Black Ghetto," *Trans-action* (Feb. 1969): 26–34. The Italians have a game similar to "playing the dozens," called *La Passatella*; for a detailed discussion see Roger Vaillards, *The Law*, trans. Peter Wiles (New York: Bantam Books, 1969). On similar type games, see Bateson and Mead's discussion of teasing, pp. 148–49 in *Balinese Character* (New York: New York Academy of Sciences, 1942) and Robert Graves on cursing contests in India in *The Future of Swearing* (London: Kegan Paul, 1936), pp. 35–40.

[71] See, for example, Riesman, Potter and Watson, "Sociability, Permissiveness, and Equality," p. 338; Cavan, *Liquor License*, p. 238; Riezler, "Play

and limited. It is played out within certain limits of time and space. Play contains its own course and meaning.[72]

This characteristic of play has also been noted by other social scientists. For example, Riesman, Potter, and Watson pointed out the problems that arise as a result of the informal party (a feature of modern America) in which both the secludedness and limitedness of play are relaxed. They give an example of one party studied that proceeded without time limits or formal invitations. A young couple gave an after-dinner party, asking people to "drop in around nine." The invitations were casual and the responses noncommittal; therefore the hosts did not know how many guests would attend or what time to expect them. They waited with a few friends from ten until one when finally a group arrived. During this interim the hosts' embarrassment had been communicated to the earlier guests. The earlier guests, however, were not concerned with the size of the party but did resent the late arrivals for changing the rhythm of the party activities and for making it cumbersome for them to leave at their convenience. Moreover, the hosts were not sure as to whether other guests might arrive. Like the earlier guests, the hosts found it difficult to shift emotional gears to take account of the expectations of the new arrivals.[73]

In his article on "Fun in Games" Goffman made a point to note Bateson's[74] observation that ". . . games place a 'frame' around a spate of immediate events, determining the type of 'sense' that will be accorded everything within the frame."[75] Goffman continued pointing out that the external characteristics that are not permitted to influence behavior in an encounter are determined by the "rules of irrelevance." He suggested that the character of an encounter is based in part upon rulings as to which properties should be considered irrelevant, i.e., out of frame, or not happening. Adhering to these rules is playing fair.

and Seriousness," p. 511; and Erving Goffman, *Encounters: Two Studies in the Sociology of Interaction* (New York: Bobbs-Merrill, 1961), p. 19.

[72] Huizinga, *Homo Ludens*, p. 9.

[73] Riesman, Potter and Watson, "Sociability, Permissiveness, and Equality," pp. 328–29.

[74] Gregory Bateson, "A Theory of Play and Fantasy," in *Psychiatric Research Reports* 2 (American Psychiatric Association, 1955), p. 44.

[75] Goffman, *Encounters*, p. 20.

Irrelevant visible events will be "disattended" and irrelevant private concerns will be kept out of mind.[76]

Goffman points out that it is possible to imagine a gathering where nearly all externally based matters are treated as irrelevant. In actuality, however, he claims that this is difficult to accomplish. Rules of irrelevance are strictly applied but only for the duration of the playing. Or as Riezler puts it:

> An area of playing is isolated by our sovereign whim or by manmade agreement. . . . No chains of causes and effects, means and ends, are to connect the isolated area of play with the real world or ordinary life. If there are still such chains they are disregarded.[77]

ORDER

Huizinga's fourth characteristic of play is that "it creates order, *is* order."[78] That order exists in play is also pointed out by Nelson N. Foote in his article, "Sex as Play."[79] Any kind of play, according to Foote, generates its own morality and values. The enforcement of rules of play is the concern of every player, since without rule observance, play cannot continue. The spoilsport is rejected. The development of rules intrinsic to the game itself, however, does not ensure that they will be the same rules outsiders would like to impose.

In addition to the above four characteristics of play, Huizinga noted two other sometime characteristics of play—permanency and secrecy.

PERMANENCY

Huizinga stated that members of "play communities," because of their intimate contact, have a tendency to become permanent even after play has ceased. Of course, not every game or party leads to the founding of a club. "But the feeling of being 'apart

---

[76] *Ibid.*, p. 25.

[77] Riezler, "Play and Seriousness," p. 511.

[78] Huizinga, *Homo Ludens*, p. 10.

[79] Nelson N. Foote, "Sex as Play," *Social Problems*, vol. 1, no. 4 (April 1954), pp. 159–63.

together' in an exceptional situation, of sharing something important, of mutually withdrawing from the rest of the world and rejecting the usual norms, retains its magic beyond the duration of the individual game."[80]

Examples of play groups becoming permanent or semipermanent are numerous. These play groups range all the way from groups or aggregates whose members come together occasionally for play purposes (e.g., card clubs, poker parties, swinging couples, group sex parties, rent parties, juking parties, TGIF parties) to those whose members' life style revolves heavily around play activities (e.g., those members of the "jet set" or "golden people" who are fulltime playboys or playgirls and many groups or members within the adolescent drug culture such as the "cats," the "mellow dudes," and the "pot heads" to mention a few).[81] The "cats" described in Finestone's article on "Cats, Kicks and Color," are an excellent example of a social type which rejects the work and familial routines of everyday life in favor of a more expressive, present oriented life style found in play activities. As Finestone puts it: ". . . the concept of play indicates accurately the type of expressive social movement which receives its embodiment in the cat."[82]

SECRECY

With respect to the second sometime characteristic of play, secrecy, Huizinga noted that the exceptional position of play is most significantly illustrated by the fact that we love to encompass it with a feeling of secrecy. Even for children the charm of play is intensified by making it a secret. "This is for *us*, not for the others."[83]

Although today a majority of public drinking establishments are not secret settings, during prohibition the speakeasies were (as their name implies) secret or at least semisecret public drinking establishments. In their study of *Middletown in Transition*,

---

[80] Huizinga, *Homo Ludens*, p. 12.

[81] Harold Finestone, "Cats, Kicks and Color," *Social Problems*, vol. 5, no. 1 (July 1957): 3–13; and, Alan G. Sutter, "Worlds of Drug Use on the Street Scene," in *Delinquency, Crime, and Social Process*, ed. Donald Cressey and David H. Ward (New York: Harper and Row, 1969), pp. 802–29.

[82] Finestone, "Cats, Kicks and Color," p. 8.

[83] Huizinga, *Homo Ludens*, p. 12.

Robert and Helen Lynd quoted an article on the city's "speaks" in the Muncie afternoon newspaper (April, 1933). The article briefly describes these illegal public drinking establishments and how they solved their problem of visibility.

> The very conditions [the strength of the W.C.T.U., Anti-Saloon League, and the churches] that made prohibition enforcement more vigorous in [this state] than perhaps in any other state, have molded local drinking houses into a veritable institution. Under such conditions, any great investment in a drinking establishment was not a thing to be seriously considered. To survive, those who sold drinks by the glass perforce had to avoid display of any kind. . . . These difficulties made [Middletown's] speakeasies what they are today—private homes to all appearances.
> . . . Virtually all of Middletown's liquor sellers live in unpretentious homes in the poorer sections of the city. . . . Most of these houses have no more than three rooms in which drinks are served. [Everybody is introduced by the host to everyone else present, the story went on to recount, with the result that] the shell of eternal suspicion which surrounds most persons in their business relations sloughs away when they enter the portals of the liquor houses. The atmosphere is one of genuine friendliness.
> . . . Except for the difference in the size of the houses, one Middletown drinking place can scarcely be distinguished from another. All have a front room furnished with overstuffed furniture. Conversation is sprightly, but somewhat subdued. Close harmony is banned unless the house is in a very isolated location. Each place has a regular clientele. Everyone knows everyone else. And the houses move to a new location every few weeks as a precaution.[84]

After-hours clubs today, like the "speaks" of yesterday, have the problem of retaining a low visibility profile in order to remain secret.

Play Theory Summary

In summary, the literature on play indicates that although time-out, unserious, playtime settings are orderly, behavior is expected to be free and independent from reality (for the here-and-

---

[84] From the Muncie, Indiana afternoon newspaper, April, 1933, as quoted in Robert S. Lynd and Helen M. Lynd, *Middletown in Transition* (New York: Harcourt, Brace, 1937), pp. 273–74.

now), noncommittal and inconsequential, apart from serious life in locality, and limited in duration. Thus time-out playtime settings are festive occasions where one is supposed to exhibit intimate, sincere, spontaneous, expressive behavior in order to have fun, relax, and enjoy oneself. Furthermore, not only do work groups and familial groups play, but many play groups have a tendency to form permanent groups even after play has ceased. Permanent as well as temporary play groups oftentimes surround themselves with an aura of secrecy.

Conclusions and Implications for the Rendezvous

The literature review on time-out, unserious settings similar to the Rendezvous called our attention to two general transsituational standing behavior patterns found in such settings: sociability and play. Because sociability and play concur and are not mutually exclusive in reality, we combine them for heuristic reasons, and extrapolate from the literature the more specific, prevalent, and recurring characteristics of the two in combination. These are:

1. *freedom*, both in initiating and terminating interaction and in terms of the latitudes of behavior permissible
2. *equality*, in that all actors are supposed to act as if all are equal in status and thus open for encounters
3. *novelty*, the anticipation that something unusual or out of the ordinary will probably occur
4. *stepping out of the real world* into a play world where behavior is autonomous and consequential only for the here-and-now
5. *space and time circumscriptions*, i.e., behavior is limited in both location and duration
6. *order*, which though more problematic here than in more conventional settings, is generated by actors in their behavioral routines
7. *permanency*, which refers to the sometime anticipation of actors that their play group will endure over time
8. *secrecy*, i.e., an air of secrecy may obtain among members

within such a setting demarcating their setting and their membership.

Although several bar studies deal with one or more of the above eight characteristics, no in-depth systematic study incorporates all of them. As member participants prior to the study and as participant observers throughout the study, we discovered that the Rendezvous setting was a time-out, unserious behavior setting where sociability and play were expected to occur as a matter of course and without question. The literature afforded us with the above eight specific transsituational characteristics with which to analyze sociability and play in the Rendezvous' various subsettings.

Though sociability and play were found to be the most general standing behavior patterns in all drinking establishments, the bar literature disclosed considerable variation in drinking places with respect to ecological location, use, characteristics of patrons, space-time properties, goods and services, rhetoric, and history.[85] Unfortunately, we did not find any study that systematically analyzed one or more public drinking establishments or after-hours clubs along all these dimensions. Because the literature on public drinking places showed variation in ecological location, use, characteristics of patrons, space-time properties, rhetoric, and goods and services, we figured that after-hours clubs might also vary along these dimensions.

We reasoned that studying the Rendezvous in terms of the similarities and differences found in public drinking establishments (kindred settings) would answer our basic sociological questions. What is an after-hours club? How is such a place possible? What goes on in such a setting? What are the consequences of these goings-on? Who goes there? When? To do what with whom? Where in the setting? Furthermore, we reckoned that an examination of these features in the Rendezvous would enable us to compare and contrast our case study with other drinking establishments. This would make possible comparisons between our setting and future studies of after-hours clubs.

---

[85] Variations in the history of public drinking places is perhaps best documented in popular articles about bars and night clubs. See, for example, Peter Benchley, "Five In Spots For the Midnight Chic," *The New York Times Magazine* (November 8, 1970), pp. 25–26, 117–22.

Chapter 3

THEORETICAL
ORIENTATION

Introduction

A REVIEW OF THE LITERATURE produced no answers to our basic
sociological questions about after-hours clubs per se. Moreover,
studies of similar unserious, time-out settings (parties, bars, and
the like) did not deal with these sociological questions in an in-
depth systematic manner, though they alerted us to some transsituational similarities and differences to examine in the Rendezvous.

The decision to conduct a case study on one specific behavior
setting, the Rendezvous, with respect to the sociological questions
led us to the selection of two complementary orientations: microsocial ecology and symbolic interactionism. In combination these
two approaches broaden our analysis to include (1) the environ-
ment-overt behavior milieu, (2) the covert behavior patterns, and
(3) how the actors, through the use of symbols, communicate to
one another social meanings and a common definition of the
situation they themselves generate, negotiate, and maintain. Similarities in these two approaches make their integration possible;
both approaches concentrate on answering many of the same
fundamental questions. The behavior setting approach (social
ecology) focuses much of its research on "*what* takes place,

50

where it takes place, and *when* it takes place."[1] If the *who* question is added, the list is similar to the who, what, when, and where used by McCall and Simmons in their study of *Identities and Interactions*. McCall and Simmons explain their reason for concentrating on these four variables: "We have chosen to focus upon these four w's for two principle reasons: (1) empirically, they are fairly clear-cut, yet (2) they are also of human importance to ordinary individuals."[2]

By drawing selectivity from two theoretical frames of reference: microsocial ecology (Barker, Gump, Moos, Wicker, Cavan, Ball,[3] and others) and symbolic interactionism (Mead, W. I. Thomas, Goffman, Blumer, McCannell, McCall and Simmons,[4] and

[1] K. H. Craik, "Environmental Psychology," in *New Directions in Psychology*, ed. K. H. Craik et al., vol. 4 (New York: Holt, Rinehart and Winston, 1970), p. 24. We do not mean to imply that behavior setting researchers do not or are not interested in who occupies settings; it is just that they stress the what, where, and when more. Also see David Riesman, Robert J. Potter, and Jeanne Watson, "The Vanishing Host," *Human Organization*, vol. 19, no. 1 (Spring 1960): 17–27.

[2] George J. McCall and J. L. Simmons, *Identities and Interactions* (New York: Free Press, 1966).

[3] See, for example, Roger G. Barker, *Ecological Psychology: Concepts and Methods for Studying the Environment of Human Behavior* (Stanford, Cal.: Stanford University Press, 1968); Paul V. Gump, "The Behavior Setting: A Promising Unit for Environmental Designers," in *Issues in Social Ecology: Human Milieus*, ed. Rudolf H. Moos and Paul M. Insel (Palo Alto, Cal.: National Press Books, 1974), pp. 267–75; Rudolf H. Moos, "Systems for the Assessment and Classification of Human Environments: An Overview," in *Issues in Social Ecology: Human Milieus*, pp. 5–28; Allan W. Wicker, "Processes Which Mediate Behavior-Environment Congruence, in *Issues in Social Ecology: Human Milieus*, pp. 598–615; Sherri Cavan, *Liquor License: An Ethnography of Bar Behavior* (Chicago: Aldine, 1966); Donald W. Ball, "An Abortion Clinic Ethnography," *Social Problems*, vol. 14, no. 3 (Winter 1967): 293–301; and Donald W. Ball, *Microecology: Social Situations and Intimate Space* (New York: Bobbs-Merrill, 1973).

[4] See, for example, George Herbert Mead, *Mind, Self and Society*, ed. Charles W. Morris (Chicago: University of Chicago Press, 1934); William I. Thomas, *The Unadjusted Girl* (Boston: Little, Brown, 1923); Erving Goffman, *The Presentation of Self in Everyday Life* (Garden City, New York: Doubleday, 1959); Erving Goffman, *Relations in Public: Microstudies of the Public Order* (New York: Basic Books, 1971); Herbert Blumer, *Symbolic Interactionism: Perspective and Method* (Englewood Cliffs, N.J.: Prentice-Hall, 1969); Dean McCannell, "Staged Authenticity: Arrangements of Social Space in Tourist Settings," *American Journal of Sociology*, vol. 79, no. 3 (Nov. 1973): 589–603; and George J. McCall and J. L. Simmons, *Identities and Interactions*.

others), we combine two levels of analysis—behavior in the Rendezvous and the social meanings in the setting.

The Behavior Setting Approach

The social ecologists have, for analytical purposes, divided the behavior setting (their basic unit of observation) into three components: (1) the nonbehavioral factors of milieu and time, (2) the standing patterns of behavior, and (3) the relationship or degree of "fit" (synomorphy) between the nonbehavioral elements and the standing behavior patterns.[5] The nonbehavioral elements include a space or bounded area, physical objects, areas or sub-settings within the general space, and temporal sequences at which events occur. The standing behavior patterns are composed of the overt, stable, recurring, taken-for-granted activities that occur as a matter of course within a behavior setting. The relationship between the behavioral and nonbehavioral elements is important because both the milieu and the temporal boundaries are circumjacent to the standing behavior pattern. Because of this close spatial proximity, the degree of "fit" or the synomorphy between the behavior and the physical environment has become an important focus for those studying behavior settings. This fit is of interest and use to designers of behavior settings (e.g., producers, choreographers, architects, interior decorators, impresarios, and so on) because they orchestrate the milieu—i.e., they create and arrange a setting and in some cases manipulate it over time as they see fit. For example, the architect creates a church building; the final outcome is worshipping in that building. As Gump points out:

> The milieu and the standing patterns of behavior, through the synomorphy that weds them, form the final environmental unit. The designer does not design the environmental unit, only its milieu. His influence is limited to that which his milieu, through synomorphy, contributes to the final standing-patterns-of-behavior-and-milieu-unit.[6]

[5] Gump, "Behavior Settings" p. 169; also Wicker, "Processes that Mediate Behavior-Environment Congruence," p. 601.

[6] Gump, "Behavior Settings," p. 270. Also see Barker, *Ecological Psychology*, pp. 29–32.

Barker notes a number of other sources that affect the synomorphy between milieu and behavior, only a few of which reside in the milieu. For example, the milieu can affect standing patterns of behavior through (1) the operation of coercive physical forces (e.g., walls limit behavior) and/or suggestive physical forces (e.g., small decorative fences reroute paths); (2) physiological processes (e.g., the need to sleep controls behavior); (3) physiognomic perception (flat open yards encourage people to run; small enclosed areas foster social grouping). Although these milieu sources mold behavior to its shape or quality, other nonmilieu sources also affecting a setting's final milieu-behavior unit include (1) social forces (e.g., authority or sanctions); (2) learning (e.g., neophytes are taught how to use a setting); (3) imitation tendencies (e.g., the desire of people to act like others); (4) the fact that behavior can mold the milieu to create synomorphy (e.g., actors in a setting may rearrange the furniture); and (5) the fact that settings select persons and vice versa (e.g., prohibitionists stay away from bars).[7] In short, we are not positing a milieu deterministic model because, as Gump points out:

> To a large degree, the relation of an individual's behavior to his milieu is carried by the setting's standing pattern of behavior; the milieu has significant, but far from exclusive, influence upon that behavior pattern.[8]

In his article on "Systems for the Assessment and Classification of Human Environments" Moos points out that the characteristics of the actors inhabiting a particular behavior setting may be considered situational variables because they partially define important characteristics of the setting.[9] Thus if one knows the nature of the actors in a setting, one can better infer the climate and the behavior patterns in that setting. Moos notes a number of important actor characteristics that should be considered in the study of any behavior setting:

1. background characteristics including sex, age, personal experience, skills and abilities
2. external reference characteristics such as race, weight, height, scars, looks

[7] Barker, *Ecological Psychology*, pp. 28–33.
[8] Gump, "Behavior Settings," pp. 28–33.
[9] Moos, "Systems for Assessment and Classification," pp. 5–28.

3. geographic and socioeconomic factors such as rural or urban residence, occupation, income, education
4. family characteristics such as marital status, number of children, number of dependents
5. social participation, number and type of group memberships, and extent of participation.[10]

Because we considered the actors in the Rendezvous to be the most important characteristic of the setting, this study involves an actor typology.

Just as Firey[11] influenced many students of the "traditional" macrohuman ecology approach to include symbols and sentiments in their theoretical model, Ball in his monograph, *Microecology*,[12] implicitly argues that microsocial ecology should be expanded beyond the milieu, overt behavior patterns, and the synomorphy between them. Ball postulates that microecology should include not only the ". . . *relationships between microspace, social actors and their space-related conduct and experience within it* . . ." but also the selves and identities so generated and maintained or altered.[13] We feel that this is a logical extension of the behavior setting approach and therefore include it in our analysis of the Rendezvous.

The Symbolic Interactionism Approach

Ball's extension of the behavior setting approach to include the generation, maintenance, and alteration of the actors' selves and identities led us to incorporate in our theoretical orientation several features of the interaction (especially the symbolic interactionism) approach. That is, we incorporate much of the symbolic nature of human interaction into our study of the Rendezvous. This includes both the symbolic nature of the actors on the scene and the rhetoric employed by the Rendezvous in order

---

[10] *Ibid.*, p. 13.

[11] Walter Firey, "Symbols and Sentiments as Ecological Variables," *American Sociological Review*, vol. 10, no. 2 (April 1945): 140–48.

[12] Ball, *Microecology*.

[13] *Ibid.*, p. 30.

to define the situation or performance for the audience. Ball defines a rhetoric as:

> . . . a vocabulary of specific purpose; that is to say, . . . a limited set of symbols functioning to communicate a particular set of meanings, directed and organized toward the representation of a specific image or impression. Such vocabularies are not only verbal but also include visual symbols such as objects, gestures, emblems, and the like.[14]

In his study of an abortion clinic Ball examined how the clinic through impression management presented to the actors a particular definition of the setting. This was accomplished by the manipulation of the various elements of the clinic's front, namely its:

> . . . (1) *setting*, the spatial/physical background items of props and scenery in the immediate area of the interaction, (2) *appearance*, the sign-vehicles expressing the performer's social status or type, and (3) those expressions that warn of a performer's demeanor, mood, and the like, that is *manner*.[15]

Thus by employing Goffman's concept of front and its constituent characteristics, Ball was able to identify the central dimensions and themes of the abortion clinic's presentational strategies. In this study we examine the presentational strategies that the Rendezvous employees (primarily the owner-manager) use in order to present to the actors the type of setting the club desires to project.

In addition to studying the purely overt objective behavior of the actors on the scene, we broaden our theoretical orientation to include the symbolic nature or more subjective interpretations associated with the expected overt behavior patterns. Our study draws heavily from the symbolic interactionism approach in that we stress those meanings that are socially created, maintained, and negotiated in order for the actors in the Rendezvous to present, sustain, and constantly update a common definition of a dynamic and rapidly changing scene.

Blumer has summarized the three major premises of symbolic

[14] Donald W. Ball, "Self and Identity in the Context of Deviance: The Case of Criminal Abortion," in *Theoretical Perspectives on Deviance*, ed. Robert A. Scott and Jack D. Douglas (New York: Basic Books, 1972), p. 170.
[15] *Ibid.*, p. 171.

interactionism. The first premise states that ". . . human beings act toward things on the basis of meanings that the things have for them."[16] By things Blumer means everything that people may note in their world, i.e., physical objects, social objects, and abstract objects. The second premise of symbolic interactionism is that the meaning of things arises from the social interaction of individuals with one another. The third premise states that social meanings are ". . . handled in, and modified through, an interpretative process used by the person in dealing with the things he encounters."[17]

From this perspective our study is concerned with the underlying meanings of the overt (and covert) behavior patterns exhibited by the actors in the Rendezvous, and how through their behavior they communicate these meanings to one another in order to create, maintain, and negotiate a common definition of the situation. We make five assumptions for this study. First, we assume that behavior is self-directed and observable at two levels, the symbolic and the interactional (or behavioral). Second, it is assumed that the actors (both patrons and employees) have social definitions of the situation that are, at least in part, evidenced by their conduct, and vice versa, i.e., that the actors' conduct will in part reflect their definition of the situation. Our third assumption is that actors in a behavior setting develop and possess rationalizations for their behavior in order to make that behavior presentable to themselves and to others. The fourth assumption is that actors in a setting through their behavior constantly present that setting to one another as the type of setting they take it to be. We also assume that actors in a behavior setting have a concrete interest at hand. By interest at hand we mean a behavior setting motivational focus ". . . which determines, in a specific situation, a person's definition of the situation and his particular objective, purpose, or other guideline of conduct."[18]

Incorporating the actors' views, interpretations, and reactions to the scene also helps us to determine to what extent the actors use the overt behavior patterns to mask any covert behavior they may be engaging in. Furthermore, combining features of the be-

[16] Blumer, *Symbolic Interactionism*, p. 2.

[17] *Ibid.*

[18] Alfred Schutz, *On Phenomenology and Social Relations*, ed. Helmut R. Wagner (Chicago: University of Chicago Press, 1970), p. 319.

havior setting and symbolic interactionism approaches[19] enables us to examine the extent to which the overt behavior patterns coincide with the expected or prescribed behavior patterns of our setting.

The Focus of This Study

Using the behavior setting as our unit of observation and incorporating several compatible features of the symbolic interactionism approach in order to answer the basic sociological questions posed, we concentrated on the following features of the Rendezvous setting.[20]

1. Entrance procedures: approach to the setting, biographical prerequisites, personal front requirements, screening process.
2. Rhetoric and space-time properties: the location of the club; the ecological arrangement of the building, subsettings, furniture, ornaments, and so on; the temporal sequences within the setting and subsettings; the type of image or impressions that the management attempts to create, present, and maintain to the actors; the goodness of fit between the milieu and the ongoing activities.
3. Use and interests at hand: the use that various actors make of the setting and its different subsettings; subsetting constraints on an actors' behavior; how actors' interest at hand influences their choice of subsetting; how actors with hidden agendas utilize the setting.
4. Standing behavior patterns: overt and covert stable, recurring, taken-for-granted activities that are expected to occur as a matter of course in the setting, and the degree of fit between them and the milieu.
5. The form and content of encounters and verbal exchanges among actors within the club's subsettings; i.e., initiations, supports, terminations, and conventional subject matter.
6. Latitudes of behavior: kinds of disruptive behavior tolerated in

[19] For a similar approach see James B. Cowie and Julian B. Roebuck, *An Ethnography of a Chiropractic Clinic: Definitions of a Deviant Situation* (New York: Free Press, 1975).

[20] What is an after-hours club? How is such a place possible? What goes on in such a setting? What are the consequences of these going's on? Who goes there? When? To do what with whom? Where in the setting?

the setting; remedial measures for interactional offenses; kinds of sanctions imposed for various types of violations. Under what conditions were what actors sanctioned by whom for what, when, and where?

7. Ground rules related to proper behavior, minor improprieties, and serious violations.

8. Typology of actors in the setting: their ascribed and achieved characteristics, their identities and perspectives, and their behavior on the scene.

Chapter 4

METHODOLOGY

Introduction

THE SENIOR RESEARCHER, initially a member participant of the Rendezvous, personally knew a number of club employees and patrons because of social contacts in and outside the club over periods ranging up to eighteen years preceding this study. While employed in a local correctional institution, he became a friend and confidant of the club's owner-manager, who was then serving a brief penal term. At intermittent intervals as a local university student, university instructor, parole officer, prison employee, and community field researcher, he interacted with many club patrons and employees in a variety of social contexts. Many patrons were known in gambling and sporting circles, dating situations, parties, and also from bar, restaurant, and night club encounters. As an aficionado of jazz music and sometime empathetic case worker among and researcher of an assortment of deviants and criminals, he became a trusted friend of musicians and bar habitués, some of whom were Rendezvous patrons and employees. He lived within four blocks of the club for a period of two years preceding the present research while engaged in a participant observation study of professional gamblers and criminal fences. Finally, in Psathas' terms, an insider, he visited in the homes of several patrons.[1]

This researcher had often been involved in the everyday lives of

[1] George Psathas, "Ethnomethods and Phenomenology," *Social Research*, vol. 35, no. 3 (Sept. 1968): 500–20.

many of the individuals he was to study and thereby was provided with inside information about them, a chance to view their behavior in process, a knowledge of the varying problematic situations confronting them, and an opportunity to understand the common sense meanings of their everyday language and activities. In all, he was a member of the club for about ten years and had established rapport with all the club's employees and many of its patrons prior to the study.

During the last two years of the initial researcher's club affiliations, he was joined by a second sociologist (who had only brief exposure to the club as a member participant) and both moved from the role of member participants to that of secret researchers, while at the same time retaining the role of hip squares as a cover. This change in purpose at hand entailed a change in stance. Previously the Rendezvous offered itself (and was conceived of) as a practical theater of action, a place to have a good time, and a setting with taken-for-granted features "out there." Now that the club was to be studied as a natural setting in everyday life, the researchers moved from a native's position similar to Husserl's "natural stance" to a theoretic stance and with past and current knowledge at hand began to retrospectively reconstruct the Rendezvous setting in such a way that its members as well as outsiders could recognize and better understand it.[2]

Because our aim was to concentrate on both the dynamic and structural features of the Rendezvous setting, two primary methodologies were triangulated—participant observation and interviewing. Initially participant observation was employed permitting the study of primary or first order data in flux.[3] As Ball, in his "An Abortion Clinic Ethnography," noted, the study of deviant behavior (regardless of how it is defined) has long suffered from a lack of primary data.[4] Most deviant behavior studies have depended upon data gathered and removed from the actual social phenomena. By themselves, official statistics (from various sources) and self-reports by participants removed from the behavior setting do not represent an unbiased sample of actors,

[2] For a discussion of the natural and theoretic stance see Jack D. Douglas, *Introduction to Sociology: Situations and Structures* (New York: Free Press, 1973), pp. 104–15.

[3] Norman K. Denzin, *The Research Act: A Theoretical Introduction to Sociological Methods* (Chicago: Aldine, 1970), p. 298.

[4] Donald W. Ball, "Abortion Clinic."

actions, or social organization.[5] Approaches similar to those advocated by Ball, Becker and Greer, Blumer, Cavan, Denzin, Douglas, and Goffman represent an alternative method for studying deviance.[6] Ball, along with the above and other scholars, proposes that we go ". . . directly to unconventional actors and their subcultures; it is only with such procedures that the natural context of deviance can be studied without the skewedness typical of the usual sources of data."[7] We follow this general approach, which is a direct outgrowth of the Chicago school of symbolic interactionism.

In our participant observations of the Rendezvous we concentrated primarily on collecting data for all eight of the study foci derived from the theoretical orientation, i.e., entrance procedures, rhetoric and space-time properties, standing behavior patterns, ground rules, nature of encounters, latitudes of behavior, use and interest at hand, typology of actors in the setting. Near the end of the participant observation period indepth interviews were conducted with several patrons and employees outside the setting in order to (1) obtain additional data on the more invariant and stable features (structural) of the Rendezvous,[8] (2) assess our participant observation reconstruction of the Rendezvous scene using native informants, (3) observe Rendezvous actors in another social context (in home environment), and (4) triangulate methodologies and data sources.[9] This complementary methodology yielded additional data on all eight focal points of the study—particularly on use, interests at hand, and the typology of actors.

[5] For an excellent discussion of the limitations of official statistics as a data source, see Jack D. Douglas, *American Social Order: Social Rules in a Pluralistic Society* (New York: Free Press, 1971), especially Chapters 3 and 4, pp. 42–132.

[6] See, for example, Ball, "Abortion Clinic"; Howard S. Becker and Blanche Greer, "Participant Observation: The Analysis of Quantitative Field Data," in *Human Organization Research*, eds. Richard Adams and Jack J. Preiss (Homewood, Ill.: Richard Irwin, 1960), Herbert Blumer, *Symbolic Interactionism: Perspective and Method* (Englewood Cliffs, N.J.: Prentice-Hall, 1969); Sherri Cavan, *Liquor License: An Ethnography of Bar Behavior* (Chicago: Aldine, 1966); Denzin, *The Research Act*; Douglas, *American Social Order*; Erving Goffman, *The Presentation of Self in Everyday Life* (New York: Doubleday Anchor Books, 1959).

[7] Ball, "Abortion Clinic," p. 293.

[8] Denzin, *The Research Act*, p. 298.

[9] See Norman K. Denzin, "The Logic of Naturalistic Inquiry," *Social Forces*, vol. 50, no. 2 (Dec. 1971): 166–82 and Denzin, *The Research Act*, pp. 297–313.

Participant Observation

"COVER" AND TIME SEQUENCE

Two sociologists collaborated in order to obtain participant observation data on the aforementioned eight focal areas of the study.[10] Prior to and for a year and six months after the researchers moved from the role of club members ("natives") to the role of secret researchers, the owner-manager, assistant manager, and five key informants were the only other actors on the scene who knew about the study. These informants cooperated throughout the project and in fact facilitated all research endeavors. The owner-manager's and assistant manager's expressed, open friendship toward the researchers while they were in the club served as an enabling research mechanism.

As "rounded-off hip squares" (safe, regular attending squares) the researchers were able to gather participant observation data on the club for a period of two years during which time at least one sociologist was in attendance at least one morning every three weeks. Attending during different days of the week (except Monday nights when the Rendezvous was closed) and frequently remaining until closing permitted coverage at various time spans within each subsetting (with a few exceptions) for each operating day.

STRATEGY

The researchers attended the club together, separately, as solos, and with a wide variety of patron types (males and females). Once the theoretic stance was assumed both recorded separately

[10] The participant observation approach for this study was similar to that advocated by Severyn T. Bruyn, *The Human Perspective in Sociology: The Methodology of Participant Observation* (Englewood Cliffs, N.J.: Prentice-Hall, 1966), especially Chapter 7, pp. 198–253. Also see Jack D. Douglas, ed., *Observation of Deviance* (New York: Random House, Inc., 1970); Jack D. Douglas, ed., *Research on Deviance* (New York: Random House, Inc., 1972); and William J. Filstead, ed., *Qualitative Methodology: Firsthand Involvement with the Social World* (Chicago: Markham Publishing Company, 1970) and William F. Whyte, *Street Corner Society* (2nd ed.) (Chicago: University of Chicago Press, 1955).

extensive and detailed notes on club events within their temporal, spatial, and social contexts, and on who did what, when, where, and with whom. Both also recorded (1) the natives' (actors') definitions and explanations of club events and (2) their own club experiences. In observing club events and actors' behaviors (whenever possible) the events which preceded and followed these events and the behaviors and explanations of their meanings by participants and bystanders before, during, and after their occurrence were noted. Research notes were written within twenty-four hours after departure from the Rendezvous. Frequently, notes had to be jotted down surreptitiously while on the scene—on napkins, match books, personal identification cards, miscellaneous scraps of paper. This necessitated the reconstruction of many of our quotations from such notes and from reports written after each visit. We were careful in the reconstructions to get the words, substance, and tone, of the conversations as close to the original as possible.

Data Sources and Triangulation

Our research notes were based on covert observations about club happenings (things said and done) while (1) participating with various types of actors in a variety of club activities (i.e., chatting, joking, round drinking, dancing, flirting, and engaging in the pickup routine at the bar; drinking, eating, conversing, listening to music, engaging in heterosexual encounters, and so on at the tables; drinking, eating, negotiating, and romancing in the booths; talking and drinking with the owner-manager in his private office); (2) observing as bystanders or spectators the behavior of other actors in various subsettings (e.g., the impromptu acts on the dance floor, the mien of musicians on and off the bandstand, the flirtations of the bar maids and cocktail waitresses with male patrons, the pickup routine at the bar and tables, and so on); (3) listening to and overhearing conversations throughout the club; (4) engaging in lengthy discussions with the owner-manager, the assistant manager, all other employees, and a wide assortment of patrons in and outside the club; and (5) escorting female patrons in and outside the club.[11]

[11] On this procedure see Howard S. Becker and Blanche Greer, "Participant Observation and Interviewing: A Comparison," *Human Organization*, vol. 16, no. 3 (Fall 1957): 28–32.

Throughout the two-year study, the researchers triangulated the participant observation data by continually comparing one another's findings. About once a month these notes were submitted to the owner-manager, the assistant manager, and the other key informants for their critical analysis, i.e., their agreements, disagreements, and suggested additions about our readings of the Rendezvous scene. Any divergencies among these sources were checked by subsequent participant observation updatings and further discussions with the key informants. At this stage few discrepancies were found among these data sources. Ultimate minor divergencies (e.g., demographic characteristics of patrons, outside status of patrons, and so forth) were adjudicated by the owner-manager and assistant manager.

The Interviews

KEY INFORMANTS

The researchers explored the feasibility of the research approach with the owner-manager and the assistant manager over a six-month period prior to the beginning of the study. These sessions included several informal, lengthy (one to two hours) discussions at the Rendezvous during closing hours. Both the owner-manager and the assistant manager agreed to go along with and support the study, and moreover volunteered their services as key informants and special respondents.[12] As key informants and special respondents they supplied us with information relevant to the study's strategy problems. For example, they supplied historical data about the club; detailed the club's operating procedures including the selection and supervision of personnel; rendered biographical data on different kinds of club actors; aided in developing the actors' typology; introduced the observers to club employees and to a variety of patrons; assisted in the selecting, locating, and contacting of interviewees; indicated the club's basic ground rules, sanctioning procedures, rhetoric strategy, entrance procedures, security measures, and patron status hierarchy; re-

[12] For a discussion on key informants and special respondents see Raymond L. Gordon, *Interviewing: Strategy, Techniques and Tactics* (Homewood, Ill.: Dorsey Press, 1969), pp. 106–7.) (This book has an extensive bibliography on interviewing.)

ported the events and the nature of special encounters occurring in the club settings inaccessible to the researchers (e.g., businessmen's booths, private parties in the owner-manager's office); helped interpret the actors' social meanings and behavioral activities in the club. Furthermore, as mentioned earlier, club observations, both verbal and written, were submitted to these informants for their critical comments at one-month intervals throughout the study. They also examined and commented on the accuracy of our interview materials.

The services of five additional key informants and special respondents, three regular patrons (one male night club owner in the city of the Rendezvous' operation, one male musician, and one female entertainer) and two club employees (one barmaid and one cocktail waitress) were also secured three weeks prior to the project with the assistance of the owner-manager and assistant manager. Though not utilized as frequently and as intensively as the first set of key informants, they obtained information pertinent to the goings-on in several inaccessible settings (women patrons' lounge, men and women employees' rooms, private booths, and the owner-manager's private parties); served as validity checks for club observations and interview materials as well as for the other key informants' reports; turned us on to (i.e., facilitated social mobility into) a diversity of club activities, patron types, social encounters, and social cliques; helped us discover and interpret club activities related to hidden agendas and covert behaviors; supplied biographical data on many actors in the setting; helped us to observe and interpret other actors' behaviors in the club (e.g., heterosexual encounters and the pickup routine); helped establish an employee and patron status hierarchy, and so on. Each key informant was asked not to discuss the study with anyone else inside or outside the club. Beyond the necessary discussions about the strategy of the study between the owner-manager and the assistant manager, we are convinced the key informants kept in confidence their contributions to the research project.

REPRESENTATIVE RESPONDENTS

SELECTION PROCEDURES

The owner-manager and the assistant manager in conjunction with the researchers selected thirty patrons and fifteen employees

to be interviewed for the study. These potential interviewees were
selected on the basis of their (1) representativeness of the club actors, (2) confidentiality, and (3) overall knowledge of the Rendezvous scene. Before the interviews started, club observations had disclosed the first-order categories of actor types that are discussed
in the typology of actors section at the end of this chapter. The
interviewees were purposely selected from all of these first-order
categories. Confidentiality refers to the selectors' estimation of the
potential interviewee's willingness and ability to keep quiet about
the research project. Eligible interview candidates were those
patrons and employees who had been on the Rendezvous scene
for at least two years.

Two-hour interview appointments with the forty-five selected
actors were scheduled at their homes by means of telephone, personal Rendezvous contacts, or through and by the owner-manager
and assistant manager. The researchers explained to each of these
candidates that he or she had been observed in the Rendezvous
without his or her knowledge for a two-year period as part of a
study of the Rendezvous. Each was asked to participate in the
interview phase of the still ongoing research project and was personally assured anonymity by the owner-manager, the assistant
manager, and the researchers. Most appeared to be honored and
privileged to be a part of the study. All agreed to be interviewed.
Two-hour interviews were conducted with each of the forty-five
actors over a period of about three months.[13] Because of the
length and nature of the interviews (e.g., open-ended questions
were used), it was necessary to schedule a second two-hour session
with each respondent. The total interviewing period was placed
at about eight months.

Five cases (patrons) were ultimately excluded from our analysis
because they did not make themselves available for the second
two-hour interview session.[14] Procrastination based on a busy daily
round rather than negative feelings toward the interviews or the
interviewers was at issue here. The table below shows a detailed
breakdown of the forty respondents included in our final analysis.

[13] For a discussion of a similar approach to depth interviewing in combina-
tion with (and following) participant observation see James M. Henslin,
"Studying Deviance in Four Settings: Research Experiences with Cabbies,
Suicides, Drug Users, and Abortioners," in *Research on Deviance*, ed. Jack D.
Douglas, pp. 35–70.

[14] These five cases included two night people, two female aides to businessmen, and one call girl.

Number and First Order Category of
Interview Respondents

Type		Number
Employee		
Cocktail Waitress		5
Barmaid		3
Musician		3
Bouncer		1
Lookout Man		1
Women's Patron Lounge Attendant		1
Cook		1
	Employee Total	15
Patron		
Night People		7
Entertainer	(3 males)	
Agent	(1 male)	
Musician	(1 male)	
Night Club Owner	(1 male)	
Bar Owner	(1 male)	
Hip Square	(2 females, 3 males)	5
Party Girl		4
Call Girl		3
Male Thief		3
Female Thief		2
Man on the Take		1
Businessman		0
Female Aide to Businessman		0
	Patron Total	25
	Total for All Actors	40

INTERVIEW SCHEDULE

The interview instrument consisted of five major sections: (1) biographical data, (2) typology, (3) identities and perspectives, (4) club use and behavior in the setting, and (5) unsolicited information.

The biographical data section comprised a mixture of specific structured and unstructured questions about the respondents' ascribed and achieved characteristics, i.e., age, sex, formal education, occupation, social class origin (parents' background), marital status, marital ties, current residence, juvenile delinquency history, criminal history, and deviant behaviors (drug use, alcohol use, criminal companions, sex practices, and the like). Juvenile delinquency and criminal histories were cross-checked with official secondary sources available to the researchers (local police records, juvenile court records, correctional institutional records, F.B.I. Abstract of Criminal Records).

In the typology section the respondents were given a copy of the rough patron and employee classifications (obtained through participant observation and from interviews with key informants), and they were asked to respond critically to these first order categories.[15] Next each respondent was requested to categorize himself or herself within this scheme.

The third section consisted of two parts, identities and perspectives. Identities included both open-ended questions and topics about the respondents' role identities and self-concepts. Role identities were determined by role prominences as stated by respondents, with particular attention given to their self-designated Rendezvous identity. Additional prominent identities were ascertained by such questions as "Who are you? Who else are you? If you had to give yourself only one of these labels, what would it be?" Respondents were then requested to discuss each self-designated identity with respect to the following: the degree of prominence of each role identity, the degree of self and social support they received for each major role identity, the degree of intrinsic and extrinsic gratification they derived from each major role identity, and the personal commitment to and investment in each of their major role identities.

Perspectives referred to life themes, life styles, and world views held by Rendezvous actors and were determined by discussion topics. The topics included personal traits and codes of behavior required by the respondents' peer groups (probes here were primarily directed toward peer groups associated with prominent role identities), general life style (recreational, occupational, familial), and views toward conventional society.

The fourth part, club use and behavior in the setting, consisted of a series of open-ended questions. Examples are: What uses do

[15] For a discussion of first order types vs. constructed types, see Marshall B. Clinard and Richard Quinney, *Criminal Behavior Systems* (2nd ed.) (New York: Holt, Rinehart, and Winston, 1973), pp. 12–13. In brief, first order types are "existential types" or typifications constructed by member participants (natives). As opposed to first order constructs, second order types developed by social scientists are based on their observation of the scene and their theoretic stance.

you make of the Rendezvous? Do you ever use the club for any special or unusual purposes? What do you expect to happen at the Rendezvous as a matter of course? What kinds of people do you expect to meet there? What do you do with different kinds of people there? Do you ever have contacts elsewhere with people you meet at the Rendezvous? If so, what do you do with them outside the club? (For additional questions, see the next section on Data Collection Techniques for the Major Areas of Study).

Unsolicited information, the final part, comprised recording any pertinent knowledge about the Rendezvous setting volunteered by the respondents but not specifically requested in the interview schedule. Toward the end of the interview, the respondents were asked to elaborate retrospectively on their unsolicited reports. Finally, we asked each respondent to tell in his own words what the Rendezvous was all about with respect to his everyday life. After the interview each respondent was asked not to discuss their interview or mention the study to anyone else. To the best of our knowledge, this request was honored.

Data Collection Techniques for Major Areas of Study

ENTRANCE PROCEDURE AND RHETORIC AND SPACE-TIME PROPERTIES

Purposely through time the researchers entered the club in the company of a variety of membership groups—first-timers and regulars (hip squares, party girls, entertainers, male thieves, and so on)—to gain a systematic knowledge of the club's entrance procedures and rhetoric. Particular attention was given to the interaction between those screened and those screening, and the comments of first-timers about their impressions of the club's front. On the basis of observation, interviews with the owner-manager and assistant manager, and detailed measurements a blueprint of the entire physical and ecological layout of the Rendezvous was constructed (see pages 78 and 92). Over time, through participant observation and discussions with key informants, the distribution and flow of actors in the Rendezvous setting were recorded, i.e., the actors' temporal and mobility patterns in each subsetting and among the subsettings.

Through direct observation and participant observation the investigators noted how the management and the employees manipulated elements of the club's rhetoric (its setting, appearance, and manner) to project to the patrons the kind of setting they (the management and the employees) desired it to be. In turn, the patrons' reactions to this attempted impression management were examined, i.e., the patrons' readings, interpretations, and negotiations of the management's projections. In this endeavor particular attention was paid to both the verbal and behavioral responses of all actors toward the presented front.

USE AND INTERESTS AT HAND

In the area of use and interests attention was directed to the uses made of the club and its various subsettings by different kinds of actors over time; how the actors' interests at hand influenced their selection of subsettings; how the subsettings selected actors; and the kinds of behavior (involving hidden agendas) occurring throughout the club. Uses made of the club and its subsettings were determined by the observers' personal use of the club as native member participants, participant observation, discussions with the key informants, and the interviews. Some pertinent interview questions follow: Why do you go to the Rendezvous? Where in the club do you spend most of your time? What do you do in this setting? How much time do you spend in other settings? What do you do in each of these settings? What days do you generally go to the Rendezvous? What time of the morning do you go there? How late do you stay there?

STANDING BEHAVIOR PATTERNS

Two criteria—frequency of occurrence across time and situations and systematic import—were used to determine whether or not a particular unit of behavior such as round drinking, dancing, or joking was part of a standing behavior pattern, in this case sociability. Recurring activities such as dicing for drinks or flirting that were not followed by sanctions and did not disrupt encounter situations or the regular flow of events were defined as taken-for-granted patterns in the setting.[16] Because the literature disclosed that sociability and play are the two primary activity patterns found in legal drinking establishments (i.e., that most of the recurring activities or particular units of behavior in bars comprise a standing pattern of sociability and play), we were interested in determining the presence of these two behavior patterns in the Rendezvous. In this endeavor the behavior patterns in the Rendezvous were examined with respect to the eight indicators of sociability and play derived from the literature (see page 48).

We were also interested in the synomorphy (mesh) between the milieu (rhetoric and physical environment) and the club's patterns of behavior. Data sources for this focal area were derived primarily from participant observation and discussions with the key informants.

The Form and Content of Encounters

We also concentrated on the form and content of both focused encounters and brief, unfocused social contacts. With respect to form we centered on: Who typically initiates encounters with whom? How are encounters generated? (i.e., what are the social cues, rituals, and body language involved?) How are encounters maintained? What degree of closure prevails in ongoing encounters? How long are typical encounters? What procedures do actors utilize in terminating encounters? Regarding content, the focus was on conversational style, topical themes, and the gravity of verbal interchanges. Answers to the preceding questions were derived through and by social participation and encounters with various types of actors in all subsettings (with the exception of the businessmen's booths, the women patrons' lounge, the women employees' room, and the owner-manager's and secretary's offices during private parties). As strategically situated snoopers in the club's subsettings the researchers viewed and listened in on various types of encounters and verbal exchanges among other actors.

---

[16] The strategy here was similar to that of Sherri Cavan, *Liquor License*. Also see Julian B. Roebuck and S. Lee Spray, "The Cocktail Lounge: A Study of Heterosexual Relations in a Public Organization," *American Journal of Sociology*, vol. 72, no. 4 (Jan. 1967): 386–96.

LATITUDES OF BEHAVIOR

The extent to which actors were permitted to deviate from the overt and covert standing patterns of behavior was also observed and noted. The conditions under which actors were sanctioned by whom for what, where, and when were recorded. Interviews with key informants provided an additional source for information about latitudes of behavior.

GROUND RULES

Ground rules of a restrictive and enabling kind accompanying proper behavior, minor improprieties, and serious violations were ascertained by noting the sanctioning and nonsanctioning of behavior, personal experiences of ground rule enforcement, and interviews with key informants (especially the owner-manager and assistant manager), employees, and patrons.[17]

TYPOLOGY OF ACTORS IN THE SETTING

To clarify who comes to the club to engage in what social action with whom, when, and where, and to ascertain the important personal characteristics of club actors (since these characteristics were considered important situational variables for understanding the club's milieu), an actor typology was developed.

The following sequential procedures were employed in developing the typology: (1) First, by participant observation, we noted how actors typed themselves and others in the club. (2) Second, this rough classification was submitted to the seven key informants for their critical comments (at this point some subtypes within the category "Night People" were added). (3) Third, this first order classification (native constructs) was presented to the fifteen employees and twenty-five patrons during their interviews for further critical comments. They accepted the classification and typed themselves within the schema. (4) Fourth, these first order

---

[17] Our definition and use of the term "ground rules" is similar to that of Goffman's as presented in *Relations in Public: Microstudies of the Public Order* (New York: Basic Books, 1971), pp. x–xiii.

categories were explored along three theoretical dimensions. Here we relied heavily on and triangulated data from all our methodologies, i.e., participant observation, key informants, interviews (both information obtained about the respondent himself and information the respondent provided about others in the club), and secondary sources. (5) Finally, our constructed typology was presented to the key informants for a final validity check. Only minor modification, mostly by way of additions along the three dimensions, were necessary.

PATRON TYPES

During tenure in the club as member participants and later as participant observers, we discovered that the actors categorized themselves into several subcategories falling within two general types: patrons and employees. These first order constructs were categorized by the management, the employees, and the patrons themselves into several membership groups (groups assumed to be more or less homogeneous). This labeling process involved several data sources: actors' knowledge about themselves and others in and outside the club; what actors said about themselves, and what others said about them; how actors perceived one another; presentations of self; what actors interacted with whom, when and where in the club; what actors did in the club. The following widely agreed upon categories emerged from this process: hip squares, night people, call girls, party girls, businessmen,[18] female aides to businessmen, male thieves (professional criminals), female thieves (professional criminals), and men on the take.[19] These patron types (based on the actors' first order constructs) were utilized by the actors in: (1) recognizing, designating, and referring to individual patrons; (2) describing and telling stories

[18] The term "businessmen" was used by the actors in the club to refer to organized criminals who were engaged in both illegal and legal business activities.

[19] It should be noted that, unlike employees, it was not possible to type every patron who entered the Rendezvous at one time or another during the research project. This was true for two reasons: (1) a few patrons entered the club only once and then only for a short period of time, and (2) some few patrons although attending several times were not classifiable because other actors could not obtain adequate biographical data on them. In both cases, these "questionable" guests were preliminarily placed in the hip square category.

about individual patrons; and (3) affording club status to individual members.

Employing this first order typology as a base, we developed a constructed typology for such analytical and sociological purposes as to gain a more systematic and broader knowledge of patron types and to better understand the climate of the Rendezvous setting. The first order patron types were studied in relation to three sociological dimensions: (1) achieved and ascribed characteristics; (2) identities and perspectives; and (3) behavior on the scene. The first two dimensions were included to permit an in-depth understanding of who goes to the club. Because one's identity is inextricable from one's behavior, and because we were interested in who does what with whom, when, and where in the club, a behavioral dimension was added. Relying heavily on participant observation, key informants, and interview data each patron category was developed along these three dimensions in order to arrive at our constructed patron typology.

In the first dimension we included age, sex, marital status, education, occupation, social class origin, residence, physical attributes, speech patterns, dress patterns, delinquency history, criminal history, and deviancy history. The second dimension consisted of identities and perspectives as related to life biographies. Identities refer to prominent role identities and self-conceptions relative to subcultural perspectives. Perspectives refer to world view, major life themes, life style, and stances toward conventional and unconventional society.[20]

Behavior on the scene, the third dimension, included time intervals spent in different subsettings; activities engaged in; types of actors interacted with; synomorphy (degree of fit) between actors' behavior, and the physical and symbolic milieu of the setting.

EMPLOYEE TYPES

Utilizing the same method in the classification of employees as that employed for patrons, we noted that the actors in the club

---

[20] Our conception of role identities is similar to that of George J. McCall and J. L. Simmons in their *Identities and Interactions* (New York: Free Press, 1966), pp. 63–193. The use of perspectives parallels that of John Irwin, set forth in his book *The Felon* (Englewood Cliffs, N.J.: Prentice-Hall, 1970), pp. 1–15.

categorized all employees (except the lookout men) according to their work roles in the club. These occupations corresponded to those found in kindred legal settings. Moreover, we found that all the club's employees had worked at similar jobs in legal establishments. Rendezvous employee categories follow: owner-manager, assistant manager, barmaids and cocktail waitresses, jazz musicians, bouncers, lookout men, cook, hatcheck girl, ladies' room attendant, and secretary. Lookout men performed duties outside the club so only the employees and a few patrons were aware of their existence. Thus this category was derived primarily from employee typing. As in the development of the patron classification, each employee category was developed along the same three dimensions.

Chapter 5

RHETORIC, SPACE-TIME PROPERTIES, AND USE

Introduction

THOUGH THE SOCIOLOGICAL QUESTIONS we posed at the outset of the study and the focal areas we examined to answer them are dealt with throughout the text, in this chapter we concentrate primarily on: What is an after-hours club (in this case, the Rendezvous)? What happens when and where in the Rendezvous? The focal areas at issue here are (1) *entrance procedures,* (2) *rhetoric and space-time properties,*[1] and (3) *use and the actors' interests at hand.* (The focal areas of this study are discussed in Chapter 3, pp. 57–58).

[1] For a sociological conceptualization of rhetoric and space-time properties in a natural behavior setting see Donald W. Ball, "An Abortion Clinic Ethnography," *Social Problems,* vol. 14, no. 3 (Winter 1967): 293–301. Like Ball we extend Goffman's delineation of front and its constituents of setting, appearance, and manner, originally a framework for analyzing the presentation of self, to an establishment and its actors. See Erving Goffman, *The Presentation of Self in Everyday Life* (Garden City, New York: Doubleday Anchor, 1959), pp. 22–30. Our format of analysis follows roughly the patterns established by Sherri Cavan in *Liquor License: An Ethnography of Bar Behavior* (Chicago: Aldine, 1966). As explained in the theory section, our analysis also draws from other social psychologists and includes, among other things, a typological dimension.

Entrance Rhetoric: Actors' Introduction to the Rendezvous

The unmarked Rendezvous Club is in a three-story, brick, detached, three-family residence in a quiet, lower-middle-class neighborhood three miles from the city's dominant business district. The location is changing from a residential to a mixed residential-commercial configuration, and the club and its milieu blend with the other surroundings. Patrons come in cabs or on foot from a busy thoroughfare two short blocks away. For security reasons parking facilities are not provided and disembarking from vehicles in front of the club is discouraged. External environs convey the impression of a respectable, safe space configuration. One first-time patron in the company of a group of regulars, while walking to the club, remarked:

This place looks safe . . . you'd never know it was here. I don't see any cop cars or people on the street. Are you sure we can have some fun in here?

Patrons gain entrance by descending wide stone steps to a shielded side entrance framed by a heavily girded door. These accouterments, along with the faint sound of jazz music, communicate expectations of secrecy and unserious activities.

Admission follows the speakeasy routine. The would-be patron, after pushing the buzzer, is observed and screened through a peephole door window by a doorman-bouncer formally dressed in tuxedo. Recognized patrons are promptly admitted to the foyer and then escorted through a closed door ten feet straight ahead that opens into the entrance hall (see Figure 1). At the other end of the entrance hall, a twelve-foot straightway, there is another closed door that opens onto the club's primary theater of action. Hats, coats, wraps, and other personal belongings are deposited with a checkroom girl who occupies a small, open-faced chamber on the left side of the hallway adjacent to the club proper. Male patrons are required to wear coats and ties, and women are ex-

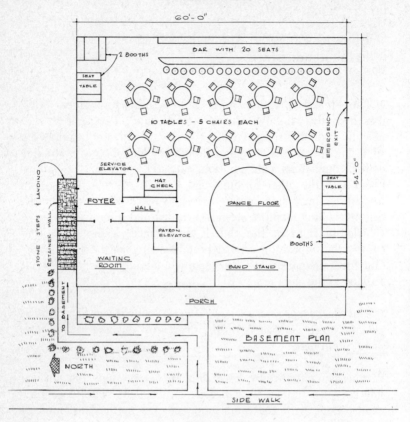

FIGURE 1

pected to be at least semiformally attired.[2] First-timers in the company of known regulars are generally admitted to a waiting room situated to the right of the foyer for further screening. Unknowns not in the company of regular patrons and undesirables are denied entrance and are politely asked to depart from private property.[3] The club's screening chores are made easier because

[2] Occasionally regular esteemed "high rollers" (big spenders) are permitted to enter without ties and some female regulars are permitted dress latitudes.

[3] People under twenty-one, college kids, hippie types, street drug addicts and pushers, notorious and unsuccessful petty and habitual criminals, low-class street thugs and barroom brawlers, fugitives from justice, law enforce-

many potentially undesirable patrons are unaware of the Rendez-vous' existence; many cannot afford the scene; some would not find the scene to their liking; still others know that they would be neither welcomed nor considered respectable (normal, regular, worthy) there.[4]

The decor in the foyer is reminiscent of that found in plush hunting lodges. A tiled foyer measuring approximately 10 by 10 feet and a thick, red-carpeted hallway 5 by 12 feet are embellished with wrought iron light fixtures, mahogany wainscoting, antique weaponry (swords, pistols, and rifles), and arrangements of English and Scottish clan coats-of-arms. A high plastered ceiling with wide mahogany beams and antique gaslight pieces convey a private, clubby atmosphere. The entrance routine, the attire of the doorman and patrons, the spaciousness of the entryway, and the plush, masculine, "aristocratic" decor define for the patron and employee audiences alike a respectable, exclusive, luxurious behavior setting similar to that of some legitimate and prestigious private club settings. Commented Harold, one affluent first-time patron:

I knew I was in a classy place when I saw that doorman in the monkey-suit and all the fancy hardware and that thick carpet. Being with those well-dressed people, I knew somehow it was all together—my kind of place.

The waiting room is a wall-to-wall carpeted salon, furnished with comfortable red leather upholstered sofas and chairs, that serves as a stopover for some patrons en route to the inner club and as a screening site. End tables located beside each chair and sofa provide cigarettes, ashtrays, canapés, and bonbonnières. A serving table with hors d'oeuvres graces the center of the arrange-

---

ment personnel not "on the take," or those not on friendly terms with successful criminals or employees of the club, police informers, and noisy drunks are considered to be undesirables.

[4] For analysis of respectability as a problematic relational category in behavior settings, see Donald W. Ball, "Self and Identity in the Context of Deviance: The Case of Criminal Abortion," in *Theoretical Perspectives on Deviance*, ed. Robert A. Scott and Jack D. Douglas (New York: Basic Books, 1972), pp. 158–86; Ball, "The Problematics of Respectability," in *Deviance and Respectability: The Social Construction of Moral Meanings*, ed. Jack D. Douglas (New York: Basic Books, 1970), pp. 326–71. For example, many people feel embarrassed or out of place in some behavior settings. They may not know how to act, what to say, how to dress, and so on.

ment. Here, under hospitable and pleasant conditions, first-timers in the company of supportive others are courteously questioned about their identity and may be asked to produce identifying biographical materials such as driver's licenses, credit cards, and company identification cards.

According to the management, our observations, and the interview materials, the potential patron's ability to confirm ties with regular patrons or employees of the club marks a crucial biographical test for admission. Actually the "hip front" (including knowledge of the offbeat world, speech, dress, and mien) presented is equally crucial for entry. Those few found unacceptable are told politely that the club is private and that they may not attend at this time—and are then ushered out. Those accepted are ushered through the entrance hall leading to the inner club. Greeting and screening routines are conducted in a quiet and formal but gracious fashion. The management presents a decorous front as if it is presiding over a rite of passage. Voices are somewhat hushed, and the backslapping and noisy hilarity frequently witnessed at the entrances of many unserious settings is discouraged. Quizzical and studied looks are directed upon those patrons who by their exuberant talk and actions make light of the entrance procedure. We noted that these screening cues were usually effective in maintaining a serious entrance procedure.

Thus by a rather sophisticated entrance process an occupationally deviant management and staff consistently and illegally present to a group of "situationally deviant" patrons a "respectable" behavior setting—or more precisely put, the appearance of a respectable setting. Patrons, unlike the staff, have no career interests in the club; however, they are offbeat in terms of the odd-time recreational hours they keep (1:00 A.M. opening time to 7:00 A.M. closing time) and in the company they keep. All inevitably carouse at the club in the presence or company of some secondary deviant types such as call girls and criminals.[5] Though some deviant and criminal collectivities utilize the setting for serious activities, most actors appear to use it most of the time for unserious behavior; and all actors have a vested interest in helping to maintain the club's front as a respectable, unserious behavior

---

[5] Secondary deviants are people who have organized their lives around deviant behavior. They identify themselves as deviant and espouse unconventional values. Edwin M. Lemert, *Human Deviance, Social Problems, and Social Control* (rev. ed.) (Englewood Cliffs, N.J.: Prentice-Hall, 1972).

setting whatever their purpose at hand. As a regular reported during his interview:

Different people go to the Rendezvous for different reasons. They go there one time for one purpose and another time for something else. It all depends on what they're looking for at the time, see? If you want to you can do it all up at one time—like drink, eat, do business, and still get laid. Most people go to have a good time. And whatever you got in mind you act like you're out for just that. You have to put up a respectable front. Otherwise, the place would turn into just another dive, and the police would close it up. If everybody shows a little class, it helps everybody else, understand?

The Bar Subsetting

THE SCENE

Patrons enter and leave the club's action center through the same door, which is situated at the end of the entrance hall. This physical feature provides for security and patron management, as well as for aesthetic effects. One step forward from this widely arched doorway and a scan from left to right provides a panoramic view of the club's internal physical layout, scenery, and activities. Rich mahogany woodwork and simulated marble topped tables, leather upholstery, red wall-to-wall carpeting, simulated gaslight electrical fixtures, pastel hunting prints superimposed on dark paneled walls, and several murals depicting Victorian women in various stages of undress—all depict a risqué, hunting club motif throughout the club couched within a traditionally respectable frame. The ceiling complements that of the foyer and the entrance hall by way of white plaster and mahogany beams.

After entering the main theater of action patrons may choose to go left around the tables to the bar, which is parallel to the east wall of the club and is the focal center of behavior for many actors and the place to see and to be seen. As one regular remarked to another at the bar:

Anyone who is somebody will show here at least once a week. They know where the action is. To be in the swim you gotta see

*and be seen. Look at old Charlie over there with two fine honeys.
Who needs two? Hell, either one could screw him to death in five
minutes. He's just gotta make the scene.*

The 20-stool, parallel bar is a polished, well-lighted, high and
thick, brass trimmed, formidable mahogany structure that offers
the maximal physical and social exposure for social encounters
and the least private seating arrangement in the club. A heavy,
ornate, full-length back-bar mirror crisscrossed at its base by hand
carved, wooden shelves laden with a myriad-colored assortment
of liquor flasks furnishes an elegant optical device that reflects
the entire mise en scène—the posh mahogany-brass-steel-glass bar;
three voluptuous barmaids dressed in flimsy, red micro skirts and
halters, black mesh hose with a red garter belt, and dressy striped
sandals; and fashionably dressed men and women sparkling with
expensive accessories and jewelry.[6] These animate and inanimate
symbols suggest to the actor an unserious, odd-time, sexually stimulating though reputable scene. As one customer remarked to his
comrade at the bar:

Those broads [barmaids] *may as well take that blouse-like thing
off. You can see everything anyway. They come on strong* [talk]
*but nothing here comes cheap. The whole thing looks sexy but
straight. This place looks more legit than many legit places I've
been in.*

Employees and patrons then simultaneously cooperate with
one another to sustain the definition of a respectable club setting.
We noted that patrons typically spoke to and treated the employees as though they (the employees) were legitimate service
workers similar to those employed in plush, legitimate cocktail
lounges, bars, and private clubs. In turn patrons were addressed
and dealt with as worthy (respectable) patrons by the employees.
During a music break, the ensuing remarks were exchanged be-

[6] As Simmel reports, members of some groups express their esthetic excel-
lence by adorning themselves with stylish clothing and jewelry that serve as
symbols of general esteem for themselves and their group. By conservative
standards the club patrons' personal adornments are flamboyant. The men
wear flashy bejeweled rings and accessories, and the womens' decollétages,
coiffures, and jewelry are bold if not avant-garde. See Georg Simmel, *The
Sociology of Georg Simmel*, trans. and ed. Kurt H. Wolff (New York: Free
Press, 1965), pp. 342–44.

tween Jeanne, a garrulous cocktail waitress, standing at the bar
awaiting a drink order and Ted, a musician employee who was
seated next to Buck, one of the observers:

Jeanne: *This place has it all over the Derby. I work there four
nights a week, and it's a drag. This place has class. Well-dressed
customers who don't mind spending money. Important people in
and out of the life. And a boss that pays, and you know, good
working conditions. Besides, I don't get hustled and pawed over
like a bitch. Eveybody at the Derby is on the take or on the make.*

Ted: *Yeah, I know what you mean. I make twice the dough
here that I do in legit joints. The bread is fine, and I don't get
the hassle from the management or the squares that I get at other
gigs. Sometimes it's fun working here because I feel more at home
than out there in that sea of squares. Even the squares here are
half human. But Jeanne* [as he put his arms around her and playfully squeezed her breasts] *I don't buy that hustling bit.*

Jeanne [languidly slipping his embrace]: *Oh Ted, don't put me
on. It's different in here. You know what I mean. But you're right,
people here even smell good.*[7] *And so polite too, but everybody
has a hell of a good time. You know just any ordinary barmaid
or musician couldn't make it here. Those jerks at the Derby would
be wasted here, man. Wasted.* [turning to Buck] *Don't you agree?*

Buck: *You know it.*

SEATING ARRANGEMENT

The lateral seating arrangement at the bar requires that actors
sit abreast of each other. Small, self-contained groups sit along-
side one another, the members on each end tending to turn inward toward the center (bookending) to maintain ongoing encounters without the intrusion of others. Groups of five or more
generally form a bar cluster of three or four seated and several
standing actors. When all bar seats are occupied, male groups
and single males usually stand behind occupied bar stools, one
or two deep, while consuming their drinks; and, though they may

[7] Largey and Watson report that odors, whether real or alleged, are often
used as a basis for conferring a moral identity upon an individual or a group.
See Gale Peter Largey and David Rodney Watson, "Sociology of Odors,"
American Journal of Sociology, vol. 77, no. 6 (May 1972): 1021–34.

move between occupied bar stools in order to purchase drinks, they rarely stand between unknown, seated bar patrons.

Unescorted and escorted women utilize bar seating space in much the same way as men. Though they have equal access to all bar areas and no stigma is attached to them wherever they might position themselves, with or without male or female companions, rarely do they stand, because male patrons insist on giving them seats.

Bar patrons customarily space themselves one or two stools away from people they do not know or those whom they wish to avoid. Three empty bar stools was noted to be the maximum distance over which actors would attempt to initiate and maintain encounters. Actors more than three bar stools away who wish to engage in lengthy conversation move next to one another. This procedure is also the rule should one unknown buy another a drink. In cross-sex encounters that involve physical movement, the obligation for changing location is, with rare exception, the male's.[8]

Several spatial features provide support for bar encounters at the Rendezvous. The close physical proximity of actors to each other, the lack of precise physical boundaries, and the physical mobility (at close range) of actors who move into and out of the bar setting facilitate frequent, brief, and fluid social encounters among those acquainted and unacquainted. Even groups desiring exclusivity are potentially open to conversational approaches from barmaids, cocktail hostesses who stand at the bar awaiting table drink orders, actors who move in and out of the bar, and actors who sit, stand, or move in and about this subsetting. Some actors who move about, in, and out of the setting leave markers (cigarette lighters, cigarettes, money, and so on) on the bar to designate and reserve their seats. In their running conversations with several groups and individuals around the bar these floaters tend to foster and link group encounters between those known and unknown to one another.[9]

[8] This distance for initiating and maintaining encounters and the male's obligation to move confirm Cavan's findings for legal bars. See Cavan, *Liquor License*, pp. 89–95.

[9] For definitions of different types of encounters, see Erving Goffman, *Relations in Public: Microstudies of the Public Order* (New York: Basic Books, 1971), p. 25.

USE

Various collectivities of actors were observed to utilize the bar in the same way and in different ways over time. Many male patrons talk, laugh, and joke with the cheerful, polite, and coquettish barmaids. Such encounters are usually generated in a light and sexy vein, though at times they may digress into earthy direct propositions and parries. The protective barrier of the bar promotes verbal sexual exchanges. Barmaids usually dodge direct, persistent, and serious propositions with verbal "cutoffs" that call for corrective behavior and serve as reminders that the behavior setting is unserious by making a joke of them, changing the conversation, feigning acceptance jokingly, diverting attention to another female, feigning comic disbelief, and the like. The following are some of the overheard replies made by barmaids to various male patrons who attempted to arrange dates after closing hours:

Tiger, you've got to be kidding. Be serious and tell me more about those clowns you played poker with last night.

Sure baby, I'll go with you after we close. You know, that's when I really come on.

Baby, you've got to be kidding. One night with me, and you would never be the same again.

Tiger, I'm just one of the hired help; just a decoration. Why don't you hustle one of those girls over there. The sexy brunette looks like your type.

Groups of well-acquainted males from two to five in number frequently sit with and stand behind each other at the bar to drink and converse. Occasionally they eat, play box-dice for drinks, kid around with the barmaids, seek pickups, or negotiate serious matters. Drinking among male group members usually follows a ritualistic reciprocal gift drink routine called round drinking, i.e., each team member in turn buys a set of drinks for the group.[10] Female patrons usually sit at the bar with their male companions when escorted; when unescorted they typically sit in twosomes or threesomes with pickup purposes in mind.

Patrons utilize this setting as a convenience bar, an accessible

---

[10] For a detailed analysis of round drinking and gift drink rituals, see Cavan, *Liquor License*, pp. 113–32.

place to talk, unwind, and drink during after-work hours; a sexual marketplace, pickup spot; a serious drinking site; a home territory bar, a home away from home; or a temporary hideaway or haven (for those who occasionally prefer a secret and exclusive bar setting). Some patrons come to extend a night's entertainment beyond that originally planned. Still others treat this configuration as a stopover station or rendezvous spot where they await the assembly of other group members. Several types of actors, as is subsequently detailed, may talk shop and negotiate serious matters here.

We noticed that the early morning round of activities at the bar did not vary appreciably from day to day; however, there were some differentials in bar happenings, number of customers present, and type of clientele in attendance throughout each operating day (shift). These variations are described later on, but a few examples for illustrative purposes follow. The bar tends to be more crowded from 2:30 to 4:30 A.M. than at any other time (with seated and standing customers). Groups of revelers who have just closed down legitimate bars and who wish to extend the evening for a few more drinks come early, 2:00 to 2:30 A.M., and leave early, 3:30 to 4:00 A.M. Squares, irregular patrons, prefer weekend attendance, whereas certain types of regulars prefer weekdays. Regulars spend longer periods at the bar than do irregulars—and depart later. Pickup activities and the presence of women at the bar are more in evidence earlier in the morning (1:00 to 4:00 A.M.).

The noise, hilarity, and mobility of the hurly-burly bar setting reaches a peak about 4:30 A.M. during weekdays. After this, things appear to wind down. The crowded bar thins out, pickup activities decrease, and those remaining knot up in more discernible segregated groups. Verbal joshing diminishes and actors appear to take one another seriously. Trips to the restrooms decrease in frequency, and both men and women seem to be less concerned than formerly with personal appearance, as evidenced by the condition of their hair, clothing, and make-up. Drink orders begin to slow down and food orders (rare at the bar before 3:30 A.M.) increase dramatically. This winding down process tends to increase as closing time approaches. This changing tempo and modification of activities, though observable, is much less in evidence during weekend shifts and occurs a little later, after 5:30 or 6:00 A.M.

The Nightspot Setting
(Dancefloor, Tables, Bandstand)

The Scene

Incoming patrons must first enter the nightspot setting, which is suffused with a jazzy atmosphere. Their eyes first meet with the dance floor upon which one of several performances may be taking place: an animated montage of couples dancing to the band's musical routines; unrehearsed, comical skits, pantomimes, or acts; impromptu musical numbers; or mock strip acts. At times joined by employees (cocktail waitresses) patrons engage in these antics on an elevated circular dance floor, which is empty at sporadic intervals in deference to jam sessions in progress on the bandstand. The cast of middle-aged men and attractive young women interact in a heterosexual and, for the women, a somewhat "dated" scene, since they generally prefer a more current style of music and dancing. Four attractive vivacious cocktail waitresses, dressed similarly to the barmaids, add color to the spectacle.

The central dais, moderately illuminated by two low-hanging chandeliers, is flanked on the left by two rows (five to a row) of dimly lighted, round, five-chaired tables. The moderate lighting effects afford prominence to actors onstage. We found that the contrapositional table seating arrangement imposed a face-to-face position on table groups while simultaneously demarcating them from other groups in the setting. Thus patrons at tables are physically and visibly more removed from others than are patrons at the bar. Patrons have a tendency to turn in toward the tables during conversational encounters, thereby turning their backs on those seated at other tables. This practice further isolates them. Thus the physical attributes of this internal array present little support for encounters between those unacquainted or those acquainted seated at separate tables, but on the other hand promote closed interaction among self-contained groups seated at the same tables.

The five-chair seating arrangement provides for occupancy by two couples and allows space for an extra or for floaters and cocktail waitresses who occasionally join table groups. Table patrons, unlike bar patrons, are offered ready access to the moderately lighted dance floor and a clear view of its activities from a dimly lighted vantage point. The following remarks exchanged between two cross-sex couples (Alex and Maria and Charles and Rena) occupying a table with one of the authors show how the internal arrangement and the expectancy of restricted mobility checks sociability between table groups.

Alex: *We were right here for two hours the other night and didn't know you two were around.*

Rena: *Well, we were only two tables away and saw you. But we were with some people and didn't think you wanted to be disturbed.*

Maria: *At least you could have dropped by and said hello.*

Charles: *We considered it, but the tables were loaded with people. And after all, you acted like you wanted to be alone.*

A bandstand, an essential instrumental component of the subsetting, is situated to the right of the dance floor, parallel to the west wall and clearly demarcated from actors on the dance floor and at the tables. Musicians here, as elsewhere, prefer to be separated from other audiences while playing.[11] As one musician quietly remarked to another musician during a break at the bar, "Man, it's a pleasure doing this gig. We're so far away from those clowning squares."

In addition to a physical ordering that hinders interaction between groups, indiscriminate table hopping among those unacquainted is discouraged by the management. Patron groups, therefore, who choose the nightspot setting are usually committed to interaction among themselves and to restricted movement that consists for the most part of ingress to and egress from the dance floor. Though some group members occasionally move to and from the bar to chat with acquaintances, drink orders are invariably given to cocktail waitresses, thus minimizing table-to-bar traffic. Flow on, to, and from the dance floor, to and from the bar, and into and out of the setting through the club's entry door entails momentary face-to-face contacts, but the absence of a milling area reduces ambulatory interaction. Even face-to-face confrontations among those who are acquainted but who are not

---

[11] See Howard S. Becker, *Outsiders: Studies in the Sociology of Deviance* (Glencoe, Ill.: Free Press, 1963), pp. 95–97.

together at the club are typically of brief duration, punctuated by momentary physical pauses and fleeting, verbal exchanges, nods, "hellos," "how-are you's" and "how-goes-it's."

USE

We recorded that different collectivities of patrons appropriated the nightspot setting in one or more ways at the same time, or in one or more ways at different times: for intimate verbal and/or physical interaction; dancing; listening to music; impromptu acts on the dance floor; pickup purposes; serious business negotiations; drinking and eating; observing the ongoing scene. There is no programmed entertainment other than dance music and occasional jam sessions, but the dance floor, the acts upon the dance floor, the tables for spectators, and the music that is played by sets lend a production aura to the scene. As one table patron put it, "There is always the feeling that something exciting may come off."

So far as we could tell nightspot routines and activities did not vary appreciably throughout the week in form and content; however, activities did vary over time during each shift. Arranged and sometimes spontaneous jam sessions closed down activities on the dance floor and tended to unify a large listening audience, including patrons at the bar. In fact the nightspot scene was more crowded during jam sessions than at any other time. The tables are more crowded on weekends than during the week, at which time they more frequently accommodate dating couples. Squares, escorted and unescorted, enter the setting more often during weekends than during the week. On weekends squares come early (1:00 to 2:00 A.M.) and stay late (closing time). During the week they come early and leave early (about 3:00 A.M.). Squares and other irregular patrons dance more frequently than regulars.

Throughout the week the nightspot setting appeals to self-contained groups of regular patrons who prefer to remain together and who wish to avoid numerous contacts and encounters with others that might disrupt their togetherness. They desire a quieter place than the bar. The mobility, spatial arrangements, and noisy sociability of the bar setting foster problematic disruptions that are less likely to occur in the nightspot setting. The tables are more likely to be filled with couples and those interested in dancing, listening to the music, and pickups from 1:00 to 5:00 A.M.

whereas the more serious negotiators (in criminal activities) tend to occupy the tables later on (5:00 to 7:00 A.M.). As is the case at the bar things begin to wind down after 4:30 or 5:00 A.M. on weekdays. There is less dancing and clowning activity on the dance floor, and patrons' mobility within and to and from the setting decreases. Drink orders also decrease, and food orders increase. The tempo of the band is modulated and becomes more suitable for background music than for either dancing or for listening pleasure. The musicians take off longer periods between sets. Patrons and the cocktail waitress talk less and speak more softly, seriously, and less animatedly than earlier. Patrons begin to thin out as an increasing number leave the club, and those remaining tend to become less concerned with their fronts and what goes on around them. The setting's gaiety subsides and gives way to a more relaxed and melancholy atmosphere. Some patrons appear half asleep or in a dream-like state. On weekend shifts, as in the bar, the winding down process for patrons and employees commences later—around 6:00 A.M. The employees appear less fatigued and affected by the winding down process than do the patrons.

Open Booths

THE SCENE

Beyond the dance floor four banquette style booths are situated in the southwest corner parallel to the south wall. These six-seated, high-backed, dimly lighted booths screened by a curtain of beads hanging from the ceiling to the floor are fashioned from mahogany and red leather upholstery. This veiled subsetting facilitates the most intimate encounters found in the club and affords the least opportunity for contacts with outsiders, because the physical attributes diminish visibility and reduce audibility. Seating arrangements here provide for close, lateral, and contra-positional body-to-body and face-to-face contact. Physical features enable if not foster intimate interaction within exclusive groupings and simultaneously promote physical and social separation from ongoing activities and persons outside as well as within this sub-setting (the other booths).

Use

Regular patrons as couples or teams routinely occupy these booths. Typically they are appropriated by regular couples who engage frequently in heavy petting, intimate verbal exchanges, and sexual intercourse, or by serious negotiators. Occupants may initially choose this setting; they may move in from the nightspot setting; or they may move in from the bar setting. Cross-sex couples once in the booths rarely change settings. Serious negotiators (e.g., those dealing in illegal transactions) move in and out of this setting as their interests at hand change. They use the booths frequently (more often on weekdays than weekends), but they do not remain there for long periods of time as do couples.

It was reported to us in interviews that the activities in the open booths remain routine over time; however, they were observed to be more crowded on a cross-sex basis during weekends than on weekdays. Routinely they get more play between 3:00 and 5:00 A.M. on weekdays, after which time they are often empty. During weekends they stay full until closing time.

Private Booths

The Scene

Two banquettes similar in physical structure to the open booths, including a curtain of beads, are located in the northeast corner of the club, beyond the north end of the bar.

Use

This setting furnishes a home territory place for a group of self-designated "businessmen" who are reported to be organized criminals.[12] Movement in and out of this habitat is at a minimum. Although activities here are primarily unserious in nature, business

[12] These reports were substantiated by our other data sources, i.e., criminal records, interviews with key informants, and discussions with other actors (not businessmen) in the setting.

activities are said to be conducted. Conversing, drinking, joking, eating, and flirting comprise the major activities taking place. Variations in use over time depend on the composition of the group and will be discussed later.

Backstage Regions

INTRODUCTION

The first floor above the main theater of action houses several backstage areas for various types of actors (see Figure 2). Some backstage regions are either inaccessible to the patron audience

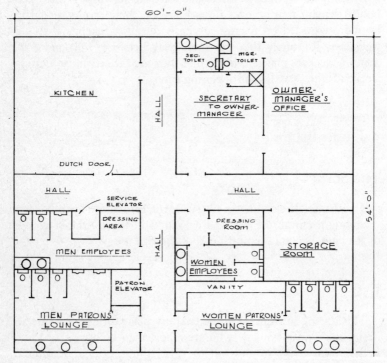

FIRST FLOOR PLAN

FIGURE 2

or off limits to certain types of actors. Some actors in some of these areas may be somewhat off guard with other actors and prepare for their next performance in the main theater of action. Some other actors may work (e.g., cook, women patrons' lounge attendant, owner) relax, or play (e.g., guests invited to owner's private office) in some of these restricted regions. Various backstage regions are used by different actors for different purposes at different times. The owner-manager uses his office for work purposes at times, and at other times he utilizes it for private parties. Backstage regions on the first story are accessible to the club's actors by a patrons' elevator situated to the immediate right of the hallway entry door in the club proper. A service elevator (employees' elevator) is located at the northwest end of the nightspot setting. The first floor above the club is traversed by two wide halls, one running from north to south and another running from east to west.

MEN PATRONS' LOUNGE

The men patrons' lounge is situated in the northwest corner of the first floor facing the east-west hall. Combs, brushes, and other toiletries are available, but there is no attendant. Restricted to male patron use it has a clean, aseptic, roomy, solid, functional appearance. Gold colored tile tones down its white-walled stark appearance. We noted that patrons entered this area in a business-like fashion and left hurriedly in the same manner as men use public bar restrooms. Social contacts were brief and brusque, eye contacts were avoided, and social encounters were held to the minimum. The total absence of chairs or benches does not contribute to prolonged encounters and renders the term "lounge" a misnomer. Patrons were less messy than in public bars and spent longer periods of time in self-grooming here than in public bars.

WOMEN PATRONS' LOUNGE

This spacious chamber built into the southwest corner of the first story directly across the hall from the men patrons' lounge affords a long vanity with stools, two sofas, two chairs, toilet facilities, and a full-time lounge attendant who helps patrons with their grooming tasks. The decor in the carpeted lounge is frilly Victorian. Though it is primarily functional, female actors reported that they do socialize here to some extent in chit-chat and gossip. Occasionally it serves as a refuge for those distraught or inebriated.

MEN EMPLOYEES' ROOM

Facing the east-west hall and adjacent to the men patrons' lounge is the men employees' room. It has tiled floors, toilet facilities, a dressing area (with lockers and coat hangers), and a long leather sofa and four chairs. Though functionally solid and comfortable, it has a barracks room, austere appearance with no pictures, carpets, or ornaments. Restricted to male employees, it is utilized by the assistant manager, the musicians, the bouncers, the cook, and the cook's helper. Employees dress, undress, and clean up here, but the employees reported that socializing is at the minimum.

WOMEN EMPLOYEES' ROOM

This bathroom and dressing room adjacent to the women patrons' lounge opens onto the northwest hall. It is furnished with a dressing room equipped with a vanity, coat hangers, and lockers. This combination toilet and dressing facility is more than adequate from a functional point of view but is not decorated. Women employees, barmaids, cocktail waitresses, and the women patrons' lounge attendant utilize this facility for functional purposes. They say it is not used for extended social encounters and that the little time spent there is used for dressing and undressing.

OWNER-MANAGER'S AND SECRETARY'S OFFICES

The owner-manager's and secretary's expansive adjacent offices form a rectangular space stretching from the southeast corner to the east-west hall and to the north-south hall on the west side. Only one door, opening onto the north-south hall from the secretary's office, permits entrance. Just one door connects the secretary's office with that of the owner-manager. This office arrangement provides for a great deal of privacy. The secretary's office is equipped with the usual furnishings—desk, typewriter, calculator, file cabinets, copy machine, and the like. Additionally two large leather sofas and four leather chairs flank the walls. Mahogany paneling, plush red carpeting, and a beamed plaster ceiling continues the club's decor. A private toilet with lavatory and a separate, enclosed shower room provide for extra comfort. The shower is a real necessity for those participating in private, cross-sex parties in the owner-manager's office to be discussed later on. A part-time secretary performs clerical, stenographic, and bookkeeping chores here three afternoons per week during closing hours. From time to time, usually late in the morning (4:00 to 6:30 A.M.) with the owner-manager's consent, this room is appropriated for private parties.

The connecting owner-manager's office follows in part the style set in the secretary's office with similar leather furniture, red carpeting, and wall and ceiling structure. He also has a private toilet with lavatory but no shower. A large, plush, mahogany, brass trimmed, executive type desk occupies the center of the room. The desk affords a private telephone and a built-in wet bar. A wall safe covered by tapestry is located behind the owner's desk chair. Three walls are flanked by long red leather sofas accompanied by end tables and low, elongated coffee tables. A few classical and colorful nineteenth-century productions hang on the walls. The decor here is Mediterranean. This chamber is used for business transactions as well as for private parties, and the form and content of social interaction depends upon its use at the time. During closing hours it is used strictly for business affairs; during the club hours it is used alternately for serious work and for pleasure. It is reported by key informants that "businessmen" may also use it from time to time for pleasure or for conference purposes.

Conclusion: The Total Configuration

The rhetoric employed by the actors, both patrons and employees, tends to sustain and reinforce acceptable ongoing behavior within an illegal, space-time configuration. The management and staff present an affluent clientele of early morning players, revelers, and other actors with a semisecret, exclusive, differentiated, exciting, comfortable, secure, "respectable" drinking and frolicking haven devoid of any cheap or illegal counteracting stereotypic imagery. Employees by occupational designation (e.g., barmaid), work site (e.g., behind the bar), dress, mannerisms, vocalizations, gestures, postures, and services rendered symbolize to patrons and to themselves a group of legitimate actors engaged in conventional work roles. The patrons appear to accept the rhetoric "given" and the legitimate selves presented to them; and they in turn present their own legitimate identities (as worthy patrons) to themselves and to others in different subsettings in the club—this respectable presentation despite the fact that they are fully aware of the illegal nature of the entire playtime behavior setting. Patrons, then, as well as employees make this setting available to one another as the kind of setting they define it to be, i.e., they produce through their own activities that which they "take for granted" is really out there.[13]

The club's spatial features, physical objects and accommodations, entrance routines, and goods and services routines promote the physical demarcation and distribution of patrons and their activities in the setting, including the type and quality of social encounters that transpire there. Special ordering divides the club proper into *four contiguous quadrants of action:* the bar, the nightspot setting, and two different booth subsettings where various types of actors engage in various types of activities over time. One backstage region, the owner-manager's private office, in addition to serious functions provides for private parties—a partytime configuration within a wider party-time or playtime context, a party within a party for a select inner core of Rendezvous actors.

---

[13] We are not concerned here with the actors' consciousness but rather with how impressions are created and sustained; with how actors' impressions determine the way they will act toward others and how others will act toward them; and with how the scene that they create manages their activities. The ultimate referent here is the reading of conduct. Management and staff by design work hard at impression management, a necessary part of the business they are in. Employees and patrons then provide reciprocal impressions to one another about the respectability of an illegitimate behavior setting. Both sets of actors seem to "play themselves straight." See Sheldon L. Messinger, Harold Sampson, and Robert D. Towne, "Life as Theater: Some Notes on the Dramaturgic Approach to Social Reality," *Sociometry*, vol. 25, no. 1 (Mar. 1962): 98–110. Perhaps as actors learn to play the respectability role, they learn to project it convincingly to others. On this point see James M. Henslin, "Sociology of Everyday Life," in *Introduction to Sociology: Situations and Structures,* ed. Jack D. Douglas (New York: Free Press, 1973), pp. 227–49.

Other backstage regions offer a support base for the main theater of action, the club proper.

An actor's behavior in the Rendezvous is contingent upon several features, including among others rhetoric, space-time properties, the club's goods and services, and his or her interests at hand. The club's ecological and physical settings in which actors locate and situate themselves provide for differential patrons activity, exposure, and accessibility that vary somewhat over time. The actor's interest or purposes at hand (e.g., initiating social encounters, negotiating seriously, dancing, picking up a girl, getting picked up, remaining in a self-contained group, drinking seriously) and the space-time configuration at the Rendezvous narrow his subsetting selection. This interest at hand also affects how he positions himself within that locale. Once in a setting one's conduct is directed or circumscribed by the setting's features. Of course, one may move with a change of interest to other settings or even attempt (and on occasion succeed in) rearranging a setting. However, in general there is a great deal of fit between behavior and the milieu.

In answer to our sociological questions (What is the Rendezvous? What happens when and where in the Rendezvous?) we found the club to be a voluntary, "exclusive," plush, early morning, unserious behavior setting that is convenient to an odd-time, affluent group of patrons. It affords a variety of goods and services in several subsettings, subsettings in which a number of different activities occur over time in a "respectable" safe, space-time configuration. As Cavan's and other bar studies demonstrate, we likewise noted that most of the overt behavior units (activity patterns) such as drinking, conversing, verbal joshing, dancing, petting, horse playing, acting, dining, flirting, picking up sexual partners, and round drinking constituted in the main a standing behavior pattern of sociability and play.

In contrast to many other unserious settings, for example the public bars studied by Cavan, the Rendezvous requires a serious entrance procedure of its patrons—a procedure that connotes secrecy, illegality, exclusivity, and simultaneously contributes to a more novel, circumscribed, illicit and exciting but safe playtime setting. Actors at the Rendezvous appear to be more concerned with a respectable front than many actors we have observed in other unserious settings, including those researched in public bars. We also witnessed a greater degree of temporal change in behavior, mood, and atmosphere at the Rendezvous than is reported in the literature on other bar settings. Finally, the Rendezvous offered more backstage regions for study than many other unserious settings we had observed.

Chapter 6

SOCIABILITY AND PLAY IN THE FOUR SUBSETTINGS

Introduction

THIS CHAPTER PURSUES further the sociological questions: What happens in the Rendezvous? Where in the setting do these happenings occur? Additionally, we address the question: What are the consequences of what goes on at the club? Answers to these questions were obtained from focal areas (4) *standing behavior patterns* and (5) *the form and content of encounters and verbal exchanges among actors* (see Chapter 3, Theoretical Orientation). The owner-manager and the other key informants informed us at the beginning of the study that the Rendezvous was designed for sociability and play purposes—in their terms, "a place for good people to play, socialize, dance, and drink in." The bar literature confirmed that the major activity patterns occuring in public drinking establishments make up a standing behavior pattern of sociability and play.[1] Because our preliminary participant observations also indicated that most of the overt activity patterns (drinking, dancing, conversing) taking place in the Rendezvous' various subsettings appeared to comprise a standing behavior pattern of sociability and play, we decided to check our

[1] For a discussion of sociability as the autonomous form or play-form of sociation, see Georg Simmel, *The Sociology of Georg Simmel*, trans. and ed. Kurt H. Wolff (New York: Free Press, 1965), pp. 43–57. Also see Sherri Cavan, *Liquor License: An Ethnography of Bar Behavior* (Chicago: Aldine, 1966), pp. 49–66 for an analysis of public bar sociability.

observations on this point. More specifically, we examined encounters and the various units of behavior (activity patterns) in the club's subsettings in terms of the presence or absence of eight criteria of sociability and play found in the literature: freedom, equality, novelty, stepping out of reality, space and time circumscriptions, order, permanency, secrecy (see page 48, Chapter 2). Next, a comparison was made of variations in sociability and play found in each subsetting. Simultaneously, we looked for any additional standing behavior patterns present in the club.

The Bar

An Open Region

The bar is the most open region of the club's four subsettings. Here patrons unacquainted and acquainted have the right to engage one another in conversation and the tentative obligation to acknowledge, if not accept, the overtures of sociability offered them. For the most part actors expect the bar to be a time-out setting where what is said and done will be regarded as important only for the present and of little consequence. Their remarks and behavior in the bar designate play and sociability. As one patron remarked to one of the researchers at the bar:

Man this bar's a gas. You talk to lotta people about a bunch of nonsense. But it's lotta fun. You put people on, and you tell and listen to lotta jokes. You can always find someone to play games with. I mean someone to argue with about somethin' or other. Like sports or broads or somethin'. You kick it around with several people during your stay, but most of it's for fun. But it don't mean nothing when you step outside.

Bar patrons vary in their relationships to one another. Some are unacquainted. Some are only slightly acquainted. Many are unlikely ever to become associates elsewhere. Still others are close friends. Even patrons of unequal social status whose lives overlap outside the bar are open to one another for conversation at the Rendezvous bar.

On the other hand, though patrons here (like patrons in public drinking places) are open persons, no one has to engage in social encounters with others. Furthermore, no party to an encounter has a familiarity license to probe into another's confidential and personal preserves. Moreover, conversations may be terminated at will with impunity by any member of a conversational group. The social intercourse scenario at the Rendezvous bar, then, is indeed unserious and problematic—that is, indeterminate. As a patron commented during his interview:

What you do and say in the bar depends on the situation. If you're with friends, that's one thing. You get chummy, but with others you talk junk. You got a lot of freedom to talk to a lot of people or leave them be. Usually you talk to people you know outside regardless of who they are. You're not with your family, and you're not on the job. And what you talk about is a bunch of nothing anyway. You find a lot of interesting people to talk to. You find them there and you leave them there. You break off the talk when you want. They understand. They feel the same way. The Rendezvous bar is one thing. The outside world is something else. But remember that it depends on the situation. Who you're with and what you're looking for. You want a broad? You want to buy something? You want to just shoot the breeze?

The subsetting's divergent usage and membership promotes a degree of status leveling and thus openness for sociability.[2] Because patrons come from several different collectivities (different occupational and social class groups) some of whom are occasional customers, regular customers, habitués, guests, or neutral persons (those whose presence is tolerated), no one membership can dominate—that is, close others out of bar conversation and activity. Should any patron be unable or unwilling to make social contacts with any particular group or to participate in any one activity, there are other groups and activities available to him. In short, one's social viability is not determined by one's interaction with any one exclusionary group. The following comments recorded in an interview illustrate the openness of the bar as well as status leveling.

When I go to the club, I sit at the bar where there are all kinds

[2] Simmel notes the sociability game is played as if all actors were equal. Objective external attributes, such as wealth and social position, and personal traits of actors are partially submerged as factors in sociability. Simmel, *Sociology*, pp. 45–50.

*of interesting people to talk to like entertainers, hustlers, squares
—you name it. Everybody is friendly at the bar.*

Features of secrecy further accentuate status leveling and sociability. Unlike a public bar, the Rendezvous is an exclusive setting
where the patrons assume that the screening practices have
weeded out undesirables and brought together "respectable"
actors with similar recreational interests. While at the club patrons
are members of a semisecret society—a society where their outside
biographies and differential personality traits are partially leveled.[3]
Behavior in this protected and partially leveled environment is
somewhat removed from outside rules and therefore is relatively
free from future consequences. More so than in public bars, the
expectancy at the Rendezvous in Goffman's terms, is "dramaturgical loyalty"—i.e., in this case what occurs at the bar will not
be divulged by the actors outside the club.[4] As Freddie, a regular
bar patron, remarked to a group of friends at the bar:

*I feel free as a bird here because nobody is going to say nothing
about what I'm doing. No boss, no holy Joes. No wife. Jesus
Christ, what else could a man ask for? Not that I want to do
anything crazy, really out of line, like some of those nothings you
see crosstown at the Kitty Cat. I just relax and have a ball. To
hell with yesterday and tomorrow like that tent maker Khayyam,
or whatever his name is. Now if I did at the Kitty Cat what I do
here it would be all over town the next day.*

Patrons who wish to avoid contacts with others signal their
unavailability for encounters in several ways: by posturing or arranging themselves in a closed manner, avoiding eye contact with
outsiders, only briefly acknowledging greetings and salutations,
ignoring or nodding off remarks by intruders, affixing attention to
immediate surroundings and tasks. For example, John, a regular
serious solitary drinker, customarily walks straight to the bar
where he nods to the barmaid and immediately sits down hunch-
ing himself slightly forward resting each elbow on the edge of the
bar. He directs his attention straight ahead or downward toward
his drink, cigarettes, cigarette lighter, and change, warding off all

---

[3] Simmel notes that the "de-personalization" of members of a secret society
promotes relative equality and freedom among its memberships. *Ibid.*, pp.
372–75.

[4] Erving Goffman, *The Presentation of Self in Everyday Life* (Garden City,
N.Y.: Doubleday Anchor Books, 1959), pp. 212–16.

overtures from others with nods or grunts without moving his body or head toward them. He communicates with the barmaids by lifting his empty glass when in need of a refill. Actors who desire separation from the open sociability game at the bar frequently avoid it by sitting at the tables or in the booths.[5] Solos (single males), however, regardless of their purposes at hand rarely sit at tables or in the booths unless they are staking turf while awaiting the arrival of other group members.

GENERAL ENCOUNTERS

OPENINGS

The problem of bar actors involved in starting, sustaining, and ending social encounters is how to achieve the desired degree of social and personal proximity to others for conversational purposes without suffering moral loss, i.e., designation as an unworthy or disreputable actor in the setting.[6] Though in an open region, the socially situated bar actor has to present an acceptable front to others and at the same time make readings on others to accomplish his interests at hand—generally sociability. And though the multiplicity of Rendezvous bar actors and audiences contributes to sociability in a general sense, their diversity requires that actors seeking encounters vary their presentations of self. The success of this diversified presentation process is not guaranteed since the patrons come from different backgrounds and do not necessarily share the same set of values or similar stock of knowledge. Moreover, it is difficult to appear worthy to a sequence of different kinds of people and groups. Therefore, composure, respectability, and sociability are problematic in this setting.

Encounters between those not acquainted are ordinarily accomplished by remarks, queries, or declarations that actually serve as ritual forms or moves requesting conversation. Typically a patron within conversational range of another patron with whom he

---

[5] For a discussion of game-theoretic frameworks, especially "relationship games," and game typology, see Stanford M. Lyman and Marvin B. Scott, *A Sociology of the Absurd* (New York: Appleton-Century-Crofts, 1970), pp. 26–69.

[6] See Donald W. Ball, "The Problematics of Respectability," in *Deviance and Respectability: The Social Construction of Moral Meanings*, ed. Jack D. Douglas (New York: Basic Books, 1970), pp. 326–71.

desires an encounter directs toward this person casual comments about the bar, the weather, sports, music, barmaids, or cocktail waitresses. Should the approached patron respond with more than a brief nod, gesture, or verbal acknowledgement, the initiator receives a cue to answer—and with this exchange an encounter begins. Positive responses by the recipient usually include a turning of the body toward the initiator, friendly eye contact, and a pleasant open-ended reply. Patrons were also observed to initiate encounters by open declarations to the bar that were answered by any of several patrons or barmaids. Encounter patterns frequently consist of remark, counter remark, interchange, silence, remark, counter remark, and so on.[7] Prolonged silences are treated as conventional endings. Thus, as patrons must exert conscious efforts to avoid encounters, they must also work to promote and maintain them.

Barmaids in the Rendezvous normally introduce those unacquainted who appear to desire company. Moreover, as they move in and out of encounter groups while performing their chores up and down the bar, barmaids' verbal exchanges serve to unite disparate conversational groups. Similarly, patrons known to some bar customers sometimes encourage encounters among unknowns by exchanging remarks with several conversational groups, thus linking those unacquainted into social interaction. Unusual incidences or happenings at times evoke a momentary, central patron focus that often results in group encounters, e.g., some girl tries to dance on the bar.

As in public bars patrons at the Rendezvous sometimes converse and interact with each other without exchanging names, thereby avoiding a symbol of acquaintanceship; however, protracted conversations customarily involve introductions (at least on a first-name basis). Frequently, when names are exchanged, either patron offers to purchase the other a drink. Sometimes gift drinks are purchased during encounters prior to introductions, and in this case names are commonly exchanged when the drink is delivered. In either case the gift drink, a symbolic token, marks a change in relationship from interactant to acquaintance.[8]

The acceptance of a gift drink is virtually obligatory and if declined requires a "good account," e.g., "Thanks, but I must

---

[7] See Cavan, *Liquor License*, p. 57.
[8] *Ibid.*, pp. 119–22.

leave soon"; "Thanks, but I've had it." Recipients are obliged to interact with donors at least until the gift drink is finished. Subsequently, recipients might reciprocate the gift drink, signaling a desire to continue the encounter, or they might disengage. Alternately those newly acquainted often play a box dice bar game for drinks after exchanging names, in which case there is no mutual conversational or gift drink obligation.[9]

Rendezvous bar encounters are problematic, and mere social contact does not ensure their birth or duration. For example, George, an irregular patron, obviously intoxicated, staggered up to the bar near a group of regular patrons with whom he was not acquainted and asked in a loud and demanding voice, "Don't you boys think it's a little drunk out tonight?" He was greeted with dead silence. His comical query constituted a ritual move requesting an encounter. The undesired and unexpected silence defined him as an unworthy (presumptuous) person in the setting. He quickly moved to the other end of the bar, and after consuming one drink in a standing position, nodded toward the barmaid and quickly departed, leaving $3.00 in change on the bar. The audience of regulars whom he had accosted exchanged brief, knowing looks during the interruption, but continued to talk as if nothing untoward had happened. After his exit, the barmaid who had deftly but silently served him commented to the offended group, "What a clown." A few other patrons silently nodded, and the incident then was history to all present.

Another excerpt illustrates the success of a declaration followed first by a response and then an encounter. Jacques, a regular, nonchalantly walked up to the bar and exchanged cordial greetings with Joan, a barmaid. During one drink he tentatively glanced at a group of three males seated to his left with whom he was not acquainted. Upon noting a lull in this group's conversation, he tentatively remarked in their direction, "It sure is cold out." Joe, one of the threesome, replied with a smile, "Yeah, cold as a whore's heart." And Max, another group member, chimed in, "Yeah, cold as a witch's tit." Subsequently, the new group of four

---

[9] Gift drink rituals and ceremonies are associated with a variety of forms and meanings that comprise an essential part of patterned behavior and sociability in the club. Male patrons treat women as well as other men, while women may treat other women. Club employees occasionally treat patrons and in turn may be treated by patrons. Men invariably treat female companions and proffer gift drinks to unknown females with whom they desire interaction.

discussed the weather among other things for about 45 minutes. Jacques was accorded worth and respect in that he was supported as a speaker and thereby treated as normal in the setting. The form not the content of his declaration was at issue. Jacques' trivial statement was a ritual act in the guise of saying something that could be interpreted as valid by the audience—something that showed respect for social interchange.

Some requests for Rendezvous bar encounters are blocked by "cutoffs," "putdowns," and cracks. Tommy, an irregular patron, obviously intoxicated, walked up to a group of three men seated together at the bar and introduced himself in a loud voice, "My name is Tommy. To whom do I have the honor of speaking?" Fred, one member of the threesome, after a cursory, sharp look at the intruder, replied, "I can't help it, I didn't name you, Jack." He then turned his back on Tommy, who quickly went to the other end of the bar.

RECIPROCAL SUPPORTIVE EXCHANGES

Encounters at the Rendezvous are of variable duration and are frequently sustained by supportive interchanges, i.e., rituals and verbal exchanges that affirm and keep a conversation ongoing. Participants in encounters here as elsewhere are expected to cooperate with one another by tentatively accepting the definition of the situation (e.g., a mutual definition of the encounter as unserious).[10] Ritual offerings operate to designate and extend one actor's involvement with and connection to another. Newly acquainted Rendezvous bar patrons sometimes provide one another with small goods and services, such as cigarettes, lights, matches, the correct time, directions in and outside the club, and gift drinks—all of which are supportive ritual offerings.

Bar actors might nourish encounters by casually commenting on or asking trivial questions about the passing scene. It was noted that any person, place, or thing might offer a conversation piece, e.g., barmaids, the dance floor, lighting fixtures. Frequently encounter members courteously introduce one another to nearby friends and thereby extend their conversational group in membership and time. Bar patrons also continually exchanged "grooming talk"

10 See Goffman, *The Presentation of Self*, pp. 9–10.

with one another in the guise of passing compliments about appearance, wearing apparel, and tastes. Such talk frequently lends support to encounters. Even the combination of greetings and farewells at the bar were observed to comprise supportive ritual behavior.[11]

ENDINGS

The openness and unseriousness of the Rendezvous bar situation that facilitates conversations and encounters simultaneously tend to shorten them. The weakness of conventional closure rules promotes the fluidity of bar encounters, and the lack of bar actors' commitments to one another fosters encounters of a tentative and superficial nature. We found that parties to encounters withdrew at will but that the recipient of a gift drink usually remained with the donor until he had finished the drink. When disengaging, the recipient usually thanked the donor. Gift drink reciprocity usually occurs; a drink calls for a drink in return then or at a later date. Patrons usually closed out encounters in more ceremonial fashions by awaiting appropriate moments (lulls in conversations that legitimized the impending termination), and then saying something like, "It's been nice talking to you, but I must leave now." However, as Cavan found in public bars, formalities were not necessary.[12] For example, Rendezvous bar patrons were seen to withdraw from encounters by protracted silence, movement to another location, the engagement of another actor in another encounter, or departure from the bar with or without a nod or goodbye. Departures from bar stools signal encounter endings unless markers are left or unless one states intentions of returning, "I'll be right back. Have to go to the restroom." Once closed, future encounters between the participants (on that occasion or later) generally require a repetition of the ceremonial opening moves.

[11] Ritual conversational offerings alone, however, do not comprise supportive interchanges. A recipient must accept and acknowledge them, thereby signifying that a relationship exists between giver and receiver as the performer implies, i.e., that the performer is worthy and that the recipient is appreciative. As Goffman notes, supportive interchanges are interpersonal rituals since the form indicating a relationship rather than content is of primary importance. See Erving Goffman, *Relations in Public: Microstudies of the Public Order* (New York: Basic Books, 1971), pp. 105–36.

[12] See Cavan, *Liquor License*, pp. 54–60.

THE NATURE OF BAR TALK

Bar talk at the Rendezvous is normally small talk because the casual remarks, statements, queries, and declarations utilized to open encounters stimulate brief, trivial conversational topics that incur no commitments, such as the weather, sports, popular music, sex, gossip, and the like. In sociability terms the talk at the bar becomes its own purpose, a ritual for interaction. In Simmel's terms, ". . . the topic is merely the indispensable medium through which the lively exchange of speech itself unfolds its attractions. . . ."[13] And because bar talk has no objective ends beyond the sociability of the here-and-now, it tends to be transitory and noncommittal. This does not mean that bar conversation may not be amusing, witty, and even interesting. Frequently it is, but content is seldom its raison d'etre.

For example, the following typical encounter at the Rendezvous illustrates the triviality and transitory nature of bar talk. Joey, a criminal lawyer, Louis, an electrician and sometime hustler, and Fritz, a "rounded-off" square, sat at the bar talking about the sexual attributes of one of the cocktail waitresses. Mike, an unacquainted seated nearby, volunteered the following interjection during a conversational lull:

Mike: *I know her* [Diane the waitress] *from way back. She works from six to two over at Cecilia's.*

Joey: *So she works at Cecilia's. She's new here, right?*

Mike: *Yeah, she moonlights here. Good kid.*

Louis: *Is she straight?*

Mike: *Yeah, she's not a hustler. Most of the time she has a boyfriend around.*

Antonio [another unacquainted male seated to the right of the team]: *Well, it's good to know it's not going to waste. She's got it all. And in the right places, too.*

Fritz [while outlining an imaginary hour glass in the air]: *Yeah, I think she has pretty eyes, too.*

This expanded encounter group continued conversing about sex, the weather, and sports for about one hour. Then Mike and Fritz picked up two females at the bar and moved to a table. Joey, Louis, and Antonio remained chatting together at the bar.

[13] See Simmel, *Sociology*, p. 52.

Shop talk, usually involving commitment and closure, is engaged in at a minimum at the Rendezvous bar because of the diversity of the actors there as well as the unseriousness of the setting. Conversationalists typically take turns at the talking game, and though some are recognizably far superior to others in their verbal ability, most offer *conversational gifts* appropriate to the background expectancies of their audiences.[14] Talk outside the context of background expectations uttered wittingly or unwittingly is not well received. It may not even be understood.

Rendezvous bar talk becomes more serious for those patrons who seek goals other than sociability, e.g., negotiators of various types who commonly disguise their nonsociable purposes, patrons who play different games at the same time, intimate friends who may discuss family problems. Yet the playful and dynamic scene characterized by episodic encounters impinges upon all present, whatever their interests at hand.

The bar patrons' general expectation that bar conversation is unserious and circumscribed in time and space generates one of the Rendezvous' basic rules about bar encounters: patrons who are engaged in bar conversation with other patrons are not obligated to acknowledge any relationship with them at another time in the same or in another setting. This corroborates Cavan's findings in public bars on this point.[15] Fred and Michael, with whom one of the observers had talked and exchanged gift drinks several times at a nearby public convenience bar, were seated three bar stools away from him at the Rendezvous. Yet for an hour neither indicated any recognition of his presence. Similar failures to acknowledge acquaintances in more formal settings would be taken as social insults.

Even friends who share close relationships outside the Rendezvous are under no obligation to recognize one another there, though they are more likely to do so than are bar acquaintances without outside relationships.[16] Patrons well known to each other

---

[14] By background expectancies, we refer to those sets of taken-for-granted ideas and properties of common understandings in everyday life that permit the interactants to interpret the conversational gifts in the first place. See Harold Garfinkel, *Studies in Ethnomethodology* (Englewood Cliffs, N.J.: Prentice-Hall, 1967), pp. 36–42.

[15] See Cavan, *Liquor License*, p. 64.

[16] According to Simmel, modern man shares differentiated friendships that relate to specific spheres of mutual interest rather than intimate friendships that encompass all aspects of the personality. Friends' and acquainteds'

usually acknowledge one another's mutual presence by at least an exchange of nods and smiles upon arrival or departure.

SPECIALIZED CROSS-SEX ENCOUNTERS

PICKUPS

Though the Rendezvous bar subsetting is primarily oriented toward sociability among male patrons, several of its features generate pickups, i.e., noncommercial, transient, sexually oriented encounters between those initially unacquainted who become acquainted without a proper introduction. Because women at the bar are virtually on an equalitarian basis with men, the ground rules guiding their behavior are similar to those guiding male behavior. These rules together with certain spatial and physical properties encourage cross-sex encounters. Females comprise 15 to 20 per cent of all Rendezvous bar patrons at any one time, and most of them enter the setting without male escorts.

The general expectation among bar actors (as disclosed in the interviews) is that women without escorts are open to encounters, unless they signal their unavailability or discourage the pickup activity pattern. Unlike other bar social encounters, the pickup is characterized by sexual flirtation. In pickups there is also a move from sexual flirtation and conversational exchanges to an exclusionary social commitment—at least for a period of time. Cross-sex conversations sometimes did and sometimes did not result in pickups, and pickups at times were witnessed to dissolve into mere casual conversation. Pickup routines frequently included negotiations pertaining to future mutual availability; however, most appeared to be present oriented.

We noted that men and women seeking pickups usually signalled mutual interest and availability by sustained eye contacts, smiles, open body postures, and cues indicating unattachment. The male after receiving positive eye contact signals (e.g., the female holds his eyes with hers; winks, smiles) frequently caresses the intended quarry by eye caresses directed to her lips, throat, breasts, and body. Upon receiving additional positive signals he frequently moves (sitting or standing) near the interested party

---

"mutual spheres of interest" may not extend to the bar. See Simmel, *Sociology*, pp. 325–26.

in order to talk to her. Females were observed to induce pickups by holding a man's gaze, i.e., by catching and locking in his eyes before they could slide away. Once they captured the male's attention, they often engaged in one or more of the following come-on techniques (over a period of time): crossing or opening legs in order to expose thighs; rolling hips, lips, and shoulders; stroking thighs, legs, or breasts; arching back and thrusting breasts forward; licking and pouting the lips; adjusting garments to expose body; playing with the hair, earrings, and other accessories; stroking up and down on drinking glass with fingers; tipping or holding an empty glass.[17] Women many times engaged in one or more of the following behaviors while seated beside males they were trying to pick up: touching him on the hand, face, leg, or shoulder; brushing her breasts, legs, knees, or hips against him; asking for small goods and services (e.g., cigarettes, lights, direction, the time).

Males frequently sent gifts drinks through the barmaids to women as a part of the pickup routine. When the recipient accepted and acknowledged the drink by turning toward the donor, smiling, and nodding her thanks, he immediately joined her. When she accepted the drink and indirectly communicated her thanks through the barmaid, she signified her temporary unavailability. The male in most pickup moves was noted to be the ostensible instigator. The four-to-one male to female ratio at the Rendezvous bar reinforces this customary expectation that men approach women for encounters rather than vice versa; however, females are active and equal players in the game, the outcome of which they ultimately control.

Once the pickup was established, it was noted that the parties to it typically moved to another club setting, i.e., the nightspot setting or the booths. Reports in the interviews made clear that whatever the outcome, an evening of flirtation or ultimate sexual intercourse, neither party was committed to any additional future course of interaction; that neither had to be concerned about any reputational problems incurred since what happened after the pickup would not become public information. The pickup routine was described as unserious sexual play.[18] As Frank, one male

---

[17] For a further discussion of body language utilized in pickups see Julius Fast, *Body Language* (New York: Pocket Books, 1970).

[18] Nelson N. Foote, "Sex as Play," *Social Problems*, vol. 1, no. 4 (April 1954): 159–63.

patron, put it during his interview (attested to by several others):

> *I'm a married man and can't afford to pick up a chick in a lot of places. Too many people know me and would talk. The girls at the Rendezvous aren't going to talk. You can be with a girl there without worrying about it being all over town the next day. The type of girl you find at the Rendezvous has more class than most broads, and they're out for the same thing I am.*

Angelo, another married patron, submitted:

> *I've been picking up girls there since the place opened, and I've only heard that love junk from one dizzy broad. The girls there don't want to get involved. I mean no long-term thing. They know the story. And they don't talk. They know we don't talk either. It's all the real thing—I mean fun.*

The Rendezvous bar pickup routine sometimes resolved into a play form of erotic sociability similar to Simmel's play form of coquetry.[19] Women play up alternately allusive promises and allusive withdrawals to attract the male but stop short of that which is tantamount to sexual surrender without depriving him of all hope. The male is often an eager player because of (and not in spite of) the female's vacillation. Both "sweet-talk" each other in a playful, amusing, and flirtatious sociability game for its own sake without concern for any definitive sexual goal. Of course the consequences are frustrating when one or another player in this two-way game is playing "for real" while the other is playing "for fun," as the example of Raphael and Laurie's bar encounter disclosed. Raphael walked hurriedly to the bar, ordered a drink, and struck up an animated conversation with Sussie, a barmaid, while occasionally glancing at his watch:

Sussie: *Got a new watch?*
Raphael: *No, dammit, I've just got an hour.*
Sussie: *For sure?*
Raphael: *For sure.*
Sussie: *You got time for another?*
Raphael: *Yeah, doll, and give that redhead over there a drink, too.*
Sussie: *But the time, lover?*
Raphael: *To hell with the time. Give her the drink.*

[19] See Simmel, *Sociology*, pp. 50–54.

Subsequently, Raphael moved down the bar and introduced himself to Laurie (the redhead), with whom he had been exchanging flirtatious glances while talking to Sussie. After two rounds of drinks, during which time he continually glanced at his watch, Raphael stood up:

Raphael: *We've had enough booze, honey. Let's split and go do it.*

Laurie: *Beautiful, shall we go to my place or yours?*

Raphael: *Hell, if you're going to argue about where, let's forget it.*

HETEROSEXUAL ENCOUNTERS AMONG THOSE ACQUAINTED

Acquainted, unattached males and females in the bar were frequently seen to approach one another directly for encounters without preliminary rituals. Possessing biographical data on one another and liking one another, there was no need for ceremony. Such encounters among acquainted actors who unexpectedly meet at the bar generate heterosexual sociability. For those who attend the Rendezvous unescorted (according to interview reports) there is usually no expectation of meeting any one particular acquaintance, but rather there is the anticipation that one might run into any of several acquaintances of the opposite sex—a contingency that enhances the prospects for cross-sex bar sociability. As one female patron said, "It sweetens the pot."

READINGS AND RELATIONSHIP TAGS

Rendezvous bar actors' accounts about their encounters in the bar include information about how they made social readings on the identities of others and on the social relationships among others.[20] They claimed they had to make these readings in order to engage in encounters. As one patron interviewee stated:

You got to take a reading on the people in the bar. Not the whole life story, but something, man. If you keep your eyes and ears open you usually get enough of a print-out to talk to most guys at the bar. Once you get to talking you fill in as you go along. You fill each other in, see, but you sift things out. You don't tell

[20] For an analysis of tie-signs indicating social relationship, see Goffman, *Relations in Public*, pp. 188–210.

the story of your life. Who wants to hear anybody's troubles. You wing it if you know what I mean. It becomes an automatic.

As Simmel and Goffman found elsewhere, for viable social interaction to occur actors must infer biographical data about others on the basis of what others say and do in a particular social situation.[21] Our bar patrons claimed that they made readings continually on one anothers' identities and bar relationships.

Indicators of social and personal relationships at the Rendezvous as elsewhere include biographies, symbolic objects, behavior, and expressions. Bar actors have at least a limited biographical knowledge about other acquainted bar actors that sustains and cases interaction with them in this setting. At the bar and during the interviews, bar patrons informed us that they gathered information about unknowns at the Rendezvous in several ways: by noting unknowns' conduct and appearance at the club, listening to what unknowns said about themselves, recording what others said about unknowns, observing with whom (and how) unknowns interacted, noting how unknowns treated and were treated by others, checking the discrepancies between unknowns' fronts and what they knew or could find out about them in and outside the club.

Rings, shared and well-marked personal belongings, body proximity, facial expressions during conversations, and the physical proximity of drinks frequently indicated bar actors' togetherness and relationships, i.e., boy friend, girl friend, comrade, employer. We registered that several behaviors helped designate who was together and the intimacy of that togetherness at the Rendezvous: hand holding; holding of personal belongings; lap sitting; arm locking; embracing; fondling; hand squeezing; kissing; mutual and intimate eye contacts; smiles; body postures and gestures.

Conversational form, content, emotional intensity, and degree of openness to others for encounters frequently signified the relationship name of those patrons perceived to be together (acquaintances, friends, fellow employees, partners, brothers in crime, playmates, fathers, sons, sisters, single couple) as well as relationship intimacy (casual, chilly, conflictive, friendly, intimate). Careful observers at the bar compared and contrasted several relation-

---

[21] Simmel, *Sociology*, pp. 322–24; and Goffman, *Presentation of Self*, p. 105.

ship signs in their endeavors to read correctly other actors' identities and social and personal relationships. Actors reported that it was often important not only to determine who was in a social group but who within a social group was with whom. For example, in a circle of five consisting of two men and three women, who is the unattached female? The latter type of reading was of paramount concern to singles seeking pickups.

The relationship indicators used by actors at the Rendezvous in reading one another appeared to be tied in with conduct, i.e., *the conduct among those people perceived to be together.* For example, at the Rendezvous bar a wedding band might designate a married woman, but it does not divulge the relationship with her current male escort who could be her lover, employer, employee, marriage counselor, pimp, John, psychiatrist, hairdresser, professor, probation or parole officer, pupil, friend, or even (though rarely) her husband. Assumed symbolic objects and outward appearances alone do not denote the relationship existing between or among actors. Conduct in the form of how they act toward each other must be observed and interpreted. Social relationships at the Rendezvous bar as in other socal settings are dynamic; they begin, run their course, eventually end, and are even rejuvenated at times. The unseriousness of this setting is such that one's acquaintance tonight could become one's sexual playmate tomorrow, one's sexual playmate tonight, or someone else's sexual playmate tonight or tomorrow. As one male actor informed us during his interview: "Good readers are winners; slow readers are losers."

Nightspot Setting

ACTIVITIES

Like the bar, the nightspot setting varies in usage and patron membership; however, it is primarily oriented toward heterosexual interaction on a couple basis. Drinking here was often discovered to be a side involvement subordinate to other activities such as provocative and endearing heterosexual conversation. These exchanges were frequently punctuated with such demonstrations of affection as kissing, fondling, and embracing. Eating, smoking, dancing, listening to music, and impromptu acting on the dance floor were other activities that typically went on in an unserious romantic context.

Certain spatial properties make for a degree of conventional closure, thus screening out many interruptions. Actors here were found to have less to negotiate than bar actors, and they were also more frequently committed to one another than were actors at the bar. Most table patrons come to the club together and remain together more so than do bar groups. One and two couple groups (sometimes accompanied by extras) comprise the most numerous and prevailing group memberships at the tables. Four-somes, two couples, generally interact on an intracouple basis. When male or female extras are present, interaction tends to be more on an intergroup basis.

On the other hand, unlike many other nightspot settings that provide programmed entertainment, a sizable minority of patrons in the Rendezvous nightspot setting are unattached (approxi-mately 20 per cent whose sex distribution is about equal). This minority group is dispersed approximately in the setting as follows: male or female extras seated at tables occupied by one or two couples; several males seated together at one table; several females seated together at one table. Since there is no headwaiter, tables are available on a first-come, first-served basis. Though table hopping is discouraged, acquainted persons sitting at different tables are allowed this privilege. These features combined with the gift drink and dance routines permit cross-table encounters and pickups among those actors who are acquainted, and at times among those actors who are not acquainted.

Men at the bar, in a similar vein, occasionally interact with un-attached women (without male escorts) at the tables through the gift drink routine. Once the female accepts the drink, the male approaches her table and asks for a dance or for permission to sit with her. Frequently, the inviter and the invited ask the cock-tail waitresses for readings on each other prior to the invitation or acceptance of the gift drink. Therefore, the cocktail waitresses play an important mediating role in "proper introductions." They usually know many patrons well and assume the responsibility for facilitating pickups among people whom they deem compat-ible, and for discouraging pickups among those judged otherwise. Though this kind of service is condoned by the Rendezvous man-agement and anticipated by the patrons, all involved expect cocktail waitresses to receive tips beyond the normal range in return for these undertakings—which they routinely get. Cocktail waitresses also socialize with table groups, and when not busy, sit and drink with them, especially when there is an unattached male at a table who desires female company.

We observed that unescorted females could choose to maintain temporary or permanent self and/or group containment by accepting or rejecting one or more drinks or dance offers from one or more men at one or more times. They employ various social cues similar to those utilized in bar pickups to indicate their degree of availability and receptivity to heterosexual encounters. As in the bar, cross-sex encounters vary in length and intensity and may or may not result in pickups. Pickups customarily involve spatial and membership group changes, i.e., coupling-up makes for changes in space occupied and in group encounter membership. Unattached male or female patrons who see unattached counterparts in this setting occasionally approach each other directly by changing table memberships (moving from one table to another). This type of direct approach is seen less often here than at the bar because of spatial barriers and because actors at tables, even though unescorted, may be tied in with self-contained groups—and with actors who may not wish to be disturbed.

The rules that enable and constrain sociability in this subsetting are primarily geared toward heterosexual encounters, though occasionally dealers in illegal goods and services (sellers and buyers) make use of a table or two. Some actors expect and obtain group closure; some others expect an open situation that they may or may not subsequently close. In any event, closure is not automatic. A certain amount of bar sociability spills over to the tables (especially those close to the bar) because there are no physical barriers separating these two subsettings. Thus the actors must work (although not as intensely as at the bar) to create and maintain the setting that they desire, depending upon their interests at hand.

TABLE TALK

Though table conversations were detected to be more private and intimate than bar conversations, most were filled with either romantic discourse or trivial subject matter about the passing scene in the club. The observers, usually sitting as extras with one or two table couples with whom they were well acquainted, perceived the typicalness of snatchy, romantic remarks interspersed with embraces and kisses, an occasional dance, a cigarette, a swig of a drink, or a sandwich. At intervals between such endearing remarks as "I love you," "It's good to be together again," "No one turns me on like you," "Hold me tight, baby," "I know, I just can't wait," "Kiss me again," "When will we get together again?" "I'll never let you go," and so on, one hears sketchy and disjointed talk about a variety of mundane topics. For example the patrons talk about such things as the music, the musicians, the dancers and actors on the dance floor, the light and sound effects, theirs and other people's dress and personal adornments, different kinds of drinks, others' state of intoxication, the bar, cocktail waitresses, food, and sports, movies, clothes, cars, money. Frequently they also discuss their sex life together, how good it is, and how much better it is with each other than with others. Sometimes they gossip about other people's sex life.

When interacting on a table group basis rather than on a couple basis, they may talk shop, remark on the passing scene, tease one another, gossip about their mutual friends, tell each other sexy jokes, and josh each other about sexual tastes and sexual experiences. Table groups of unescorted women converse most about the men in the club and their chances of getting picked up. Otherwise they engage in small talk about clothes, jewels, cars, makeup, music, their sex lives, and the men who turn them on. Table groups of unescorted men talk about sex, the women in the club, female patrons and employees; and they discuss criminal activities and negotiate illegal deals at the tables.

Open Booths

ACTIVITIES

Observation and the interviews disclose that couples who enter the setting of the open booths usually remain there until they leave the club. Some males infrequently venture to the bar for brief chats with acquaintances and then return to their girls in the booths. Booth couples dance now and then. Couples frequent the four southwest corner booths to engage in sexual negotiation and heavy petting up to and at times including sexual intercourse. Drinking and at times eating are definitely subordinate activities. These booths also provide seclusion for some couples who do not wish to be seen by other actors in the club. Closure definitely obtains here, and interaction is confined to cross-sex partners. Sexual intercourse is more likely to occur when only one couple occupies a booth. Occasionally serious nonsexual negotiations occur in this setting, e.g., illegal transactions in stolen property. We noted that cocktail waitresses rarely enter these booths until they are summoned for drink or food orders.

BOOTH TALK

Conversational topics here are similar to those at the tables (i.e., sexually oriented). However, structured properties that screen out many distractions and a minimum of outside interruptions promote conversational content of a more intimate nature than that found in either the bar or at the tables. Verbal interchange is more serious, intent, couple focused, and less snatchy than that without. Conversations also tend to be lengthier and more detailed in nature than that overheard in other club settings. Even personal problems of a transsituational type are talked over sometimes, though most of the discourse alludes to, reflects, or stimulates heterosexual activity, e.g., "I'll never forget the first time you did me. . . ;" "Wait, I'll unzip. . . ;" "Give it all to me baby, now, I can't wait. . . ;" "Remember that time in the telephone booth . . . it's better here."

Private Booths

ACTIVITIES

Two northeast corner booths serve as a home territory setting for a select group of "businessmen" who drink, eat, dice, and socialize with each other and their girl friends. Closure rules operate, and outsiders enter only upon invitation. Sometimes, upon invitation cocktail waitresses and unattached women join this group for brief periods of time. Unlike the case with the other booth setting, cocktail waitresses frequently check these booths for service orders. Like the other subsettings, there is an expectancy here of playtime behavior, and interaction usually occurs at a superficial, playtime level, particularly when women or other outsiders are present.

BOOTH TALK

Conversations in form are similar to those in the open booths though they tend to be of longer duration and less snatchy than verbal exchanges at the bar and at tables. Unlike the open booths, encounters here are more group oriented than couple focused. Topic content varies with the group's composition (exclusively male, mixed company, exclusively insiders, insiders and outsiders) and the situation. Since these men know each other well, engage in similar occupations, and frequently work together, serious topics are sometimes discussed, e.g., business relations, "family matters," weddings, funerals, birthdays, saints' days, comrades, the administration of criminal justice, payoffs. Like the open booth subsetting and unlike the other two subsettings, secrecy here in the private booths obtains at two levels because encounters and activities herein are screened from the other settings inside the club as well as from the outside world.

The two home territory booths comprise the most serious of the club's unserious subsettings. In addition to the physical and ecological properties, several other features, such as group homogeneity, shared in-depth biographical knowledge, and secrecy and closure foster this greater degree of seriousness.

Conclusion

With respect to our question, "What happens in the Rendezvous?" we found two standing patterns of behavior: (1) sociability and play, an overt pattern, and (2) dealing in illegal goods and services, a covert pattern. The former was clearly the paramount standing behavior pattern and was established by an examination of encounters and activity patterns (units of behavior) in the club in terms of eight criteria of sociability and play found in the ture. During this process we supplied answers to the quest ___. What happens where in the setting with regard to sociability and play? What are the consequences of these goings-on?

At the Rendezvous the style of sociability and play varied by subsettings. The bar was the most open subsetting with respect to initiating and terminating encounters followed in descending order by the nightspot setting, open booths, and the private booths. This degree of *freedom* in initiating and terminating encounters was directly related to the *equality* found in the various subsettings. *Novelty*, the anticipation that something unusual or out of the ordinary will probably occur prevailed throughout the club, though to a greater degree in the nightspot setting (e.g., impromptu acts on the dance floor) and at the bar. All subsettings in the Rendezvous permit actors to step out of reality, i.e., stepping out of "real life" to where behavior is autonomous and for the "here-and-now"—and inconsequential for the "there-and-then." The bar seemed to facilitate this stepping out of reality more so than the other subsettings, in part because the actors here generally have less biographical knowledge about one another than actors in the other subsettings. Behavior at the Rendezvous is *circumscribed in both space and time*, i.e., restricted to the confines of the club between 1:00 A.M. and 7:00 A.M. We found that many of the playtime activities in this unserious setting would not be appropriate in other settings at other times. In the club certain behaviors are limited to certain subsettings (e.g., dancing in the nightspot, heavy petting in the booths, dicing for drinks at the bar).

Although the Rendezvous is a time-out unserious behavior setting where behavior is more problematic than in more formal settings, the actors including the management, employees, and patrons through their behavior routines have generated a social *order* and an attendant set of ground rules and rituals. Order varies within the club from one setting to another. Behavior is more problematic at the bar than in other subsettings. Actors here have the greatest potential to negotiate the definition of the situation, e.g., the modification or changing of a brief heterosexual encounter into a pickup routine or the carryover of dicing for drinks into a dice game for money. *Permanency* (which refers to the sometime anticipation of actors in play groups that their play groups will endure over time), with the exception of businessmen in the pri-

vate booths, was not found among other groups in other subsettings. We did find that most actors had a vested interest in maintaining the Rendezvous as a odd-time, time-out, unserious setting
for sociability and play. *Secrecy*, another sometime characteristic
of sociability and play, existed at two levels in the Rendezvous:
(1) the behavior in all the subsettings was secret in nature (i.e.,
veiled from the outside world) and (2) the booths provided for
secrecy within the club.

The second standing behavior pattern, dealing in illegal goods
and services (usually to be delivered or performed at some other
time), although established and expected to occur as a matter of
course and without question, was covert in nature. Behavior within
this pattern (e.g., buying hot clothes and jewelry) was expected
and required to take place surreptitiously under the guise of sociability and play—or to be transacted privately in the booths or in
one of the backstage regions such as the owner's private office.
Behavior within this pattern was serious and consequential for
both the present and future—and much more important for those
actors with serious interests at hand than those without hidden
agendas.

Rendezvous actors at the same time or at different times may
engage in one or both of the above standing behavior patterns.
Furthermore, we found that though sociability and play at the
Rendezvous are separate from reality, they are for many actors
related to and anchored in the real world. For example, some
entertainers and musicians while socializing in the club exchanged
information about the nightlife world including job opportunities.
Likewise criminals and some other actors kept abreast of what
was going on in the underworld.

Chapter 7

LATITUDES OF BEHAVIOR AND GROUND RULES

Introduction

THIS CHAPTER DEALS PRIMARILY with the sociological questions: What goes on in the Rendezvous setting? What are the consequences of these goings-on? The focal features of study in this endeavor were the *latitudes of behavior* and the *ground rules* related to proper behavior.[1] (See focal areas (6) and (7) as set forth in Chapter 3, Theoretical Orientation.) We surmised that these findings would help us in determining the *standing behavior patterns* in the Rendezvous (focal area 4), i.e., the stable, recurring, taken-for-granted activities that occur as a matter of course in the setting.

Permissive Behaviors and Social Control

The patrons' playtime expectations at the Rendezvous, where much of what happens is inconsequential to things that count outside the club, were found to promote not only sociability but also to facilitate a wider leeway of behavior than that expected or permitted in more serious settings. Moreover, we found that a

[1] We are primarily concerned with patrons' behavior in this chapter. Improper employee behavior is discussed in the employee typology chapter.

wider variety of expressive behaviors were more tolerated at the Rendezvous than in legal bars: a great deal more sexual flirtation, heterosexual familiarity and sexual joshing; more singing, joking and clowning activities on the dance floor by patrons and employees; and much more "showing out" behavior (bragging, signifying, exaggerating, posing). However, certain behaviors were more likely to be prohibited than in public bars: fighting, violence, heavy gambling, soliciting for prostitution, and overt trafficking in illegal goods and services. It was feared these behaviors would bring heat from the outside and cause disruptions within the club. We also heard less hard-core profanity and obscenity throughout the club than we had noted in public bars. Sexual language here was couched in a more romantic and respectable form than sexual language we had overheard in public bars.

All types of Rendezvous actors were found to be concerned about some social control of behavior at the club. The owner-manager and all regular employees share career stakes in the club's preservation. Sometime employees, moonlighters, have a monetary concern in its continuation. Various types of patrons hold vested recreational interests in the club's survival, and for them as well as for others there is always the available option of dealing seriously. The management and employees pointed out in the interviews in different ways that behavior had to be controlled at the Rendezvous to avoid public exposure and disapproval that could lead to costly, embarrassing raids, arrests, and legal prosecution. Though the fix is in with the police, "the club," in the words of the owner-manager, "has to police itself." This meant, according to him, "keeping things nice and orderly and avoiding things like violence and drugs that would bring heat."

Patron interviewees, though they claimed to feel safe, made a point of the necessity for all actors "to play it cool" at the club to avoid inside hassles and outside heat. "Play it cool" in their terms meant self-control, the avoidance of violence, and the presentation of a sophisticated front.

Illegal licensers reported to receive protection money (payoffs for permitting the club to function) possess monetary, career, and sometimes recreational interests in the club's continued operation. The owner-manager told us that these licensers are very much concerned about the control of social behavior in the club and the transaction of illegal business there. They wish to make sure that the illegal negotiations in the club are kept secret. Any exposure of the club is a threat to them.

The comments of Rendezvous actors in the club to one another, their comments to us, and their statements in the interviews suggested a concern with two general levels of behavior: (1) proper behavior at the club defined in terms of enabling and restricting ground rules that facilitate ongoing pleasant and rewarding activities; (2) problematic behaviors in or outside the club that threaten the club's ongoing activities.

Proper Behavior

It was assumed that patrons had to have some knowledge of the range of activities open and closed to them in order to behave properly in the club. Interactional guidelines appeared to be constructed by the actors themselves. These guidelines tell actors what they might expect of others and the way they might be expected to respond to the behavior of others. The owner, for example, by impression management helps in this direction. The rhetoric throughout the club promotes an aura of respectability within an illegal, playtime, space-time setting—*the impression of a regular place for irregular people.* Screening procedures serve as part of this rhetoric in that they eliminate the presence of those considered unworthy or disorderly and those considered likely to become disorderly. Simultaneously, screening procedures, along with other presentational strategies (e.g., good service, high prices, plush private club decor), tell the actors that they are worthy patrons in a respectable place. Because the cast of actors, the setting, and the scenario are presented as respectable, proper behavior from all is expected by all. Patrons and employees expect themselves and others to behave properly while having a good time. Proper behavior is facilitated by the attendance of worthy patrons who come to the club with a legitimate purpose in mind, to have a good time. The normal appearance of having a good time calls for the presentation of a pleasant, courteous front throughout the club, and additionally, an air of social accessibility, especially in the bar subsetting.

Extensive observation triangulated with participant observation and interviews (especially with key informants) yielded the following do's and don't's in the Rendezvous. To avoid an alien role one does not stare at other people; make furtive, awkward movements; encroach upon others' immediate physical surroundings and personal belongings. Actors respect the privacy of social groups that wish to be left alone. In a conversational group one takes his turn, which is indicated by "go ahead" social cues such as nods in one's direction, questions, eye contacts coupled with speech pauses, and the like. When entering a conversation, an actor sticks to the prevailing subject and avoids drawn-out dissertations. The speaker concentrates on current events in the club and other "light" topics, avoids distracting side talk, screens out conversation about one's status and roles outside the club, and refrains from probing into the outside personal lives of others.[2] One apologizes or gives a good account[3] of himself to any person whom he offends or is about to offend.

Club observations clearly showed that the code of proper behavior was sometimes broken but that most actors resorted to remedial measures (i.e., some form of apology or account) when they transgressed the code and thereby paid it deference even in its violation.

Minor Improprieties

As in other bars, a variety of self-indulgent and untoward acts frequently occur in the Rendezvous without sanction,[4] though they may or may not be approved by all actors present.[5] We discovered that such acts were taken for granted throughout the club so long as they did not cause run-ins or interfere seriously with

[2] For an elaboration of discretionary measures employed with acquaintances and friends, see Georg Simmel, *The Sociology of Georg Simmel*, ed. and trans. Kurt H. Wolff (New York: Free Press, 1965), pp. 320–26.

[3] For a definition and analysis of various types of accounts and how they are negotiated, see Stanford M. Lyman and Marvin B. Scott, *A Sociology of the Absurd* (New York: Appleton-Century-Crofts, 1970), pp. 111–43.

[4] Sanction is used in a sociological sense, that is, to designate a reward or punishment used by actors to encourage or discourage the repetition of a particular behavior in a given setting.

[5] Sherri Cavan, *Liquor License: An Ethnography of Bar Behavior* (Chicago: Aldine, 1966), pp. 67–87.

other actors' ongoing activities. Patrons sometimes became intoxicated to the point of losing motor control and, consequently, fell off bar stools, went to sleep, stumbled around, fell on the floor and up against others. Men and women displayed open and marked affection for each other (e.g., fondling and embracing) and engaged in heavy petting—and occasionally sexual intercourse in the open booths.

Sexual activity in the open booths is condoned if concealed. In most cases specific intimate sexual contacts are not known about in the club, though most actors are aware that intimate sexual interaction does occur there. Patrons are not expected to call to the attention of others any knowledge of their sexual exploits in the booths, i.e., talk about their sexual behavior there or make undue noises during their sexual activities that might evoke outside concern. The assistant manager submitted the following remarks during an interview:

So long as lovers in the booths keep their game to themselves, we could care less. After all that's what the booths are for. At least one reason. We don't put up with any gang banging or a hell of a lot of noise. We can't stand for a train of people going in or out like a whore house. We don't want the booths messed up either. Now if some couples get it on in a quiet way—so, what else is new? But we can't stand for any sexual athlete blabbing about his screwing in the booths all over the place. It's really no big hassle. People in here know how to act. Once in a while we have to call a couple down. You know when they make too much noise, or when they have too much to drink, and come out without all their clothes on. But we have the situation under control. We send them back in and make them dress, or we send a cocktail waitress or a bouncer in to help them.

Commenting further on rules connected with booth sexual behavior and expressive behavior throughout the club, the assistant manager remarked to one of the researchers in the owner's private office:

We don't have trouble with the businessmen's booths. They keep quiet, and don't get really with it with girls. We'll even send a drunk broad who's a little messed up—you know her clothing and make-up—upstairs with a cocktail waitress. In the women's lounge she gets fixed up by the maid. We'll do the same for a man—you know, have a bouncer take him up for a rest and a clean-up job in the men's lounge. When they come back in later, sober, we tell them once is enough. No more or out they go. Don't get me wrong, the sex thing is no big thing. So long as they show a little class. Most of them are just clowning around anyhow.

Actors engage in a wide range of exuberant, expressive behaviors with impunity: talking and laughing loudly, singing, back slapping, mock fighting, telling sexy and earthy jokes, quarreling or arguing, playing clowning tricks, exchanging profane but endearing greetings and farewells. For example, one observer overheard the following exchange at the bar:

Hello, Pasquale, you old bastard, where in the hell have you been hiding out?
Who knows? Three steps ahead of the cops.
Bullshit, you got the police, the district attorney and the grand jury in your pocket, so who gives a damn about the cops?

The concern here, as in the case of expressive sexual behavior, is with behavioral consequences that might disrupt the setting. The owner-manager explained to one observer at the bar:

They come here to have a ball, so you go along with them. That's what the place is for—for people to have a good time. They feel a little freer here than in a public bar. After all, they're with their own kind, and they don't have to be on guard all the time because they know they're in good hands with us—like Allstate. So they're going to drink more here and really get it on with the broads. If it's for fun, fine, but when they get mad and take each other seriously, we have to step in and cool it off. We can't have a couple of gorillas tearing up property and blocking other people's acts.

Interactional Offenses and Remedial Measures

The close, unavoidably frequent face-to-face contacts among actors at the Rendezvous in a crowded, commingling, fluid behavior setting increase the chances for social mishaps and run-ins. The intoxicated condition of many actors probably adds to this contingency. Most offenses we witnessed in the club, however, of either commission or omission were typically minor, trivial, transitory, social piques that did not leave lasting ill effects. They consisted of inadvertent pushes, bumps, shoves; the usurpation of others' seats at the bar or table; careless mishandling of others' belongings; spilling of drinks on anothers' person or territory; mistakenly picking up others' drinks; burning someone's person or property with a cigarette; knowingly or unknowingly flirting with another's girlfriend or boyfriend; forgetting or neglecting to pay for an obligated round of drinks; neglecting to introduce one party to another when an introduction was in order; statements or expressions interpreted as gaffes or insults by coparticipants.

Since these offenses at the Rendezvous typically involved slight affronts to someone's self-respect rather than to someone's serious property rights, they usually received ritualistic, remedial measures such as automatic apologies or accounts along with portrayals of regret on the part of the offender.[6] The offender usually presented a remorseful front to the offended, claimed respect for the rule that his actions violated, dissociated himself from the broken rule, and promised that the transgression would not recur. The offended party usually accepted the offender's account (explanation or claim of mitigating circumstances) or apology (assumption of responsibility accompanied by remorse), thereby giving the contrite wrongdoer relief and simultaneously preserving the scene for everybody concerned. Other actors with vested interests in the encounter usually attempted to facilitate these remedial measures by helping the offender justify his actions that were interpreted negatively by the offended party. These ritualistic forms were some variant of "I'm sorry" and at times generated serendipitous encounters by paving the way for pleasant acquaintanceships.

The success of remedial measures depended upon the defender's finesse in requesting and obtaining the victim's relief. Remedies and reliefs were exchanged by gestures as well as by words. When offenders failed to offer remedial ritual, victims either overlooked the slight or challenged the offender, who then did or did not offer an acceptable remedy. A few victims pointedly refused to accept a remedy or gave sarcastic remedial renditions. Negative variants sometimes led to quarrels but rarely to physical fights. When remedial exchanges failed between offender and offended,

[6] For a theoretical analysis of remedial interchanges, see Erving Goffman, *Relations in Public: Microstudies of the Public Order* (New York: Basic Books, 1971), pp. 108–66, 183–87.

sanctions were typically imposed by other patrons or employees. Other patrons would "cool them down" or physically separate them. Club employees sometimes presented both offender and victim with a gift drink telling them to "drink up and forget about it."

Serious Violations

The patrons, employees, and management wishing to perpetuate the behavior settings in the club without inside or outside interference sanctioned behaviors they thought would victimize them in any way or interrupt their ongoing activities. Serious behavior violations were reported in the interviews to be of three kinds: fights and violence, overt and direct trafficking in illegal goods and services, squealing to the police or city officials about the club's operation. Violence in the form of fights between or among patrons and employees was taboo. Aggressive stands accompanied by pointed and caustic, obscene or profane language; damage to the club's or a patron's property; and rowdy, aggressive actions that abridged the rights of others were also sanctioned by patrons and employees. Sanctions of run-ins usually occurred in the form of third-party interruptions between two wrangling participants. They were usually told to shake hands and "forget about it." When necessary, bouncers attempted to quell disturbances by "cooling down" the situation, i.e., by appealing to the offender's sense of propriety and fair play, issuing cease and desist orders, and negotiating patrons' differences. When all else failed, the bouncers resorted to force, physically restraining belligerents or aggressors against persons or property, physically bouncing offenders out of the club. Usually requests to leave were sufficient, such as "Why don't you go home, Charlie, and sleep it off? We'll see you tomorrow." Physical force was rarely necessary and always applied with a minimum of intensity.

Illegal goods, services, and overt criminal activities (beyond operating a club and selling drinks after hours) are prohibited by the Rendezvous. Such activities are the use, possession, or sale of drugs; wagering on anything other than drinks; openly buying, bartering, or selling stolen property; house prostitution or the open soliciting of prostitution. These interdictions did not preclude the presence of various criminals and hustling types, nor were they intended to do so. However, they did appear successful in preventing overt and direct criminal and hustling activities. Patrons reported in the interviews that they meet various hustlers and criminals in the club with whom they negotiate illegal deals for some other time and some other place. Some examples are bookies with whom they place bets, fences from whom they buy stolen goods (hot clothes, jewelry, whiskey, and so on), gambling house operators with whom they gamble, officials and police officers with whom they negotiate protection as well as other services, con men whom they employ to "set up" others, enforcers who enforce for them, thieves who steal for them, and professional prostitutes with whom they negotiate sexual liaisons for themselves or others. The point is that although the Rendezvous is sometimes used as a clearing house for criminal activities by some actors, its front must be straight. Therefore, behavior connected with criminal pursuits must be veiled there. If not, it is negatively sanctioned. For example, following the ejection of a call girl patron from the club, the owner-manager explained to one of the observers in a table group:

Manager: *I hated to ask her to leave. She's a regular and everybody likes her, but I warned her over and over not to hustle in here.*

Observer: *Yeah, but it's hard to tell who's hustling who sometimes.*

Manager: *I don't want to hear it. She don't have to throw her ass around with a price tag written on it. She could show a little class. And then who'd give a damn? It don't look right to some other people in here, and you have to be careful about hustling. You just can't run an open hustling joint. If you allow a bunch of hookers to work right out in the open, a lot of good people will stop coming. The police and the public would close you down if you tried that. She just shows off her ass too much and pushes it on too strong. Christ, with what she's got, she don't have to come on so strong.*

Observer: *O.K., I get your message. Are you going to let her back in sometime?*

Manager: *Let her back in? What do you take me for? Some kind of social worker?*

Observer: *Well, whatever's right.*
Manager: *Maybe so, if she learns how to act right.*

Patrons who either pry too closely into the personal affairs of
others at the club or who gossip too freely about what goes on
there (in or outside the club) are ostracized. According to the
owner, this kind of talk "gets around" and "gets back to me."
Employees give these "loud mouths" and "finks" poor service and
the cold shoulder. Other patrons shun them. The word is passed
around that "so and so" talks too much, and subsequently "so and
so" is ostracized from social encounters. Transgressors of this type
are rare (one or two a year), and informal sanctions usually drive
them out of the club. A few who refuse to heed the message are
told by the management to stay away. Any patron who is discovered giving any information to the police, city officials, or the
press about the Rendezvous is immediately barred from club attendance. In certain cases, depending upon the identity of the
squealer, other unpleasant things await him. The owner-manager
addressed the point in an interview:

*We don't as a rule have any problem with informers or
squealers. The reason is simple. The professional informers and
those who get paid for piece work can make more money on our
side than they can with the police. Informers know who to inform
on anyhow. They want to live and be happy like everybody else.
Why should they want their heads knocked in? We don't have to
enforce anything. Our patrons are our enforcers. Nobody likes to
see a good thing screwed up. Once in a while some damned do-
gooder or some honest cop, or some guy that gets mad at us for
some reason, like we had to throw him out for whatever, will talk
too much to the wrong people. We get the word pretty fast and
work something out. Nobody's ever testified in court against us
yet. Who pays any attention to an informer anyway? Who's going
to support his song? If I find out about a squealer, he gets a message to get lost—real lost.*

Summary

The Rendezvous permits and even fosters wider latitudes of
expressive behavior, especially sexual behavior, than that found in

public drinking establishments. Some utilize the club as a clearing house for criminal activities without fear of sanction. Playtime to them at the club may be a side involvement used to camouflage more serious activities. For others, the major involvement is playtime activity, with the prospects of selling or buying illegal goods and services a side involvement. For the majority of the actors, the setting is a playtime setting. Obviously, this unserious setting is more unserious for some than it is for others. The setting's unserious, semisecret, protective features, combined with the actors' "code" of proper conduct and sanctioning procedures, promote these behavioral latitudes.

Actors at the Rendezvous seem to have more diversified and compounded stakes in maintaining and protecting their setting than do actors in public bars. They appear to lend one another greater support in this endeavor than do public bar actors. For example, they maintain a courteous front of having a good time, engage in remedial measures to prevent run-ins, sanction one another, maintain silence about the club's activities, camouflage nonsociable purposes, and enforce the club's secrecy rules. Cooperation among different types of actors with differing sets of interests makes the scene possible. In short, they all work to maintain social order in the club.

Chapter 8

PATRON TYPES

Introduction

THIS CHAPTER IS PRIMARILY CONCERNED with the sociological questions: Who goes to the Rendezvous? When? To do what with whom? Where in the setting? The eighth focal area of study, *typology of actors in the setting* (see Chapter 3), furnished the most specific answers to these questions. Here, in line with recent studies on deviants, we go to the actors themselves for knowledge about their identities, self-conceptions, world views, and social meanings.[1] Moreover, we attempt to reconstruct the Rendezvous setting through and by the perspectives of the different types of actors in the setting on the basis of their verbalization and behavior—fronts, conversations, social encounters, gestures, body

[1] Some sociologists note that the study of deviance is moving increasingly in the direction of participant-observer studies and toward theories of deviance based on such research information. There are wide gaps in our knowledge of deviance and perhaps the best method for getting the information we need is participant-observer studies of the case-study type on deviance in the open. Deviance so labeled by formal rule-making and rule-enforcing bodies may tell us more about labeling procedures than about deviants and deviancy. Captured respondents without their natural habitat may be gorillas in the zoo, not in the jungle. See the following participant-observer studies in the "open" tradition: William F. Whyte, *Street Corner Society* (Chicago: University of Chicago Press, 1955); Howard S. Becker, *The Outsiders* (New York: Free Press, 1963); Elliot Liebow, *Tally's Corner* (Boston: Little, Brown, 1967); Lewis Yablonsky, *Hippie Trip* (New York: Western Publishing, 1968); Erving Goffman, *Behavior in Public Places* (New York: Free Press, 1963); Laud Humphreys, *Tearoom Trade: Impersonal Sex in Public Places* (Chicago: Aldine, 1970). See also Jack D. Douglas, ed., *Observations on Deviance* (New York: Random House, 1970) for an excellent collection of recent research on deviance in the open.

language, and activities. Some interview materials were utilized for biographical and illustrative purposes. Within the typological schema, we were not only concerned with differentiation among actors but also with their social articulation and their fit (or synomorphy) with the Rendezvous setting. As explained in Chapter 4 on methodology, we derived the typology from first order categories (the types suggested by the actors themselves), which were then analyzed along three theoretical dimensions: (1) ascribed and achieved characteristics, (2) identities and perspectives, and (3) behavior on the scene. In this chapter we present the patron section of the constructed typology. The next chapter deals with the employee types.

Hip Squares

Ascribed and Achieved Characteristics

Hip squares are a relatively young (ranging from twenty-one to forty), well-educated (most have completed college), affluent, middle-class group of mixed marital status revelers who play conventional roles in the straight world.[2] Square women (most under thirty) are younger than square men and are most frequently without marital ties. All squares are educationally equipped to work at the white-collar level, and most are employed in middle to upper echelons of business, government, or professional positions. Especially is this the case with men. None have working class backgrounds, and most are products of stable, urban, conventional, middle-class homes. All currently reside in respectable, middle-class residential neighborhoods.

Squares have no career interests in the club or in any other underworld activity, though some are acquainted with a few criminals in gambling, sporting, and recreational contexts. None report juvenile or criminal records, unwed parenthood, criminal abortions, or behavior problems during youth and adolescence.[3]

[2] By pristine standards, very few would qualify as truly hip. For an excellent discussion of the process of becoming hip, see J. L. Simmons and Barry Winograd, "The Hang-Loose Ethic" in *Deviance, Reality, and Change*, ed. H. Taylor Buckner (New York: Random House, 1971), pp. 365–67.

[3] This checks out with the official records we examined.

Though all drink and some use soft drugs (primarily marijuana)
now and then, none appear to be addicted to any drug. Vivacious,
physically attractive, well heeled and well dressed (tending toward
the mod style), squares are quite knowledgeable about jazz and
popular music, food and drink, clothing, sports, T.V., cinema and
cafe society, night club entertainment, and the "swinging" heterosexual scene (for the most part in middle-class contexts). Speech
patterns among them vary from conventional forms to the hip
vernacular.

IDENTITIES AND PERSPECTIVES

Squares view themselves as a sexually liberated, light-hearted,
hell-raising, swinging group of part-time players who though
anchored in the conventional world have ready access to the hip
world.[4] A self-styled "in crowd" of swingers, they occasionally play
marginal roles in the unconventional world without commitment.
When "the ball is over" they return to their real world, the conventional world, without contamination. Squares identify with a
particular occupation, class and family position, support private
property rights, denigrate theft, and verbalize the values of working for a living and obeying most of the legal codes. Social participants in the wider conventional society, they attend established
churches, belong to fraternal, service and civic organizations, and
vote and align themselves with established political parties—commonly with the Republican Party.

Though somewhat rebellious or ambivalent in their positions on
sex, morality, and the Protestant ethic (e.g., hard work, frugality,
and preparing for the future), squares identify with and support
the basic social institutions. Not quite ready to settle down and
play their conventional roles to the hilt, they desire the pleasures
and excitement of an off-beat play world as well as the security
of the conventional world. Squares' conventional role identities
receive a moderate degree of self and group support. And so far,
they appear successful in having it both ways.

[4] Similar in certain respects to Walshok's sexual swingers, they maintain
conventional commitments while participating segmentally in a deviant sub-
culture. See Mary Lindstein Walshok, "The Emergence of Middle-Class Deviant Subcultures: The Case of Swingers," *Social Problems*, vol. 18, no. 4
(Spring 1971): 488–95.

BEHAVIOR ON THE SCENE

Squares are irregular patrons who visit the club most frequently on Fridays, Saturdays, and Sundays.[5] Typically, they gain initial entrance to the Rendezvous in the company of other hip square patrons. Most come in groups of two to four couples a little after 2:00 A.M. (when public bars close) and occupy tables in front of the bandstand where they interact among themselves, i.e., converse, smoke, drink, snack, and occasionally dance within a self-contained group. When unescorted, solos and team members of either sex usually sit at the bar. In commenting on seating arrangements and space, one male square reported in the course of an interview:

It's not our club, and most of the time it's crowded. Most of the time we sit at one of the tables in front of the bandstand. You kind of get the message that's where they want you to sit. I mean a table or two is usually open there. The cocktail hostesses point the way, but they don't actually escort you. If I come in alone or with a buddy, I generally sit at the middle of the bar. Either end of the bar is usually taken up by a group of regulars. Of course, there are exceptions. You have to pick your way. With square girls, it's different. I mean if they come in without escorts. They sit at a table anywhere or at the bar.

Square couples usually stay for three or four hours whereas unescorted squares enter and leave more sporadically, usually remaining for longer periods of time than couples. The height of this membership reaches 15 to 20 on weekends and five to ten on weekdays. Beyond the major service provided (booze and food), squares mention several reasons for attending the club. All say they come to "listen to good music" and to see the impromptu acts on the dance floor. Some say they come to view a bunch of off-beat characters whom they perceive as exciting pariahs and deviants. As one square submitted while being interviewed:

You see all kinds of exciting characters at the Rendezvous. Characters you wouldn't believe in real life. You see show people, gamblers, musicians, criminals, whores, pimps—all kinds of way-

[5] Irregular patron refers to an attendance pattern of less than once per week.

out people jumbled together. Once in a while, I like to go down and see them jump. They're out of sight. But not the kind you'd want a steady diet of.

Most say they occasionally attend the club in order to relax from the pressures of everyday life and frolic anonymously among exciting people "who know how to live it up." Some say, "It's the best place to go after the legal bars close." Still others report they impress out-of-town guests with a trip to the Rendezvous. In this vein one male square specified in an interview:

Uncle John gets to town about once a year. He features himself to be one of those aging playboys who's been everywhere and seen everything. But really he is a square from one of those small towns in the provinces. Get the picture? Man, do I get a kick out of taking him to the Rendezvous. He thinks it's one of the seven wonders of the world. What a blast. It gives him something to talk about back home.

Though this membership's language is frequently couched in the argot of the hip, most regulars and employees take a chary view of "the plastic outsiders," particularly of newcomers.[6] A standing joke among habitués is that hip squares come to see various "way-out" types at the club and erroneously take one another for unconventionals. As one regular stated during his interview:

Those damn stupid squares come down here to look at the animals in the zoo, and take each other for monkeys and tigers. Man, they turn me off. They're all monkeys and lambs, but think they're tigers. They try to act hip, but it's all a bunch of shit.

Neophyte squares view employees as instrumentalities and interact with them only in a segmental, impersonal fashion. Typically, they do not receive prompt service despite their big tipping. Many regular patrons acknowledge them as neutral persons or nonpersons worthy only of civil inattention. In this connection, one neophyte square commented to one of the observers at the bar that on some occasions he felt like he was invisible, that the barmaid was looking straight through him. A few squares who attend the club over long periods of time are successful in projecting themselves as worthy actors in the setting. These few, referred to as

---

[6] A regular designates a patron who attends the club at least once a week.

"rounded-off squares" by regulars, are awarded wider latitudes of behavior and higher club status than common squares. Most squares, however, are not concerned with becoming "in" members of the Rendezvous since the club to them is a sometime, frolicking setting where both patrons and employees are mere agents and props. While being interviewed, an articulate square woman remarked:

It's a fun place to go. And sometimes I meet an interesting man. Even if I go to bed with him, it's no big thing. I mean, I live in a different world. People there never become anything to me [in real life]. It's just a ball sometimes to go down there and play around. It's like a theater where the actors are servants.

Neophyte square men infrequently come stag because they are more acceptable and considered less dangerous (less likely to be informers or undercover police) when accompanied by females or other well-known patrons. When unescorted, they sit quietly at the bar and interact among themselves and with others only when approached. Rarely do they take part in the various spontaneous behaviors engaged in by many others in or out of the bar setting. Neophytes find it difficult to pick up females, and when they do "score," it is generally with square females or female thieves.

Squares enjoy less freedom of movement throughout the club than other patron groups because they know less about one another (squares in other groups) and less about other patron memberships than is the case with regulars. Squares' dearth of biographical knowledge about squares (outside their exclusive group) and other patron groups prevents a square-group cohesiveness. This lack of information also limits their interactional potential with other patrons. Once seated, male squares usually remain in place drinking, talking, eating, listening to the music, and smoking among themselves. Despite their irregular attendance, some squares are usually present. Rounded-off squares, although enjoying greater freedom of action, still retain the square label. The assistant manager confirms the label but also indicates the acceptance of squares as necessary patrons. As he explained to one of the observers at the bar:

If they've been around a while and behave themselves, they're O.K. So we treat them right. But they only get in so far with us [employees], and they never get anywhere with important people.

Come to think of it, show people just put up with them. Square broads I can take easier, but squares are still squares. We need them. They spend a lot of dough. They add a respectable front. They're good bait because the other patrons feel more at ease with a few around. That way they know the club is not just another hangout for crooks. The cops see it the same way. Anyhow, the squares know their place.

Square women gain easier access to the club and enjoy a wider latitude of behavior than square men, particularly when they are not in the company of male counterparts. Once known to the club employees, they frequently come in groups of two to three women and usually sit at the bar where they drink, smoke, and talk among themselves and with some regular male patrons. Barmaids and cocktail waitresses treat them in a politely formal way and avoid (if possible) social encounters that include them. Rarely do they introduce them to other patrons. If and when a square woman is picked up at the bar, she commonly moves to the nightspot setting. Here, in addition to engaging in further sexual negotiations, they listen to music, drink, eat, converse, watch the action on the dance floor, and dance. The unescorted membership at any one time varies from three to five and is more susceptible to direct pickup overtures than other female memberships. They are considered less worthy in the setting than other female types, and most male patrons assume they come to the club, more so than other females, to get picked up. The following interview responses of one square female make this point clear:

Square girls are really out of place. Many of the other girls don't like us. They look upon us as outside poachers. So does most of the help. They give you that knowing look which says you're cheaper than they are because the only damn reason you are there is to get picked up. They want you to know that they know you're outa place. The men really move in fast. They figure if you didn't want to get picked up, you wouldn't be there. Most of the time they're right, but sometimes we just like to be left alone and enjoy what's going on.

Other female memberships in the club view square women as outside, unfair competitors, and remain aloof from them on a one-to-one basis. A call girl, a member of another type group, declared to one of the observers in the nightspot setting:

Those square bitches make me sick. They shouldn't be allowed in here. They got everything going for them out there. Why do they want to come down here to our place? They're a bunch of curiosity seekers. They come in here and try to impress all the men. You'd think they'd be satisfied. Their men must be no good. Otherwise they wouldn't be throwing their ass around in here.

Square females and males from other memberships occasionally find themselves together in mixed group situations at the tables or in the booths. This usually occurs when a group of male patrons picks up an assortment of females from different membership groups (e.g., call girls, party girls, and squares) and brings them together in a new group situation. Though square women appear to be accommodated in such an arrangement, very little inter-action beyond nods of introduction and recognition goes on be-tween them and the other women. Generally speaking, conversa-tion in these encounters occurs between men and women, and men and men. Very little woman-to-woman interchange transpires. One square female pointed out to an observer drinking at the bar:

About the only time we talk to other girls is when we get invited into a group where they are. Or, you know, if a bunch of guys pick up different girls and then bring us together. I know they feel uncomfortable. I do too. I don't speak their language. Now with a man, it's different. I can talk to most any kind of man.

The preceding and other similar statements by patrons and employees at the club and during the interviews demonstrated that conversations and social encounters between men and women from different membership groups occur more frequently than social encounters among women of different membership groups. For the most part, conversation among squares and between squares and other patrons tends to be light chitchat geared to sociability and is unrelated to situations outside of the club. On the other hand, squares may arrange (and sometimes do arrange) to purchase (at some other time in some other place) illegal goods and services at the club, e.g., stolen property such as furs, clothing, jewelry, coins, whiskey, cigarettes, appliances, produce, building materials, sex, protection, muscle. In such cases, club employees typically play an intermediary role. One rounded-off square male elaborated on this contingency to one of the researchers while seated at a table in the nightspot setting:

Sure we come to play, but other options are always open. Say you want to pick up a case or two of good Scotch at a bargain. Or you are looking for a certain kind of ring or watch. Well, you can find it. Of course, you don't go asking around out loud. Just pass the word to one of the bouncers you happen to know pretty good, or to somebody who knows the bouncer. The message gets through and you can make a good deal. You may have to wait a few days, but it'll be arranged. There's always something available. You know, some good deal on something that you hadn't thought about, or planned on. The news of the merchandise gets to you. And if you don't want it, maybe somebody you know does. If you can get a $300 watch for two bills, why not? The square broads deal too. Everybody in here is a player of one kind or another.

SUMMARY

Squares appear to be situational deviants who occasionally use the club as a place in which to covertly violate publicly accepted norms without being publicly processed as deviant and play anonymously at being hip.[7] They can shuck off their routine masks and add new ones, embroider their biographies, and seek new sexual experiences without fear of serious consequences. The Rendezvous is relevant to squares only when they are taking part in it. Behavior there is time-out behavior that is of no serious import to their outside biographies, responsibilities, and work roles. In short, what they do at the club does not count at some other time at some other place. On the other hand, the club may function as an illegal marketplace for some squares who wish to purchase illegal goods and services.

The Rendezvous caters to this type's serious as well as unserious purposes at hand. Though squares are not insiders, nevertheless their very presence adds some respectability to the club and at the same time contributes security to the setting. The management, employees, and deviant patrons can always point to the squares as straights when accused of participating in a disreputable setting. Additionally, they comprise a sizable group of the club's big

[7] For a discussion of this type of deviance, see Albert J. Reiss, "The Study of Deviant Behavior: Where the Action Is," in *Approaches to Deviance: Theories, Concepts, and Research Findings*, ed. Mark Lefton, James K. Skipper, Jr., and Charles H. McCaghy (New York: Appleton-Century-Crofts, 1968), pp. 59–65.

spenders and a purchasing group that contributes to the setting's marketplace for illegal goods and services. Therefore, they support the viability of the Rendezvous' ongoing activities. Though enjoying only marginal membership in the setting without full integration into its activities, they are affixed to its milieu. In brief, they compose a necessary membership group—a group that knows its place on the scene and plays its part according to the script that is accomplished by all the actors. In short, squares are important actors in the setting.

Night People

ASCRIBED AND ACHIEVED CHARACTERISTICS

This patron membership of night people is employed in legitimate nightlife establishments to entertain or serve others: entertainers (e.g., singers, comedians, dancers, show girls, ventriloquists, impressionists, acrobats, actors, actresses); musicians; entertainment impresarios; emcees and agents; owners, managers, and employees of night clubs, theaters, restaurants and bars. The latter subcategory includes a sprinkling of maitre d's, bartenders, bouncers, cocktail hostesses, waiters, waitresses, cigarette and camera girls, and strippers. Entertainers, musicians, emcees, entertainment agents, and owners and managers of night clubs and bars are numerically predominant among this type. Though many of these patrons are migratory (i.e., they work in a number of clubs outside the city from time to time), most are locally connected in the nightlife industry. Out-of-town night people in this category are usually temporarily employed (one week or less) in local establishments.

Though this patron type varies in age (ranging from twenty-one to sixty), sex (from 50 to 60 per cent males), education (from grade school to college graduate), marital status (single, separated, divorced, married—most of them currently unattached), occupational skill (from skilled artists to semiskilled workers), and social class origin (lower-class to upper-middle-class urban background), group members have much in common. Children of the night, they work when other people play or sleep, and play in exciting and risqué nightlife settings when other people sleep. Measured by respectable middle-class standards, they are unconventional and off-beat in life style. Their form of employment, work hours, work sites, speech patterns, dress, recreational pursuits, personal habits, associations, conduct, and ideology all differ from middle-class, day people. Most of them work and play in places where liquor is served and where audiences are frequently intoxicated; where swingers, players, criminals, prostitutes, hustlers, and underworld types congregate and negotiate; where both patron conduct and form of entertainment is boisterous and frequently erotic; and where gambling, loose women, prostitutes, contraband, and drugs are often available. They speak in a hip vernacular, a composite jargon spoken by musicians, show-biz people, drug addicts, and criminals. They dress in a modish, flamboyant fashion and pursue recreational activities focusing on a nexus of alcohol, soft drugs, promiscuous sex, gambling, and nightlife entertainment.

Night people go on many "busmen's holidays." When off duty they seek similar recreational settings to those in which they work. Many are employed in establishments owned or managed by criminals, and most of them at one time or another have been tied in with the underworld through and by contacts and contracts with "connected" agents and club owners. Many of their friends and acquaintances are either members of the underworld or have connections therein. Some buy "hot" clothes from criminal fences and know other criminals in social as well as work contexts. Many date and sometimes marry criminals. Still others even moonlight at criminal activities, usually involving gambling, prostitution, or drugs. Some work for criminals as messengers, connections, and couriers. Some fence stolen property, pimp or solicit in prostitution. Still others help set up marks for gamblers, con men, and hustlers. This patron group comes in contact with hipsters, hustlers, prostitutes, and a various assortment of people from the criminal world during either their work or playtime activity.

Most night people grew up in respectable, noncriminal families and appear to have had no serious adjustment problems during their formative years. Only a few (less than 10 per cent) report juvenile delinquent adjudication, though more than one-third note adult arrests (primarily on gambling and drug charges). About one-third have served time as adults, mostly for misdemeanors. None appear addicted to alcohol or other drugs. Night people vary in dwelling pattern from hotel to apartment, and residence sites from lower-middle-class to upper-class quarters.

IDENTITIES AND PERSPECTIVES

Night people consider themselves to be hip and cool and take great pride in their discriminating knowledge of the happenings, vicissitudes, and the ever changing entertainment formats in the nightlife entertainment industry; and of the patron and personnel turnovers occurring among different types of clubs, bars, restaurants, theaters, and show acts. They identify with the nightlife world of which they are a part and follow closely the careers and life histories of acquaintances, friends, and enemies (their significant others) in this world.

Meticulous in dress and appearance, they present a composed yet vivacious front. They see themselves as blasé, fun-loving, pleasure seekers who are always in good taste in dress, mannerisms, food and drink, sex, and recreational pursuits. Most take a dramaturgical view of the world; life is a stage, the arena of action, and they are the most important actors. At best, the "whole thing" (all of life) is a poor show and a kind of illusion or charade. They believe that they as sensitive, superior, and perceptive actors should get as much out of the awkward scene as possible and that the way to promotion and pay (money, esteem, adulation) is engineered by "seeing it like it is, not like you want it to be," "playing it by ear," and manipulation. For the most part, they present a smooth, glib, and slightly veiled cynical front to the people they encounter in everyday life.

Night people tend to be apolitical, nonreligious, and quite critical of the conventional world—a world that is not really what it seems to be. Though some attend church sporadically, they are neither joiners nor social participants in the conventional institutional framework. Few belong to fraternal, service, or civic organizations. None belong to conventional private clubs. Role identities inhere in their occupational and social positions in the nightlife world, their financial status, and their hip fronts. Night people view squares and the conventional work-a-day world with disdain. As one bar owner stated during his interview:

I couldn't make it in an office. Stuffy people get to me. Most guys work in an artificial situation all day. I couldn't do that. Take the insurance business. The same old thing and the same kind of people all the time. Most of my customers are in a good mood.

I sell booze which helps to keep them that way. People come to my bar to relax and unwind. They get to be real humans not like at work. You get a lot of laughs. You hear a lot of interesting stories and jokes. There's never a dull moment, and there's always some character around to keep things going. Of course, I run a bar to make money, but the way of life that goes with it is my style. You deal with people who come in to forget about the jungle outside. I feel more at home in my bar than I do at home.

Though expressing ambivalent or negativistic notions about the basic social institutions and the square world where they find themselves to be aliens, night people have learned to temporize with the conventional world, a world that has been good to them financially and one they could not do without. Most enjoy performing in their current work roles which, they say, afford them self and group support. As one musician put it to one of the observers standing at the bar:

We have to make it like everybody else. We're not missionaries or ghosts. At the same time we want to be creative. But you have to make it first. Look around and you'll see a hell of a lot of cats who were playing to or serving squares a few hours ago. They don't have eight-to-five jobs. They don't want them either or they wouldn't be here. You think people here give a damn about politics, the business world, and all that community crap? Let others worry about that junk. I'm not putting society down. I've done my cop-out too. But man, all establishment things are from nowhere. They may be all right so long as I don't belong. Most of the people you see here are strangers to the world you live in. The whole thing's a bad dream anyway. So why not get out of it what you can, and fake the rest. But you have to have the straight world. Musicians can't live off one another.

An entertainer voiced a similar position to a companion while seated at the bar:

One regular girl friend and later marriage. Then home cooking and home fucking. Don't forget the double mortgage and the two-car garage that's really big enough for only one. And the washing and drying machine, and all those Sears, Roebuck appliances on credit. Then the children and the loan at the bank. From the suburbs to work and then back to jail [home] five days a week. Man, the eight-to-five man has to be a loser, and the biggest trick

in the world. We need all kinds. Without some straights around I
couldn't make it. But I don't have to socialize with them.

Despite their unconventional fronts, most night people are
legitimately employed and are seeking status in an occupational
or business career. Most are hard-working, ambitious achievers,
and their success or hoped-for success comes or will come from
the conventional world. They represent and reflect a part of the
very rat race that they condemn.

Behavior on the Scene

Night people, Rendezvous regulars, form the largest numerical
group (40 to 50 per cent at any given time) frequenting the club.
They come in solo as well as in all sorts of combinations about
2:30 or 3:00 a.m. and frequently remain until closing time.
Because most of them work irregular hours and many return to
the work-a-day world the next evening rather than that morning,
early morning playtime is in keeping with their work schedules.
They attend the club more often on weekdays than on weekends
because of leisure time convenience. Most of them do not work
on Sundays, and many are free on Mondays, which permits them
two-day visits outside the city. Additionally, squares whom most of
them wish to avoid attend in large numbers on weekends.

A number of night people, however, are always in attendance.
Some come unescorted, some escorted; most arrive in cross-sex
groups of two to 10. Frequently, by prior arrangements, groups of
five to 10 meet at the Rendezvous. The most carefree and acting-
out group in the club, night people interact freely with all patron
groups except square men and male thieves. Even some thieves
are acceptable for brief social encounters should they be known
in or outside the club in business contexts. Most night people
engage in lengthy encounters only among themselves or with
party girls, call girls, and businessmen. Esteemed and well-known
actors to most regular patrons, they move more frequently to and
fro among the subsettings, insinuating themselves in and out of
various encounters, than do other membership groups. Three
settings, the bar, nightspot setting, and the southwest corner
booths, comprise their territory. When room permits, they avoid
the middle of the bar and the tables nearest the bandstand, which
are commonly occupied by squares.

Night people are the most sociable group in the bar subsetting where they move from one encounter group to another exchanging greetings, repartee, jokes, and gossip, shaking dice for drinks, toasting, joshing, round drinking, flirting, and play acting. Other group members and employees accept and appreciate their spontaneity, exuberance, and clever verbalizations. "After all, night people are a bunch of clowns anyway, but somehow they manage to get to you in a nice way—hell, you can't get offended," remarked a female thief to another regular patron at the bar. Conversely, by the use of various playful cutoffs (e.g., "Lover, can't you see I'm tied up," "I'll kiss you later"), eye avoidance, a studied inattention to others outside their circle, togetherness signals (huddling close and whispering), they purposefully maintain internal clique privacy at times. They frequently utilize the four southwest corner booths for sexual negotiations but like other group memberships avoid direct approaches to the two northeast corner booths occupied by businessmen. Many male and female night people are on friendly, intimate terms with businessmen and frequently join them (upon invitation).

Like others, night people infrequently discuss their external personal biographies and serious, personal, consequential events at the Rendezvous. Especially is this the case when they are interacting with patrons outside their membership. According to them, they come to the club after late work hours to play and relax among peers in an odd-time, comfortable haven away from work pressures, squares, and square society. As one patron musician at the bar put it:

Man, we have to have somewhere to go after playing to a group of duds all night [9:00 P.M. to 2:00 A.M.]. *Somewhere to unwind and play in away from the squares. What a drag.*

At times in a more serious vein night people discuss and gossip about the happenings of the entertainment world. Knowledge about personnel, innovations, openings, and opportunities in the nightlife circuit are exchanged, and occasionally professional and occupational contacts are made that prove vocationally consequential. One entertainer remarked to an observer at the bar:

Like I say, we come here to relax and have fun. Most of us are in the entertainment business, naturally we talk about what's going on in our world. We might go for months without seeing

each other on the street, but down here you bump into everybody
you know. People like us move around. How you gonna reach
anybody by telephone or a post card. You get the picture. What
I've been trying to say is we find out what's going on when we
come here. Sometimes we negotiate jobs for ourselves and our
buddies on the spot. Most likely we use a tip or pass it on for
outside use later. Most of the owners who hire come here. Some-
times they even call here looking for piano players or something.
It's not a union hall, but a kind of grape vine. Most people out of
work don't like to admit it. They just show and listen, and ask
their friends around about what's up.

Night people, especially males, engage more frequently in
marginal behaviors such as loud talking, laughing, singing, table
hopping, direct attempts at pickups, and playful scuffling than do
other memberships. These among other peccadilloes including
highly visible expressive sexual behavior such as pulling up girls'
skirts, patting their behinds, and fondling their breasts are more
likely to be condoned than similar action by other patrons. Regulars and big spenders and tippers, they are highly esteemed and
form the club's most important economic support base. Well
known and respected by the club's employees, they receive excellent service and attention. Extremely flirtatious and gregarious,
they continually engage in amorous antics throughout the lounge
that might signal either playful or committed intentions—that is
open to interpretation. Such conduct runs the gamut from winks
and endearing remarks to open sexual suggestions, hand holding,
hugging, kissing, squeezing, lap sitting, and simulated sexual gyra-
tions. They engage in more intimate sexual behavior in the nightspot setting than at the bar, and their sexual intimacies are greater
still within the booths. We are not saying that other patrons do
not express themselves sexually. They in fact do, but not with the
abandon and gusto characterizing night people's verbal and body
language. We once saw an entertainer standing at the bar lift a
girl's skirt up over her head and kiss her on the navel. She reacted
by playfully attempting to push his head farther down. At this
point, he disengaged. Several onlookers smiled and clapped softly.
One bystander patted the girl on the shoulder and told her, "You
won."

Many night people are "on the make" and though most of their
pickups at the Rendezvous are of their own membership, male

night people occasionally pick up party girls, call girls, square women, and female thieves. Females of the night people group are more discriminating than their male counterparts and as a rule restrict their outside pickups to businessmen and an occasional hip square. The higher the female's occupational status, the more likely she will restrict her outgroup pickups. Occasionally a few male and female night people are invited to the owner-manager's office as guests to a private party.

Night people take part in the amateur performances on the dance floor more frequently than do other types of actors. During these happenings, the house musicians and the dancing couples cease their activities and become audiences. Some assume active roles in the "show." Musicians may back up these intermittent, spontaneous skits with appropriate musical scores. Most amateur acts, however, are performed between musical sets. Jam sessions, which are programmed and cover longer periods of time, automatically rule out all other dance floor and band performances. The audience for amateur performances includes a varying number of patrons and employees. Ovations in the form of shouts, hand clapping, and whistling may follow each act and produce encores. On the other hand, boos may quickly terminate performances. Occasionally two or three acts occur simultaneously. During these periods, some observers attend a three-ring circus and try to catch all the acts. Others concentrate on one or two acts. In short, there may be several audiences for several acts. On the other hand, some patrons ignore all acts and continue with whatever they are doing. Strippers get the biggest play and are usually accompanied by strip musical scores improvised by house or guest musicians. These acts usually have both comical and sexual connotations but rarely progress to a complete state of nudity. One strip act usually follows another, and the girls vie with each other in the artistry of stripping as well as in the degrees of nudity. Some performers may be professional, though most are not. Amateurs receive the greatest applause. On occasion, the male friends of the strippers ham it up by jumping on the dais and joining the act.

Though most of night people's behavior revolves around sociability, sexual play, and "hamming it up," some of their conduct is concerned with arrangements at the club to purchase illegal goods and services. Some who are moonlighters in criminal activities negotiate and deal in still heavier criminal pursuits. Most night people appear to be on very friendly terms with businessmen and on speaking terms with professional criminals. Their social encounters in these two groups are kept separate.

SUMMARY

Though night people utilize the Rendezvous primarily for sociability purposes, they also engage in serious activities there. They profess to use the club as a regular recreational source and home territory bar following odd-time work hours. Additionally, the Rendezvous offers them an information center and a clearing house for "what's happening," "what's up," and "what's available" in the nightlife entertainment world and in the underworld. Night people meet and interact with friends, colleagues, employees, employers, dealers, sexual playmates, and others who may be hard to contact on the street. Serious as well as sociable encounters transpire; however, playtime activities predominate and set the prevailing mood surrounding them. All are segmental deviants, and some are pure deviants (e.g., criminally connected). Night people, the club's largest numerical patron group, are Rendezvous insiders and the most important actors from the standpoint of stage setting, ongoing activities, and performances. More so than any other one group of actors, they generate, sustain, and reflect the Rendezvous setting. Without the presence of this odd-time swinging group there would be no Rendezvous.

Call Girls

ASCRIBED AND ACHIEVED CHARACTERISTICS

Call girls, products of the urban lower-middle-class, are a group of young (twenty-one to thirty), physically attractive, chic, apparently intelligent, fairly well educated (high school graduates) career offenders.[8] They engage in systematic criminal activity operating from plush apartments and hotels, utilizing answering services, but without the aid of procurers or madams. All have

[8] Similar in many respects to the call girls described by Harold Greenwald in his book *The Call Girl: A Social and Psychoanalytic Study* (New York: Ballantine Books, 1958).

past legal work histories as cocktail hostesses, typists, secretaries, models, beauticians, manicurists, sales clerks, factory workers, dancers, strippers, go-go girls, show girls. Currently they are full-time professional call girls with no other means of support. Specialized offenders, they claim to have avoided criminal career activities outside the area of prostitution. In hustling skill, life style, and economic payoff (upward from $100 a trick, upward from $500 a night) they qualify as professional call girls. As one typical call girl recounted in her interview:

We don't peddle it for nothing. Forget the shoe clerks and college professors. They just don't have the bread. We have to have a nice pad for our clientele. Who wants to live in a dump? We have to dress in style. You can't walk in and out of some places we go [plush hotels, apartments, restaurants, night clubs] *unless you got class. And anyway, just plain screwing isn't what it's all about. You know, candlelight and wine, and all that romantic jazz. They're not paying for a lay in the hay. You have to hide the commercial angle. . . .*

Most call girls claim they grew up as unhappy children in economically adequate homes characterized by parental conflict, separation, and divorce. Though they report emotional rejection by one or both parents, they make a strong point of the fact that none of their parents or siblings were delinquents or criminals—and that their families were respectable. Sexual deviancy marks their life patterns. All say they were picked up by the police or probation officers as juveniles on complaints tied in with sex delinquency, such as being wayward minors, for running away from home in the company of males, sex with older males, gang banging. Though none have served felony time, some have been arrested as adults for soliciting or the possession of soft drugs.[9] Though none reported addiction, some have experimented with various types of drugs, and most occasionally use some type of speed drug and hash. Most are heavy social drinkers.

Call girls are currently single; however, most have been married at one time or another. Most of them have had at least one illegal abortion, and some have had illegitimate children, most of whom were put up for adoption. Though all get regular V.D. checkups, most reported one or more cases of gonorrhea (none reported

---

[9] Soft drugs are defined as drugs other than heroin or other opiate derivatives or synthetics.

syphilis). As a call girl explained to the researchers sitting at a
table in the nightspot setting:

*It's not that we aren't clean. We get regular checkups. Our
clientele is first class. But a dose is a dose. And you know V.D.
gets around to all kinds of people. The johns won't wear rubbers.
Come to think of it, nobody uses them anymore. So you see you
gotta take chances. We don't get anything often and when we
do, we take care of it like right now. We know the best doctors.
They're real greedy people, but we take care of them one way or
the other. They're not too good in bed. We'd rather pay the
freight than take it out in trade.*

Present and past adjustment problems seem to center on sex and
men, as the following typical remarks addressed to a researcher
at the bar by a call girl disclosed:

*My problem is men. I've always liked men too much. And when
you like somebody, you want to lay them. If you like three or four
at the same time, you just lay all of them. Well, that's the story
of my life. I just never could really settle down with one guy. My
problem is I gave away a fortune before I found out I was sitting
on a gold mine.*

All of the girls have had pimps (kept boyfriends, but not procurers) off and on—mostly off. The companionship factor, rather
than sex, is the emotional cement binding them to sometime
pimps. As one call girl conveyed to one of the observers at the bar:

*Most people think we have to have a pimp around. Somebody
we can look down on. Somebody to push us around. And somebody we can get freaky kicks from. What a joke. No man pushes
me around. If a man comes along I like, I'll latch on and do
things for him. But if he turns out to be a phony, or if I get tired
of him, out he goes. All that jazz about pimps being freaky is just
too much. Squares are real freaks. You wouldn't believe what some
of them do to me. And never would you believe what some of
them want me to do to them. I get enough sex from my clients.
Who needs a pimp just for screwing? We're like other girls. We
need a man around to talk to and go out with. Everybody needs
somebody.*

Though most admitted to having tried homosexual sex a few
times, all seemed heterosexually oriented. Contrary to some re-

search findings elsewhere, these call girls did not express universal contempt for their customers.[10] In fact, all said they enjoyed sex at times with some of their clients, especially with those who were not "too square," with those possessing sexual techniques and staying power, and with those who were not "too freaky" (preferring esoteric sex way beyond the so-called normal range). One call girl noted during her interview:

These books and magazine articles on call girls turn me off. These shrinks and psychologists don't know the story. And sociologists, put them in the same bag. What's all that jazz about not enjoying sex with johns? You don't get it on with everybody, but you do with some guys. The books talk like all your clients are a bunch of dummies. Negative. Many of my clients know what's going on. Besides, just because a man's not the hippest thing going, doesn't mean he doesn't know how to do you. I pick my tricks, and I try to stay away from freaks. All that garbage about saving it for your pimp is unreal. I come when I feel like it.

IDENTITIES AND PERSPECTIVES

At the Rendezvous call girls speak in the hip vernacular. They refer to themselves as "girls in the life," "call girls," "one of the girls." They claim consensus with other call girls and identify with the underworld in which they claim to have acquaintances, friends, and working connections; and they rationalize away their work as a necessary service occupation.[11] As one girl said during her interview:

We work on our own, not for any organization. We enjoy our work. Plus we get paid real good for our services. We work hard. We really turn them on. And this takes patience and skill which you don't start out with. We spend more on our lingerie than most girls spend on their backs. All the best perfume, a posh pad,

[10] See James H. Bryan, "Occupational Ideologies and Individual Attitudes of Call Girls," in *Deviance, The Interactionist Perspective*, ed. Earl Rubington and Martin S. Weinburg (New York: Macmillan, 1968), pp. 286–96.

[11] For a discussion of the functional aspects of illegal occupations in society, see Elliott A. Krause, *The Sociology of Occupations* (Boston: Little, Brown, 1974), pp. 279–95.

good sides [records], *and all that good stuff. We have to lay it out. So what's the big hang up? So who should worry about such a good thing? We have friends in different kinds of hustles. You don't think we buy our clothes from Macy's, do you? Certainly I know some biggies* [organized criminals]. *We do favors for them, but they don't own us. Let's say we have working arrangements. Like we take care of one of their friends from out of town. Or maybe screw the brains out of somebody they need to get to. Sometimes we get paid from both ends. But we can't depend on any one type of clientele. We have to make it with different types of guys. Don't get me wrong. We're not whores. We're selective, and we don't screw losers. We really feel more at ease with hustlers. Writers and artists turn us on too. We get along real good with intelligent people. Forget actors though. Most of them are too kinky. At least we're honest, and not like wives who claim they're not prostitutes. Marriage is the greatest prostitution thing going. All husbands are tricks. Sure we perform illegal services but they're necessary.*

These girls, through and by their call girl role identities, receive self-support and group support. In this role they have enjoyed intrinsic gratifications (sexual pleasure and companionship) as well as extrinsic gratifications (money and status). Moreover, they are committed to the role of call girl in which they have invested much time and energy. Call girls share a life organization including self-concept, values, meanings, beliefs, activities, and life style; and they interact together around a common enterprise. They view the world from a one-sided feminist's point of view. To them the world is a sexual marketplace where the clever, attractive, and seductive females get the most out of life by selling their wares to affluent men. As one call girl remarked to a friend at the bar: "There are dumb square broads who give it away, dishonest girl friends and wives who prostitute themselves, and honest call girls like me who know the score and live the sweet life."

To call girls all men are either tricks themselves or agents who make women trick. Therefore, wise women, call girls, by reverse psychology trick the tricksters—turn men into tricks.

They express negative feelings about the basic social institutions, especially the administration of criminal justice. One girl com-

mented to one of the researchers at a table in the nightspot setting:

*I just like to live in this life, that's all. The church and the
family and all that social institution bull is for straights. Now cops,
I could write you a book about. They're all pigs except those on
the vice squad. They're hogs. What a hungry bunch of scavengers.
All of them are on the take and make. I don't mind giving them
a little bread every week or two, but that's not enough for the
bastards. They want my body too. What a bummer. Three of
them wanted to pull a train on me the other day* [all three desired
intercourse one after the other]. *Man, they're the scum of the
earth.*

Despite a negative slant on the square world and many squares,
call girls realize their dependence on and relationships to conventional society. As one call girl explained to a researcher while
drinking at the bar:

*What would we do without all those conventional people? We
need all those dumb broads and squares. Without them we
couldn't make a dime. They need us, and we need them—that is,
their money. Life's a bitch, isn't it? One screwy merry-go-round.
You wanta ride? I'd rather ride than walk.*

They admire monetarily successful people in and out of the life.
Present oriented and committed to their current life style, they
express no change in future aspirations or career plans. When
pressed in this direction some mention vague plans about saving
up enough money to retire, about opening up a boutique or
novelty shop, about inheriting money from a rich appreciative
client, about marrying an "old dude who has one foot in the
grave." Call girls seldom participate in conventional institutional
settings, clubs, or organizations.

BEHAVIOR ON THE SCENE

Call girls are regular patrons whose club membership varies
from five to 10 throughout the week. Typically, they come to the
Rendezvous in the company of other call girls or occasionally with
boyfriends (pimps), about 2:30 A.M. and customarily stay late
(closing time). Because they generally go to work from 2:00 to

4:00 P.M. and quit between 1:00 to 2:00 A.M. (when not entertaining an all nighter), the club's hours fit their schedule. Call girls say they use the club primarily as a home territory bar, a haven away from the straight world where they can relax and be amused after work hours. One of the call girls interviewed disclosed:

We work until 1:00 or 2:00 A.M. Who wants to go to sleep then? The other bars are closed. And anyway we like the Rendezvous. The people there are a lot of fun. We usually go in a group. We don't want a hassle. The work day is over. It's a fun scene. You know, joking, dancing, and clowning around. The music's good. Everybody is so nice to us. You know we feel at home with people who don't look down on us. Most of them know who we are. So what, they accept us. Who really gives a damn what you do anyway, there. That's what makes it such a gas. Then too, we buy most of our clothes and jewelry there. And that's some saving.

Well known to, popular with, and well liked by the management, the employees, and most regular male patrons, the call girls enjoy a moderately high club status among male patrons. They receive attentive service from all employees. In turn they are outgoing and friendly toward most male membership groups and all employees. Next to the businessmen, they are the biggest tippers. Though enjoying wide latitudes of behavior throughout the lounge, call girls prefer the nightspot and bar subsettings and rarely sit in the four open booths. Occasionally they visit with unescorted businessmen in the two northeast corner booths. The following excerpt from one of the interviews illustrates the acceptability of the call girls at the club, their gregariousness, and the exciting problematic situations they encounter at the Rendezvous:

We sit at the bar where we can talk to people and watch the action. We don't go to hustle. But it's a kick to see the hustle at the bar. The guys hustle us, too. Most of them know us, and it's just a put on. But we like it. What woman doesn't? You know, all that attention and flattery. We don't take the joshing around seriously. Once in a while we'll really play a number on some guy who isn't in the know. And get picked up for what he thinks is for real. What a ball. The silent kicks we get then are too much. You know you can play it a number of different ways. You can shake him off after a while. Or if he turns out to be a good dude you can stay with him til closing, or leave with him. You can ball him for fun or for money, or kiss him good night. Chances are he's gonna give you some bread anyway. Sometimes the stud turns out to be sharper than you thought. That's O.K. too. You have a ball either way. It's a lotta fun matching wits. The beautiful thing is it's like a game. You never really know how things will turn out.

Sometimes upon invitation call girls attend the owner's private parties in his office. There they are a privileged group of insiders who enjoy the highest status. Sexual behavior here is openly expressive, permissive, and noncommercial—the essence of sex as play, without commitment. This highly secret scene, though sexually oriented, is problematic in nature. As one call girl detailed in her interview:

Once in a while the owner will have a little get together in his office. When special people are around, or when some of his friends from out of town drop in. We sit around up there and talk, fool around, and have a few drinks. The action there gets down to it. I don't mean rough stuff, but some of your clothes are coming off. You know how men are. They like to play orgy— take all the girls' bras off and sometimes their panties. And then they play around with us. You know, pass us around from one man's lap to another. Then some pair off and go into the secretary's office and turn off the lights. Sometimes you get screwed on the desk, or on the floor, or if you're lucky, one of the sofas. Sometimes even standing up. It's wild. Some of us go further with it than others, but we all play the game. Not all of us are call girls either but up there we're all equal. The men don't pull off all their clothes. Some of them will eat you up right in front of everybody. They try to outdo each other. We go along with the act—moan, groan, and carry on. I guess we try to outdo each other too. Don't get me wrong, we get our kicks. You get kind of caught up in the whole thing. Everybody else gets excited and that turns you on. There are two private bathrooms up there with plenty of towels. So we can tidy ourselves up. If we go back down it's all just like nothing happened. There's only one rule upstairs. That's whatever you do or see or hear upstairs, you don't say anything about downstairs. Not even to the people you were with. You don't say anything about who was up there or what went on. If you do, you've had it. You'll never go to another party.

When unescorted, call girls play around coquettishly with unescorted, regular male patrons at the bar, at tables, and on the dance floor. They talk, gossip, drink, smoke, dance, flirt, hold hands, and snack with (and occasionally embrace) men during these social encounters. Their expressive behavior of all types is more restrained with squares and thieves than with more esteemed males. Social encounters with women patrons are usually confined to other call girls, females thieves, and party girls. When escorted by a pimp, their encounters are generally restricted to other call girls and their pimps, male thieves, female thieves, and party girls. Other memberships hold pimps in low esteem and dodge social encounters with them and whomever else they might be with. One call girl explained her situational interaction pattern at the club to one researcher over a gift drink at one of the tables:

When we come without men there's no problem who we socialize with. That way we mingle with all kinds of people. Of course, we don't have much to do with the square women and the olive oil queens [female aides to businessmen]. *We prefer men. But if we come with a man, that's different. If the guys don't know him, they take him for a pimp. So you are just with him. Party girls, show girls, and some squares don't mind mixing in a group, but others do. We like to come without our boyfriends.*

SUMMARY

Call girl patrons form a group of career deviants who appropriate the club primarily as a setting in which to behave normally. The playtime, time-out nature of the setting, however, does not obviate some serious consideration and use. They buy stolen goods there, meet prospective clients, rendezvous sometimes with pre-arranged tricks, and infrequently pick up tricks. In any case, the happenings at the Rendezvous for call girls are problematic, as the following comment during the interviews disclosed:

I go to the Rendezvous to play. The owner and most of the other people there know that. Now I do meet men that I trick with later. And I see a hell of a lot of them that I've tricked with before. But at the Rendezvous it's mostly to kid around and have fun. Sometimes we get a little pressure from the management to be nice to some certain guy from out of town or something. We don't mind that. The only bad thing is we have to play up to some cops sometimes. Now that's a losing proposition anyway you cut it. But what you gonna do? Some tears must fall. Believe it or not, I've done it for nothing with some guys I met at the club. So who knows. You never know what's really going to happen there. It's the not knowing exactly what's going to happen that makes it more fun for me. Who knows, you might wind up in the owner's office. And that's a blast for any girl—call girl, your girl, or anybody else's girl.

Call girls, outsiders in the conventional world, are an integral part of the Rendezvous setting. Physically attractive and seductive, they contribute to the adornment of a risqué, heterosexual scene. As big spenders and tippers and also as sexual magnets for a wide assortment of big spenders, they contribute enormously to the Rendezvous' financial success. Essentially outgoing, gregarious, and democratic, they promote group camaraderie within the club, thereby tying together a large number of actors and activities. Their easy going, expressive sexual behavior on the scene helps make the setting what it really is (up front in the club proper and backstage in the owner's office). Insiders, they are actors in a behavior setting which they help create and move along.

Party Girls

ASCRIBED AND ACHIEVED CHARACTERISTICS

Party girls form an attractive, chic, single, young (twenty-one to thirty), moderately well educated (high school graduate to college attendance), swinging group of lower-middle-class working girls. Products of urban, respectable, lower-middle-class backgrounds, they are legitimately employed outside the entertainment industry as models, school teachers, beauticians, nurses, secretaries, clerical workers, factory workers, salesgirls, and airline stewardesses. Occasionally they moonlight at prostitution by turning $50 to $100 tricks (averaging one a month) through personal contacts and recommendations and referrals by male acquaintances. They operate independently from their own apartments (in middle-class residential areas) and from hotels without the aid of answering services, procurers, or madams.

Similar to call girls in certain respects in that they turn occasional tricks, they are unlike them in many ways. They differ in self-concept and identity, working status, adolescent backgrounds, and certain deviant behaviors. None report juvenile delinquent arrests or criminal records, and all state that they grew up in respectable, stable homes without serious childhood or adolescent adjustment problems. None report illegitimate children or a history of V.D.; however, about half note at least one criminal abortion. None are addicted to alcohol or drugs and all disclaim homosexual behavior. Most say they have some criminal friends and acquaintances and some knowledge of the underworld; however, they deny criminal career pursuits. Currently, party girls are present-oriented, thrill seekers who spend most of their leisure time at posh bars, restaurants, night clubs, after-hours clubs, sporting events, and resorts with affluent, swinging male companions. They claim that they met their criminal acquaintances in these leisure-time establishments through the pickup routine.

IDENTITIES AND PERSPECTIVES

Party girls are confused in self-concept and role identities. They see themselves in one sense as legitimate working girls and in another way as swingers who now and then "mix romance with finance." They place great value on looking sharp, being stylishly dressed, having a good time with men who dress well and drive luxurious cars, being seen at the most fashionable places, and making love to "important" men. Occupationally, they do not identify with call girls or other criminals, but they believe that certain kinds of vice, including prostitution, are "socially necessary." Like some white-collar criminals, they do not define themselves as criminals despite a self-awareness of occasional illegal activities (turning tricks).

Party girls express admiration for and associate with monetarily successful swingers from the straight (hip squares) and criminal worlds, generally in a "straight" context. Occasionally they turn a trick with an unknown at the behest of some affluent male acquaintance. In these cases a monetary reward is involved, the male intermediary attempting to impress, influence, or "get to" the set-up trick who seldom knows that his sex has been paid for. Party girls told us in the club and during the interviews that most of the time they "screwed" for fun.

Party girls' views toward their sometime tricks (dates to them) are neither completely exploitative nor negative. One party girl divulged to an observer while dancing with him at the Rendezvous:

I'm selective. I pick fun "dates." No creeps. I like to ball, too. They get theirs, and I get mine. Er, the money helps. All that romance without finance gets to be a drag. But I'm not a whore. I still give more of it away than I get paid for. Squares who are in the know are O.K. Forget the other kind.

The preceding remarks also reveal a rationalization for receiving money for what they themselves enjoy.

Party girls insist that they will stop "dating" (tricking) when they "eventually find the right man" and make plans for marriage; that they are not involved in other types of criminal activities; and that they have many friends like themselves "who stopped tricking and got married." Since these young women have criminal companions, turn tricks now and then, buy hot clothes, and have adopted a swinging life style on the fringe of the underworld, it is likely that some may become more deeply immersed in criminal pursuits or become professional call girls. On the other hand, it appears that some may marry straights and disengage from illegal activity. The future of party girls is problematic.

In short-term views party girls express mixed feelings about marriage and the family (things that can wait) and the other basic social institutions. They state negative positions on the administration of criminal justice and the police (pigs to them). Conversely, they voice aspirations for an eventual, conventional life in straight society—a life style they currently find boring and unremunerative. To some extent, they are social participants in the wider conventional society. Some attend church occasionally, and some belong to clubs and organizations connected with their occupations. Most are apolitical and nonreligious. Party girls' verbalizations disclose stress and marginality coupled with a yearning for respectability. As one party girl commented to one of us at the bar over a gift drink:

Maybe I'll make it. You know, marriage and children and the suburbs, and maybe not. Anyway, I'm going to have a good time while I can. You know, exciting dates and places, er, nice clothes, and a sharp apartment. What the hell, why should the right man worry about a few balls? Maybe, I hope, he will never know. Any-way, you should have some fun as you go through life. But one thing is for sure, I'll never get hooked up with a square square.

Behavior on the Scene

Party girls, regular patrons, enter the club in twosomes or three-somes when unescorted, and when escorted they come with reg-ular male patrons. In either case they come early (1:00 to 2:00 A.M.) and stay late (6:00 to 7:00 A.M.). Membership varies from five to 10 and is higher during weekends than during weekdays. When unescorted, they generally sit at tables or at the bar where they drink, snack, smoke, and chat among themselves, with the barmaids and cocktail hostesses, and with a variety of male ac-quaintances. When picked up, they generally move to the night-spot setting where they listen to the music, watch the show, dance, drink, and converse. When in the company of a man who really turns them on, they may initially sit at, or later move to, one of the open southwest corner booths. Sexual negotiations often begin at the bar and continue at the tables or in the booths. Such nego-tiations may be terminated at any time in any setting. When escorted, unescorted, or picked up, party girls may choose any one of the three subsettings as a temporary or permanent locale.

Like the members of other female memberships, party girls rarely enter the club alone because a solo status might connote unworthiness. As one party girl explained in her interview:

Sometimes I go to get picked up. Sometimes I don't. It all de-pends on my mood. But that's not the point. I mean my reason for going. The thing is no girl likes to stand out like a red flag. Like, here I am all alone. I haven't got anybody. So I go there to get picked up. Please do me a favor and buy me a drink, or some-thing. Who needs that kind of image. Men give you more play if you don't come in alone.

Party girls are on intimate, friendly terms with the management and the employees, who give them preferential treatment as worthy regulars. A flirtatious and convivial membership group, they say they utilize the Rendezvous for a regular recreational setting removed from the straight world—a place where they can habitu-ally play and relax without fear of having to engage in interaction

with squares and moral saviors. As one party girl put it to one of
the researchers in a table group:

*Here I can be myself with a group of regular people. You don't
have to act phony or fake it. I'm a swinger, and I like to be with
swingers. Here I'm protected from all those saviors out there. I
can do my thing—tell jokes, shake it up, get it on. And you know,
do it up right if I want to.*

Party girls speak in the hip vernacular and "clown around" in
a seductive manner with regular male patrons. Permitted a wide
latitude of behavior and mobility whether escorted or unescorted,
they move at will among acquaintances at the bar and the
tables and take part in group and solo, spontaneous horseplay on
and off the dance floor (singing with the dance band, comic stripping, comic pantomiming, and skit acting). They also make mock
passes at many male patrons by verbal propositions, kisses, and
embraces in conjunction with nudging, lap sitting, and fondling.
These sexual entreaties are usually preceded by "come on" body
language: open, revealing body stances, sensual movements, and
inviting eye caresses. Commenting on these types of activities, one
party girl detailed during her interview:

*We come to have a good time. We know a lot of the guys who
come in here. What's wrong with a little playtime? I like to dance,
and I used to be a good actor in high school. I like music too. And
sometimes when I hear good music I like to sing. We like to let
ourselves go. If you like someone, why not let him know it. You
know, mash it on him. Most of the time I'm kidding around, but
I'm human. I enjoy all of that male attention. Just love it, baby.
And when I meet a man that's got it. Well, that's it.*

Although the management discourages the open hustling of
tricks by any female membership, the owner-manager and the
assistant manager frequently serve as a referral bureau for party
girls and "high rollers" who are "on the make." High rollers as
well as most prestigious male patrons prefer party girls to professional call girls as pickups. For example, we heard one party girl
ask the manager for a reading on someone who had bought her a
drink. Her question, "Who is he?" was answered, "Oh, he's O.K.,
got plenty of bread, a good guy, from Chicago. My kind of
people." At times similar readings may be volunteered to a party
girl or even to a cocktail waitress with the open-ended, nonspecific

suggestion, "Be nice to him, he's all right." In such cases, the management, by nonadherence to its own rules against hustling, promotes heterosexual sociability and, therefore, the club's viability. Whatever subsequently transpires between the male and female is problematic and may be on a commercial or noncommercial basis. Reporting in a roundabout way on this procedure and its problematic outcome, one party girl stated in her interview:

I like to pick my own dates wherever I meet them. If the guy doesn't turn me on, I don't do it for love or money. I can't always tell what I'm going to do about a man I meet at the Rendezvous. Things might go right for awhile after we get together [she gets picked up], but then he might turn out to be a drag. Looks don't tell you everything. After a few drinks peoples' real selves come out. You got to check them out. I let them down easy though with a phony telephone number, or I lay a story on them about meeting them later. No one likes to be insulted. I don't go to the Rendezvous to pick up dates, but I have picked them up there. I've done it for kicks too. It just depends. Now if the owner or the manager or say one of the big boys [businessmen] recommends a party, I usually go along with him. Sometimes I ball them that night. Sometimes on another date. Sometimes never. Sometimes money is involved. Sometimes it isn't, who can tell? There are so many different things involved—like how I feel, how he feels, or what other kind of program he might have. I do work for a living. And I don't make it on my back. I trick only once in a while for rent money or for a car payment or something. Most men like to kid themselves. They don't want a whore, but a nice girl who really likes them and is romantic. You just play along with the game. One thing is for sure, you can't tell what's going to happen at the Rendezvous. You play it by ear.

Party girls' prolonged social encounters are generally with businessmen and night people. At times they also associate with male and female thieves and call girls in closed encounter situations. These social encounters do not spill over into nor do they include more prestigious groups. Social encounters with female patrons of the club include all memberships with the exception of female aides to businessmen. Encounters with other females usually occur in mixed group situations that develop as a consequence of the pickup routine. Even then most of the conversation and interaction is woman-to-man and man-to-man and seldom woman-to-woman. Party girls say that sometimes they arrange to purchase illegal goods such as jewelry, furs, and clothing.

Though party girls make up a rather democratic group in terms of their willingness to socialize with a variety of club types, they occasionally find themselves in very exclusive company in the businessmen's booths and at private parties in the owner's office. In discussing this contingency one party girl explained during her interview:

We kid around with everybody. When you're in the businessmen's booths, it's a different story. You kid around in a different way. You have to really turn it on. They don't mess around. But it's a lot of fun, and they are for real. Now and then you get invited upstairs to the owner's office if you've been around awhile, and you're not with a man. No escort but a businessman ever goes with you up there. You don't have to go unless you want. The owner and his friends are gentlemen. If you're in the right mood, you can really have a wild time upstairs. Most of the girls who go up there know each other and trust each other. So it's not embarrassing. We play around and have ourselves a little orgy. It's a different trip moving from man to man and sometimes having more than one man doing things to you at the same time. Most of the time we eventually pair off. You really get taken care of, that's for sure. You don't have to screw, but what they do to you makes you want to. Sometimes it goes further than at other times. You have a ball whether you get screwed or not. After the party is over, we straighten up and go back downstairs or home as if nothing happened.

SUMMARY

Party girls appear to be segmental deviants who use the club primarily for the purpose of relaxing and enjoying themselves without fear of having to interact with squares and rule makers—and being publicly processed as deviant. Additionally, they also make serious use of the Rendezvous setting by picking up occasional prospective tricks and by purchasing illegal goods from criminal connections. All of this notwithstanding, deviant behavior in and outside the Rendezvous appears to involve important parts of their lives (i.e., long run situational involvement of great significance to them at the time), but it does not seem to constitute a basic identity—rather, a style of deviance. Their peripheral contacts with the underworld appear to be of a segmental, short term nature. At the present time they are not seriously involved in or committed to career oriented underworld criminal pursuits. What the future holds for them in this regard is problematic.

Marginals in conventional society, party girls mesh neatly with the Rendezvous scene. In life style, behavior patterns, world view, and interests at hand they are ready-made actors for the happenings and ongoing activities at the club. Party girls contribute to this unserious setting both in the open club situation and behind the scene at parties in the owner's office. As attractively engaging females, they draw big spending male patrons to the club. In short, they need the Rendezvous and the Rendezvous needs them. The role they play at the club is an essential role for themselves, other patrons, and the employees and management.

Businessmen

Ascribed and Achieved Characteristics

Businessmen are reported to be an affluent, middle-aged (forty to sixty) group of organized criminals: owners of books for off-track betting; race track bookies; baseball, football, and basketball bookies; owners, managers, and employees of illegal gambling houses; numbers writers and numbers backers; wholesale pilferers dealing with large-scale warehoused, transported, and resold stolen goods; loan sharks (shylocking); and racketeers engaged in such activities as the partial control of protection of the trucking of perishable goods and vegetables.[12] Their criminal behavior is said to be pursued as a livelihood through an organizational structure, a code of conduct, prescribed methods of operations, and a system of protection.

Products of lower-class or lower-middle-class, stable family back-

[12] This type appears to correspond with those offenders discussed by Gus Tyler in his article, "Roots of Organized Crime," in *Current Perspectives on Criminal Behavior*, ed. Abraham S. Blumberg (New York: Alfred A. Knopf, 1974), pp. 192–209.

grounds, businessmen range in educational level from grade school to high school. Stably married, "family men," they also engage in lucrative, legitimate businesses such as real estate, trucking, loan companies, imports and exports, laundry and cleaning services, pool rooms, restaurants, night clubs, bars, theaters, vending machines, liquor stores, hotels, and motels. These profitable enterprises function as tax shelters and provide a channel for the investment and movement of illegal money. Businessmen, therefore, are successful in a combination of underworld and upperworld endeavors. They reside in upper-middle-class to upper-class residential neighborhoods and live the sweet life in terms of material possessions and comforts—luxurious homes and apartments, big cars, fine clothing, excellent food and booze, and a menagerie of beautiful women.

All businessmen have legitimate work skills at the semi-skilled level or above (e.g., in construction, the building trades, and bookkeeping) that would equip them for occupational adjustment in legitimate society. Most have been arrested and convicted as juveniles and adults for property offenses and gambling. Adult arrest histories are brief and consist primarily of misdemeanor charges for gambling. Represented by excellent lawyers on a retainer basis and reported to have connections in the administration of criminal justice, businessmen have received light dispositions: case dismissed for lack of evidence, nolprossed, criminal fine, probation, jail sentence. Most have served at least one jail sentence, and a few have served felony time. Incarcerations have been brief and staggered; thus none have been "prisonized." All are social drinkers, but none were reported to use nonalcoholic drugs. They dress severely conservatively, speak in the street vernacular and criminal argot, and appear deficient in middle-class vocabulary.

IDENTITIES AND PERSPECTIVES

Street wise, shrewd, aloof, and conceited, businessmen are superficially sophisticated in specific areas. They are knowledgeable about criminal and civil law, food and drink, sports, gambling, clothes, jewelry, nightlife, and sex, but they are limited in general knowledge about middle-class life styles, values, and standards.

Parochial, sensual, and narrowly materialistic (the emphasis is on first-class creature comforts, money, food, and sex), they view the world as a jungle where the strong and clever not only survive but prosper and rule from behind the scenes. They visualize themselves as criminal elites who have attained success in certain financial, commercial, social, and religious circles. Moreover, they rationalize away their criminal pursuits as connected with the "dispensation of necessary goods and services which the public demands and is going to get one way or the other anyhow." One businessman's comments overheard at the bar follow:

Who's kidding who? I'm just like any other businessman trying to make a buck. I offer here what is legal in Las Vegas. My odds beat theirs or the odds given by any legal gambler. I didn't start on the top you know. It's taken me years to get where I am. But some people think of men like me as ordinary criminals. I know less about street criminals than you do. I don't associate with heist-men, burglars, and con men. They are not my kind of people. The public and the cops have to be concerned with muggers, freaks and sex criminals—not with decent people like me.

Businessmen are proud of their purported success, which they account for in terms of individual initiative, brains, and courage. They express little bitterness toward the administration of criminal justice (including law enforcement personnel, the courts, and the correctional system), though they depreciate its effectiveness. The following typical statement was directed to one of the observers sitting at the bar:

Why should I feel bitter toward jail? I don't go there. District attorneys and police—who is worried about them? Those that got any brains can be had [bought] one way or another. Everybody goes for something—money, booze, broads, gambling. Don't you go for something? Just find out what a man goes for. That's all you need to know. Then it's just a question of how much of whatever he likes it takes.

Businessmen are members of and support most of the basic social institutions. As members of the capitalistic system, they picture themselves as successful philanthropic businessmen who provide necessary goods and services for a profit. Affiliated with organized religion, they see themselves as loyal, philanthropic church laymen. As "family men" they take great pride in their roles as patriarchal fathers and good providers. They neither seek membership in service and civic organizations nor belong to private social clubs. Most of them have children in or out of high school and college. They disparage lesser criminal types such as heist men, muggers, burglars, and other heavies with whom they claim no association. Businessmen live in an ambience of esteem and camaraderie among devoted family members, friends, loyal colleagues, and employees. They define squares as either hypocrites or dopes. In brief, this type forms a group of class conscious, monetarily successful, highly committed career criminals, whose role identities receive self-support as well as group support. They share a life investment in crime as a way of life which so far has paid off for them intrinsically and extrinsically.

BEHAVIOR ON THE SCENE

Businessmen, another odd-time group, usually sleep during the forenoon and work and play during the afternoon, evening, and early morning. The Rendezvous is "their place" where they spend large blocks of leisure time during weekdays (generally from 2:00 to 7:00 A.M.) engaging in conversation and social drinking with comrades, male acquaintances, and women. The owner-manager says they prefer weekdays to weekends for two reasons: they like to spend the weekends with their families, and they avoid a large number of squares by staying away on weekends. Routinely, they enter the club with male companions of their own collectivity, but sometimes they are accompanied by two types of women— female aides who are their employees, or square broads looking for kicks. Liaisons with the latter stem from contacts in rather than from outside the club.

Businessmen typically hang together in close-knit groups in the two booths situated in the northeast corner of the club, their self-designated place or territory, a designation informally acknowledged and respected by others. Markers (money and personal belongings) reinforce this claim. When alone or while awaiting companions, they may sit briefly at the bar and chat with the barmaids, other club employees, some night people (primarily entertainers and show people), and unescorted women. Typically, they avoid encounters here and elsewhere in the club with male thieves, female thieves, square males, and people on the take. Avoidance patterns include:

1. seeing but not seeing, and averting interlocking eye contacts with outsiders
2. hearing but not hearing
3. civil inattention (I see you, you see me. I'm O.K., you're O.K. We'll just leave each other alone.)
4. studied preoccupation with their own group
5. if alone, preoccupation with personal chores such as drinking, smoking, listening to music, reverie
6. "cut-off" remarks such as "Thanks but no thanks," "I'm leaving soon," "I'm waiting for someone," "I'm busy now," "So what!"
7. the direct cut, i.e., staring through others as if they were nonpersons.

Businessmen frequent the nightspot setting only in self-contained groups when accompanied by women. Though there are external differences among this membership in terms of power, status, reputation, skill, and financial affluence, those engaged in "management" and "operations" interact on fairly equal terms. For example, bookies and book owners fraternize.

Social encounters in their corner booths occur among themselves and with female companions, pickups, night people, and club employees. Guests are invited to join them by messages given through cocktail waitresses. Gift drinks are frequently offered to unescorted square women, call girls, and party girls who eagerly join them upon invitation. The gift drink, however, does not in and of itself define an invitation to the booths. A message of invitation may or may not accompany the drink. The invitation may be in the form of indirect verbal messages or signs such as beckoning gestures with the eyes, eye brows, face muscles, and head and body movements.

According to the management, businessmen say they come to the club to enjoy themselves in a high-class, safe joint away from the riffraff of society. Most of their club conduct and conversation is of an unserious nature: eating, shaking dice for drinks, exchanging gift drinks, gossip and sexual jokes, chitchat about the weather, sports, movies, music, actors, women, food, wine. They also recount and interchange ethnic stories and jokes. Acting as Casanovas, they spend considerable time in fondling and sweet-talking women patrons. Business activities (criminal activities) are infrequently seriously discussed—and never talked about within earshot of outsiders who are not businessmen or businessmen's aides. On occasion, however, it is reported that the press of outside business activity forces them to discuss some serious external matters within the club. Many receive messages there through the management. The management reported that businessmen discuss some personal and family topics such as holidays, deaths, marriages, births, christenings, children, and family reunions when among themselves in the absence of females and other outsiders.

Businessmen, a regular membership of five to 10, enjoy the highest esteem in the club among employees and regular worthy patrons. They receive attentive and preferential treatment related to their whims about food, drink, and music. They treat all employees and known female patrons in a familiar manner, but in turn receive respect and deference. On intimate terms with the owner-manager, assistant manager, and the bouncers, this type takes great liberties with female employees in the form of sexual passes and caresses, which for the most part are of the clowning variety. These passes are welcomed and encouraged in a titillating manner by the recipients.

A number of unescorted businessmen invariably attend the owner-manager's private office parties where they spend varying periods of time—sometimes returning to the booths, sometimes not. Booze is on the house at these exclusive parties. All guests must be personally and directly invited by the owner or the assistant manager. The invitations are not command performances, and invitees may accept or decline without any explanation. Most accept eagerly for two reasons: the fun involved and the honor—only very worthy actors get the call. Male guests never include the club's male employees except the owner, and rarely include membership types other than businessmen and a few night people very well known to the management. Businessmen for the most part fill up the male guest list and must pass on other males' invitations. There is an informal understanding between them and the management in this matter. Female guests never include the club's female employees, neither those currently working there nor, in most cases, former employees. Invitations to females rarely incorporate patron types other than call girls, party girls, and night people (entertainers). Call girls and party girls predominate among female guests.

The private party setting is geared toward promiscuous heterosexual behavior. The one-on-one encounter is generally the ultimate sexual pattern, but various combinations of sexual activities may precede the closing act. For openers, two or three women might "work over" one or two men, and in turn two or more men might "work over" one or two women. The loving cup routine, however, is typically initially preferred, i.e., the passing on of all the females on a one-to-one relationship (one female, one male) to all of the men. Exceptions to these patterns occur, but male homosexual behavior in the narrow sense (men stimulating men) is not expected—in fact, unheard of. The girls receive no money, but they do receive, as does everybody else, sexual fun among an exclusive group. Sex becomes sex play here in an ultimate sense.

Businessmen are said to act as unofficial overseers of the Rendezvous setting and to have a wide latitude of behavior thoughout the club. However, since this type desires to remain anonymous to many patrons, its members usually assume a low profile and present an unobtrusive mien. Rarely do they take part in the clowning antics on or off the dance floor. In an informal manner, they act as secret, unofficial guardians of the club's ground rules. Should they at any time, as individuals or as clique members, report to the management a strong disapproval of the presence or the behavior of other patrons or employees, the management listens attentively and checks out the complaint and parties thereto. Subsequently the management takes the appropriate action necessary to preserve the scene and mollify the complainant. Labeled undesirables may be asked to correct their behavior or even leave the club. Erring employees may be warned or fired, and in either case, a report is relayed to the complainant. Normally, "fingered" undesirable patrons thenceforth receive extremely slow service, "get the message," and "fade"—stop coming to the club. Such rare but real fingerings are secretly communicated to the management directly or through the bouncers.

Businessmen's complaints about patrons generally fall into two categories: (1) Some patrons don't look and act as if they belong on the scene. They may be furtive or appear too curious about what's being said or what's going on. They may "smell like cops," i.e., give themselves away in bearing, posture, or speech pattern as authoritarians or investigators. (2) Some patrons may be too loud, rowdy, aggressive, or pushy. They might not respect self-contained groups' privacy. Complaints about employees are generally related to inattentive service.

Only regular patrons who possess uncommon as well as common knowledge of the club's activities and social order know about the guardian role of businessmen. Simmel notes that despite status leveling in secret societies, distinctions are always made between esoteric and exoteric members.[13] Businessmen are esoteric members of the club, a semisecret society.

SUMMARY

Businessmen, career deviants whose lives are totally organized around crime, appear to use the club as a microcosmic reflection of a high-class, unserious, time-out, straight world setting—a setting for behaving normally. They desire to play in a respectable upper-middle-class setting beyond their reach in everyday life. Their biographies (social class origin, limited education, and stigma as criminals) would not permit them moral worth in most respectable middle-class settings. Therefore, this influential group at the Rendezvous has a vested interest in reconstructing and maintaining their envisioned replica of a respectable, plush, high-class joint. In Simmel's terms, they are playing society. Their truncated conception of behavior in respectable middle-class settings also promotes a wider latitude of behavior in the club.

Furthermore, businessmen are exclusive and prestigious members of a secret club within a club, the private office party, a sanctum providing esoteric sexual pleasures removed from most other club memberships. In addition to all this, businessmen occasionally transact consequential matters at the Rendezvous, their home away from home. As club members, their purposes at hand are mixed and vary with the club setting and composition of the membership group in which they might happen to be at any given time. Prestigious patrons, drawing cards, big spenders and unofficial guardians of some of the club's ongoing activities, business-

[13] Georg Simmel, *The Sociology of Georg Simmel*, ed. and trans. Kurt H. Wolff (New York: Free Press, 1965), pp. 374–76.

men aid in the construction, support, protection, and maintenance of the Rendezvous setting. They are key actors behind the scene.

Female Aides to Businessmen

ASCRIBED AND ACHIEVED CHARACTERISTICS

These young (ranging from twenty-one to thirty-five), single, fairly well-educated women (high school graduate to college) are employed by businessmen as salaried personnel in various illegal and legal enterprises. Though their criminal and noncriminal activities are versatile, most are engaged in office work: clerical, secretarial, stenographic, and managerial chores in real estate offices, loan companies, trucking companies, bars, night clubs, hotels and motels, liquor stores, restaurants, laundry and dry cleaners, and gambling casinos. Some keep books, type payroll sheets, record gambling bets, construct records, figure overheads, and separate winning bets from losing bets at gambling banks (offices). Still others act as bag (pickup) agents, bookies, bookie assistants and house dealers, cashiers and office personnel in gambling casinos. The same individual frequently moves from one of these activities to the other, usually progressing from clerical duties in legal establishments to more directly criminal activities in strictly illegal enterprises.

All have legitimate work backgrounds and are products of stable, lower-middle-class homes. None report juvenile delinquent or criminal records or arrests other than for traffic violations. None have solicited in prostitution nor had illegitimate children, and none are reported to have had illegal abortions. None use drugs or appear to have liquor related problems; however, all are heavy social drinkers. They are physically attractive, chic, and sophisticated in terms of dress, personal bearing (poised and graceful), cosmetic tastes, and speech (varying from correct, conventional language to a knowledgeable hip vernacular).

These female aides were initiated into crime by means of routine clerical employment in legal establishments. Later they added more direct criminal activities to their repertoires as a consequence of association with, pressure from, and/or romantic attachments to their criminal employers.

IDENTITIES AND PERSPECTIVES

Female aides are similar in life style and world view to their male employers. However, there are differences. They are less isolated from the larger society, they have less time invested in and commitment to crime, they express more problematic notions about a future in crime, and their role identities are multiple and confused. Viewing themselves as cool, clever, attractive, high-class women engaged in illegal activities at the apex of the underworld, they also see themselves as girlfriends, lovers, and would-be wives of their male employers. Simultaneously, they picture themselves to be glamorous actors in an underworld arena, an opportunistic theater of action affording wealth, exciting work, and pleasure. All wish to marry eventually.

These women verbalize a superiority in background, skill, and social class to other female criminals, and rationalize away their illegal activities as necessary services. The following remarks of one female aide were overheard at the bar:

We're not ordinary hustlers. Most of our work is like anybody else's. Typing is typing, isn't it? Of course, some of us are into the real thing. But we're not in the street passing checks, pushing dope, boosting, or selling it [prostituting themselves]. *What's wrong with gambling anyway? We give people what they want.*

Commenting on commitment to and future investments in crime, the following overheard remarks made at a table group by one aide are typical:

It can't last forever. You don't stay young forever. I know where I'd be in this business without what I've got going for me—my looks, body, and youth. Nowhere. The biggies in the business [organized underworld] *go for sharp girls. But you've got to have brains too. Dummies and pushovers* [promiscuous girls] *are out. But without the bod, forget it. I want to cut out* [get out of crime] *sometime, and get married and settle down. Maybe Louie* [current lover] *and I will make it* [get married] *one of these days. Maybe sometime he'll realize what he's really got* [her].

Paramours of their employers, they consort with one man at a time; however, some are deftly passed on from one employer to another at "respectable intervals" (6 months to 2 years) without jealous scenes or acrimony. The comments of one female aide directed to one researcher while sitting at a table group disclosed the tenuous character of these romantic relationships as well as this group's sophistication, adaptability, and finesse in letting the lover off the hook while simultaneously surviving in the criminal world:

We know they are married. So what? It's when they begin to give you that stuff about they have to go to somebody's birthday party or anniversary. Or they got to go by to see a sick friend. Or their daughters are having some kind of party. Or their wives are having a few friends or the family over. Too much of this and you know the score. He's seeing somebody else. So, what do you do? You make it easy for the bastard. You can't blame him too much. You knew the story when you started. So you find yourself another boy. But one thing is for sure. You never sleep around. If you're smart you'll cool the romance down without a big thing. You know, pretend you understand. Don't check on him. Don't face him with nothing. Beg off a few times and stay in. Tell him to go on out and have some fun. You have a headache. Or you got to see your mother. Just let it wind down. Don't bitch when he breaks a date. Accept his excuses. He'll get the message. You got to let him off the hook. Let him know you are a trusted friend and employee even though you've lost out as a girl friend. Who knows, he might come back. If not, you'll find somebody else. Would you believe he might help you find that somebody else?

Female aides, employees and girl friends of businessmen, receive both self-support and social support for those role identities in which they derive intrinsic and extrinsic gratifications. As the sexual companions of middle-aged, married businessmen they live in plush apartments, dress expensively and fashionably, frequent the finest restaurants and nightspots, drive expensive cars, receive expensive gifts, and travel with their employer-boyfriends to resorts and sporting events throughout the country. They are known and respected in the underworld and among some members of the upperworld as efficient assistants and girlfriends of "important people." Much of the respect and deference shown to their employers are also allotted to them. They say they enjoy being what they are and doing what they do.

Their commentaries designate a greater preoccupation with the gay, glamorous, romantic, and exciting life style connected with the organized underworld than with money or long-term career interests in crime. As Angela, a female aide, confided to one of the observers in a table group:

I have a good life. I work hard. But it's exciting and never dull. You're always having to figure people out and look ahead—stay one step ahead of them. But who wants a long time career? The fun and people you meet in the business. That's what makes it interesting. Look, if it hadn't been for my job I would never have met Tony. Career, career, who wants a career in a man's world? You can believe I live in a real world with real men. Of course I do what I do well, but who's kidding who? These screwy women libbers make me sick. If they lived in my world, they wouldn't want to be libbers. The problem is they don't know what real men are. If they did, they wouldn't be libbers.

These women express ambivalent feelings toward squares and most of the conventional world, with the exception of the family, an institution they strongly support. Their expressed views vary from mild contempt to antipathy for the administration of criminal justice. While consuming a researcher's gift drink at the bar, a female aide made the following observations about the police:

I have nothing against the police and the courts. And throw in the district attorney. Why should I hate them? They don't bother me. All you got to do is keep them happy. Pay them off. The only police I don't like are those glory boys, the ones that take their jobs too seriously. Sometimes even when you got them on the pad their conscience begins to hurt. You know, when they feel the heat or something goes wrong they suddenly become honest. Those are the blue boys you have to look out for. The trouble with cops is, they go straight on you sometimes.

All admire monetarily successful people in and out of the underworld and have friends, relatives, acquaintances, and close contacts in the conventional world as well as the underworld. Most are social participants in conventional society. They have family ties, attend church, vote, and belong to social clubs and some organizations connected with their occupational performances. Occasionally some go out with and sometimes even marry hip square men; however, most hang around with underworld types. The future of these women is problematic. Some may remain in crime as the consorts and employees of organized criminals and therefore face downward mobility as they grow older. Others may marry outside the underworld and go straight.

Behavior on the Scene

Female aides, regular patrons, vary in club membership from four to five and attend the Rendezvous exclusively in the company of businessmen. They usually sit with their escorts in the businessmen's booths or at the tables. Occasionally they wait for or sit with their male companions at the bar. Most of their activities and social outlets are restricted and controlled by male companions. As one female aide commented to her female friend in a table group:

I always come to the club with Carlo. We sit in a back booth or at a table. I'm with him and stay with him. He wants me to sit down and stay put. And that's what I do.

One businessman at the bar was overheard to remark while speaking to another businessman:

When I bring my girl in here she's with me, see. She ain't here for nobody to stare at or paw over. She parks her rear with me, and she stays put. Now if I want to get up and move around, O.K. And when I come back her ass better be where I left it. You gotta keep women in line. And you got to protect them. My girl understands the score.

Female aides rarely initiate conversations with patrons outside their membership, and in fact they interact with people from other memberships only at the behest of their escorts, i.e., when other patrons are invited into their circle. Even on these occasions they rarely engage in group conversations in a full sense and are more likely to be conversational bystanders rather than conversational participants. They drink, smoke, snack, "kid around," and chitchat in a familiar way among themselves and with other male businessmen as well as with some club employees (owner-manager, assistant manager, cocktail waitresses) and night people who enter their circle from time to time. Though formally polite (acknowledge introductions to, listen to, answer direct addresses) to other membership types who join their party, they tend to avoid extended conversations with most of them, particularly with unknown males. Some are on friendly terms with a few entertainers. Serious conversation is exchanged only with their escorts, friends, and other businessmen—and then only when outsiders are not present. Most of their discourse is trivial and geared toward sociability. This type never attends the owner's private office parties.

Female aides consider themselves superior to and avoid when possible most other female patrons, whom they view as sexual competition—especially party girls and call girls. Though social contacts with most employees as well as other patrons is at a minimum, they enjoy high status in the club, commensurate with that of their escorts. Rarely, however, do they ask for special service. Assuming a low profile, their behavior is more restrained than that of other female memberships. Unless escorted, they infrequently move from one setting to another, seldom dance, and rarely perform in the spontaneous amateur acts. They say they go to the club to relax with their escorts and listen to good music in a pleasant place. These overheard comments were addressed to a female entertainer by one female aide in a table group:

We come here so we can go out with our boyfriends. Most of the guys we know feel more comfortable at the Rendezvous than they do in public. They don't want any problems. Actually we feel about the same way. You don't have to worry about anybody in here. If they weren't all right they wouldn't be here. True some people come in I don't like, but you don't have to associate with them. We stick to our own group. We like to listen to the music and talk to our boyfriends and a few people we know. They [their boyfriends] know that who you're with at the Rendezvous is less likely to get around—especially if you sit in the booths.

All male employees and male patrons who come in contact with these female aides treat them with a special kind of deference. They greet and speak to them in a more formal and respectful manner than is called for in such an unserious setting; they tone down their profanity and obscenity and refrain from flirting. Sexual fun and games in the businessmen's booths are more subdued when these women are present, and females from other collectivities are less frequently invited to enter the booths when female aides are on the scene.

SUMMARY

Women aides, consorts of businessmen, are off limits to men outside their membership group. They appropriate the Rendezvous as an unserious behavior setting in which to behave normally (in a nondeviant fashion) with their married, underworld boyfriends. Though regular patrons, they form an aloof group that is not well integrated into the Rendezvous milieu. Their club behavior, social contacts, and encounters are more restricted than that of other patrons types, with the exception of men on the take. Accepted by their escorts, the employees, and the management, they are considered an alien group by most other patron memberships. Likewise, they view most patrons outside their domain as alien. Especially is this the case where most women patrons are concerned. Female aides to businessmen serve as "classy" adorning visitors in the Rendezvous setting, but they are not really of it. In brief, they are supporting upstage actors.

Male Thieves: Professional Criminals

ASCRIBED AND ACHIEVED CHARACTERISTICS

The membership of male thieves encompasses several kinds of moderately successful professional thieves who typically operate in small working groups, criminal peer groups in flux with revolving personnel.[14] Though group cohesion is strong, some members drop out and others are added; however, generally one or two leaders form an enduring core relationship. The criminal job is important in determining group association. Three or four crim-

[14] This type is similar to the professional criminals described by Andrew W. Walker in his selection, "Sociology and Professional Crime," in *Current Perspectives in Criminal Behavior*, ed. Abraham S. Blumberg (New York: Alfred A. Knopf, 1974), pp. 87–114. See also similar types of thieves discussed by Marshall B. Clinard and Richard Quinney in *Criminal Behavior Systems*, 2nd ed. (New York: Holt, Rinehart and Winston, 1974), pp. 246–62, and John Irwin, *The Felon* (Englewood Cliffs, N.J.: Prentice-Hall, 1970).

inals with certain specialties may band together for the execution of one caper. Subsequently, they may remain together or disband and possibly later reassemble for the same or another kind of criminal job. Loyalty to the mob is based on business, the particular criminal task at hand, and is somewhat independent of personal bonds obtaining among members. Thieves systematically engage in a wide variety of specialized crimes, all of which are directed toward economic gain: unorganized gambling (owners, managers, and dealers working one to two-table dice or card games), auto theft, forgery, check passing, confidence games, fencing,[15] pimping, burglary, shoplifting, robbery (usually as planners rather than executors), pickpocketing, credit card theft, short-changing, street drug retailing.

Thieves have a tendency toward specialization, and most of them have a preferred criminal activity. However, considerable criminal versatility occurs, varying with criminal opportunities. For example, when the opportunities for their specialties are available, they stick to them; otherwise, they branch out. The more successful the thief in terms of skill, scores, reputation, and the ability to escape arrest, the greater the specialization.

Thieves, products of the lower-class and lower-middle-class, are not well educated (grade school) and for the most part are without legitimate work skills. Forgers are an exception here. None reported regular employment for extended periods of time, more than one year, though most have moonlighted at one time or another at legitimate unskilled jobs. Currently, none are legitimately employed, make no legitimate work pretenses, and say that the sole source of their income is derived from criminal pursuits. All possess criminal skills that they claim they learned from thief companions and older mentors while engaging in criminal pursuits as neophytes or apprentices. They vary widely in age (twenty-five to fifty-five) and marital status. Most of them are single or divorced without family responsibilities. Most live with a series of women on a one-after-the-other schedule. Their residences are usually located in lower-middle-class areas; however, the interiors are more plush than those of the surrounding apartments.

[15] Fences in this category of thieves were much more specialized and secretive in their operations than was Vincent, the professional fence, written about by Carl B. Klockars in his book, *The Professional Fence* (New York: Free Press, 1974).

Most thieves who attend the Rendezvous have been adjudicated juvenile delinquents and spent some time in juvenile correctional institutions. Juvenile violations in the main were for property related gang offenses. All have brief adult arrest records (four to five arrests each) and have served jail time; about one-third have served felony time. Despite arrest histories and criminal processing, only small staggered bits of their lives have been spent behind bars. All are social drinkers, though few appear to have liquor related problems. Though many have experimented with various kinds of drugs and some use marijuana, hashish, and cocaine, none are addicted to heroin. Recreational pursuits revolve around women and gambling. Most gamble heavily at various games, including the horses, cards, dice, and numbers.

IDENTITIES AND PERSPECTIVES

Thieves speak in the criminal argot and define themselves as solid (honest stand-up guys), cool (nervy and composed), skillful (with finesse and criminal technique) thieves. They identify with crime and the lower eschelons of the underworld. Working at different criminal trades, they share a subculture, belong to the same criminal world, and are isolated from conventional society. They share acquaintances, friends, and criminal connections and know and negotiate with those who seek, steal, sell, and buy contraband. Residing in the same neighborhoods, they patronize the same restaurants and bars, run with the same class of women (frequently the same women), and know and deal with the same police, fences, "juice men" (loan sharks), criminal lawyers, bondsmen, and district attorneys. Most retain criminal lawyers, and all say they have paid off policemen for immunity from arrest or for the permission to operate illegally at one time or another. Thieves exchange goods and information, provide one another with social and emotional support, and render each other assistance such as physical protection, financial aid, loans, and work skills. Self-styled, successful criminals, thieves are proud of their limited prestige, success, and reputation in the underworld, monetary rewards, and life style (plush apartments, women, big cars, and flashy jewelry). As one thief commented to the researchers standing at the bar:

Anyway you want to look at it, I'm a success. Every "all right" thief in town knows I'm a stand-up guy. We're all in this together.

It don't make no difference if you steal it or sell it. I got a lot of friends in this business. I've been fencing for fifteen years and been busted only three times. You don't have to pay off all the cops, just those in your precinct. Look at my pad. You've seen my Cadillac. I live good. My women are the finest, nothing but table stuff. I lead a good life.

Though identifying with the underworld, thieves proclaim their independent work status and, ironically, vocalize an envy of and contempt for organized criminals. While drinking with an observer at the bar, Sam, a burglar, stated:

I steal more money in one week than you make a year. Sure I got partners, I have to divvy up the loot with. The fence gives no more than sixty cents on the dollar. But the small group of guys I work with aren't married to each other. If we have a disagreement over a job you don't have to go along. In fact, we break up now and then. Like, if someone in the group wants to move on. Fine, we just recruit another man. If the piano player fades, you just get yourself another piano player. The syndicate boys make more money. They got more clout where it counts. They're the big shots. We're just trying to make a good living. Yeah, they got a license to steal. They don't have to have no real skill or guts either. To hell with that syndicate stuff. The only thing those guys ever want you for is dirty, cheap work. And once you get in the olive oil business, you stay greasy for life. My name doesn't end with an a, e, i, o, or u. Now where would I go with those boys—to jail or to the cemetery. We don't worry about them. They live in another world.

Thieves believe that everyone lives in a corrupt and unjust society and that most men, particularly straights, are dishonest hypocrites. Good thieves, whom they profess to be, are "right" and "solid," that is, honest, loyal, and responsible people who pay their debts, "hold up their end of the stick" (meet obligations), keep appointments, and show when needed by colleagues. Espousing a code of honor among thieves based on the cardinal principle, "don't squeal," thieves agree that the only way a poor, honest man can achieve a decent life style in this unfair, capitalistic society is to steal. Reluctantly, they admit that the code, like all others, is broken now and then by some who don't "hold up."

Thieves say they plan to continue stealing—the thing they are good at and like to do. Future aspirations are related to hopes for bigger scores in a life of crime—or, they hope, the one "big score" permitting retirement. This type's role identity of thief receives both self-support and group support. Additionally, these actors have a high degree of commitment to and an investment in the role of thief, which provides them with extrinsic and instrinsic gratifications.

Professional thieves express negative views about all the basic institutions, especially toward all facets of the administration of criminal justice wherein most of their contacts have been of a negative nature: arrests, bonds, trials, fines, probations, paroles, incarcerations, and payoffs. As one thief stipulated in his interview:

Justice. The only justice you get is what you pay for. You got money and connections, you get justice. If not, you go to jail. That's it. As for cops, there are no good cops. All pigs are bastards. You got only two kinds: dumb pigs and smart pigs. Dumb ones don't have enough sense to take money. You can never trust a pig. Even those you pay off. If they feel the heat, they'll squeal on anyone. By anybody I mean just that—their family and friends— other pigs and the people who pay them off. It's the honest ones you have to worry about. And when they get in a squeeze, they turn awful honest—honest about taking care of themselves and to hell with anybody else. Only pricks get to be cops anyhow. Can you imagine anyone wanting to be a cop?

They are not integrated into conventional institutions. Few have family ties, none work legitimately, none attend church, and few participate in legitimate clubs and organizations.

BEHAVIOR ON THE SCENE

Thieves are irregular patrons who usually come to the club throughout the week about 3:00 A.M. and stay for only two or three hours. They say they utilize the club for a variety of reasons: for special occasions as a convenient, safe place in which to celebrate birthdays, big scores with criminal companions, and holidays; a place to "live it up" now and then when flush; a spot to entertain and impress very special dates; a place to pick up women; and somewhere to meet comrades and negotiate criminal transactions. Thieves do not view the Rendezvous as their regular kind of place. One thief elaborated to one of the observers at the bar:

This joint's really too rich for a steady diet. The drinks are too high. It's not the bread. But it seems screwy to drop that kind of bread for what you get. Who wants to be a sucker? Everybody has his hand out for a big tip. You got to dress up. A lot of people here think they are big shots. Even the whores are stuck up. But it's a swell place to be once in a while if you want to go first class. Sometimes I do business here. Whatever comes up. In our business, we have to move around and make connections. We cruise certain bars and restaurants to see "what's up." You can't lay back and wait for jobs to come to you. If I want to find a fence that I can't find on the street, I look here. He'll show sooner or later. In here, you can find out what's going on all over town—who's scoring, who ain't. Who's busted and who's about to get busted. And you get a line on different kinds of jobs.

This membership of five to 10 commonly attend in groups of two or three and sit at the bar. Even when they come with dates (usually female counterparts or women in the life), they typically sit at the bar. This is particularly the case if the nightspot setting is crowded. Thieves claim (and the employees confirm) that informal rules favor the seating of high status groups and squares at the tables. One heist man explained to an observer at the bar:

We usually sit at the bar even when we bring girls. The action is at the bar. That's where it's going for us. Sometimes if we have dates, we sit at the tables, or if we are discussing business. But the cocktail waitresses give you that look, like the tables are reserved for the high rollers and the squares. I can understand the big shots at the tables, but the squares. I reckon they want them where they can be controlled. I'd rather sit at the bar anyhow. We don't come here to make out, so we don't sit in the booths.

Intimate social interaction is generally restricted to the thief's membership. Most are acquainted with or have heard about one another from outside social or work ties. Though belonging to different types of small working groups and engaging in diverse criminal activities, thieves come from the same underworld level where their occupational routines frequently mesh or intertwine: For example, heist men, burglars, and boosters all do business with fences; thieves borrow money from the same "juice man;" thieves often use the same bail bondsman and criminal lawyer. Most of their time at the Rendezvous is spent in conversing, drinking, eating, and smoking among themselves; joshing with the barmaids; playing box dice for drinks; telling jokes; or commenting on the passing scene. Occasionally they pick up female thieves and call girls. Mixed company groups of thieves, call girls, and/or party girls interact on friendly, equalitarian terms at the bar and at tables, but rarely does this combination's sociability include or spill over into other membership groups.

Though thieves tend to avoid most other groups (especially males) for sociability purposes, they are readily available to most patrons for serious business encounters, that is, for transactions in stolen goods, services and contraband. As a rule, employees of the club (usually bouncers) act as go-betweens in these dealings by bringing together by introductions those patrons who are interested in buying or selling certain goods (e.g., clothes, furs, appliances, auto parts, TVs, radios, rugs, silver, drugs, sex, cigarettes, whiskey, coins, stamps, paintings, furniture, jewelry). Negotiations usually have to do with the actual transfer of money for goods or services to be delivered at some other place at some other time. As one thief revealed to one of the observers in a table group:

I do business here with the right kind of people. If I know a dude, or if I get properly introduced and he's straight and knows how to handle the situation O.K. The money and buyer has to be right. If I don't have what they want, I can get it. Anything, baby, anything. Just name it.

Thieves' clothes are not as expensive and stylishly cut as those of other male patrons, and they are less verbal and less glib than other types. Moreover, when without women they tend to hang together at the far south end of the bar. When accompanied by women, other male patrons avoid this area. Therefore, the thieves comprise a highly visible type at the club. According to themselves, employees, and other patrons, thieves rank just above squares in the club's hierarchial status arrangement. As one thief reported during his interview:

Cream puffs don't like to socialize with real men. We don't look and talk pretty. Most people at the Rendezvous like to deal with a bunch of hustlers and slickers. Many customers know us. They rather hang around with their own kind. That's O.K. We don't have to make it with everybody to have fun. The joint has class. Since we can zero in on just certain kinds of broads, it's a little hard in the meat department. So if you score, you score. If not, so what? The main thing is we don't have to worry about any hassles. It's safe. The place pays off. The cops here don't wear uniforms, and they come to play. They don't bug anybody in here. They keep to themselves. They're so goddamned polite they pass right by you and don't see you. You know they damn well made you. Sometimes we speak to them. You know, calling them by their names. They just nod and look the other way.

Thieves interact on a friendly and intimate level with the club's bouncers, chat and exchange gift drinks, discuss and interchange information about mutual acquaintances on the street and what's happening in the underworld, gossip about friends and acquaintances in and out of jail, interchange knowledge of and speculations about current local criminal indictments and court cases, including the roles played by various participants (those charged, the police, witnesses, the grand jury, judges, prosecuting attorneys, defense attorneys, bail bondsmen). Confidential and touchy subject matter during these encounters is either whispered, camouflaged, or exchanged in snatches at intermittent periods—especially if outsiders are within range. The similarity of thieves and bouncers' underworld interests, backgrounds, and life styles provides a basis for their intimacy. Other club employees (especially females) are courteously formal in their relationships with this patron type.

Thieves rarely dance or participate in the behaviors transpiring on the dance floor, seldom request special numbers from the band, and rarely remind the barmaids and cocktail waitresses of tardy drink orders. While dicing for drinks at the bar, one thief reported to the observers:

I know I'm no biggie in here. I don't push. I take my time. Sooner or later I get mine. It burns me a little that the big shots hustle our broads but I don't have a shot at theirs. The square broads think they piss Chanel No. 5 and the olive oil queens belong to the untouchables.

SUMMARY

Thieves comprise a group of moderately successful, professional criminals who are welcomed to the Rendezvous as a low status but symbiotically functional membership. Though they stress the use of the club as a convenience bar and a sexual marketplace, they also appropriate it for more serious pursuits: the surreptitious discussion of past, present, and future criminal activities; the exchange of tips on criminal opportunities, stolen property, fences, the police, and the administration of criminal justice; payoffs (in cash) for gambling, personal, and criminal debts, and the receipt of such payments in kind. One thief while being interviewed at home contended:

> *The club needs us as much as we need it. A lot of that carriage trade is looking for something we got to sell. So we wheel and deal, and have a ball at the same time. It's beautiful.*

The Rendezvous then offers thieves a safe, "high-class" spot where they can socialize normally (nondeviantly) in a setting beyond their social level, and at the same time opt for business transactions. Although peripheral actors in terms of club sociability, they do not besmirch the scene and, in fact, facilitate less obvious but important club functions. They interact with some patron types on fairly equal terms but know their place in relationship to those of higher club status. Though a marginal group, they fit into the scene and participate in many activities that occur in the setting. In a real sense their presence contributes to the hierarchical social arrangements (social boundaries) that are maintained by patron groups.

Female Thieves: Professional Criminals

ASCRIBED AND ACHIEVED CHARACTERISTICS

This membership of female thieves corresponds roughly to male thieves; however, their social backgrounds and criminal *modi operandi* are more limited. Like their male counterparts, they too are engaged in a variety of criminal activities: unorganized gambling (owners, managers, or dealers in one or two-table dice or card games), sometime telephone aides and runners for low-level bookies, check passers, con artists, pickpockets, fences, boosters (shoplifters), nonaddicted street drug pushers, contact women for prostitutes, employees and operators of beauty shops and massage parlors that are fronts for prostitution.

Female thieves, like male thieves, are versatile and typically operate in small criminal working groups that include both men and women. At times they work alone and in fact are more frequently loners than male thieves. Ranging in age from twenty-five to thirty-five, they are older than other female patrons of the club. Most of them come from lower-class or lower-middle-class family backgrounds frequently marked by separation, divorce, and criminality. Their educational level is low (grade school), and none are qualified for clerical or highly skilled legitimate employment. At one time or another all have worked at legitimate employment as unskilled factory workers, sales girls, domestic servants (primarily in hotels), beauticians, and practical nurses. Most of their legitimate activities, however, were moonlighting pursuits in support of criminal activities. None of this type who attend the Rendezvous are legitimately employed.

Female thieves at the club vary in physical appearance from sharp to average looking; however, they tend to overemphasize their features and charms with heavy makeup and skimpy, tight fitting, though expensive, clothing. Heavily perfumed and bejeweled with excessive costume jewelry, they "come on" strong sexually, though none are prostitutes. All are hard social drinkers. Some "chippie around" with various types of soft drugs, but none report addiction. Like male thieves, they are heavy gamblers. Though not sexually promiscuous, they appear to be losers where men are concerned in that they experience brief affairs with a series of males (one at a time) less monetarily successful than themselves, and often wind up paying the freight (supporting the male).

Some have had illegal abortions and a few have illegitimate children. Most have juvenile delinquent and criminal records involving property offenses and have served brief adult misdemeanor sentences. All have paid criminal fines, and some have served felony time. Like male thieves, they have spent only brief, staggered periods behind bars. Female thieves' level of living reflect a moderately successful criminal career. Most are divorced or separated; a few are currently married. Most reside in well-furnished lower-middle-class residential areas.

IDENTITIES AND PERSPECTIVES

Female thieves are quite similar to male thieves in their self-concepts, beliefs, values, and world view; and both male and female thieves interact around common interests in the same underworld echelon milieu. Female as well as male thieves deal with police, criminal lawyers, bail bondsmen, and loan sharks, all of whom manage to extract large sums of money from them. Moreover, most female thieves are well known to most male thieves who attend the club. Many female and male thieves consort, compete, and do business together at the Rendezvous and on the street. Female thieves speak in the criminal argot, identify with the underworld, and view themselves as professional thieves. One booster commented to both the observers at the bar while consuming a gift drink:

I know who I am. I'm a damn good thief, and haven't been busted but once in five years. I talked myself out of that with the help of that goddamned store dick. Do you know that poor bastard didn't want any bread. He wanted a piece. The slob, I gave him some scratch and told him to buy himself some cheap snatch. And that he could live on what was left the rest of the month. I told the son of a bitch, I wasn't no whore.

Female thieves resort to legitimate employment only when criminal pursuits do not prove lucrative enough to sustain them. One thief explained to one of the observers in a table group:

Most broads who think they can make it in crime are dumb or lazy. They just can't make it. Most of them should latch onto some dumb slob to take care of them, or go to work. You can bet your ass most of them can't hustle their way out of a paper bag. Even I have to moonlight sometimes. It's a bad scene. I feel more honest when I'm stealing.

These women suffer from occupational status problems and think in an upwardly mobile way. They talk about their relatively low criminal status and verbalize aspirations for larger scores and higher prestige among criminals. As Sally, one fence at the bar, pointed out to a male drinking companion:

I'm not a loser, but I want more out of life. It's gonna take time and bread. Some people are lucky and make the big score quick. Not me. I got a long way to go. If I don't make the big score, I'll still live well off medium sized pots. Don't get me wrong. I don't put myself on the line for peanuts like some common criminals.

Though female thieves express antipathy for squares, the basic social institutions, and the administration of criminal justice, they are not as doctrinaire in this respect at male thieves. As Judy, a check passer, noted while dancing with one of the researchers:

I don't have much for squares. Marriage, brats, religion and all that junk, you can shove it. But you know some cops have enough sense to take gifts. Even some squares can learn. I can take square men and some cops. Forget square broads.

Like male thieves, they depreciate criminals whom they consider of lower status than themselves; but unlike their male comrades in crime, they admire organized criminals. As one female thief contended while being interviewed:

You find a lot of phonies in all walks of life. I got nothing for bums and amateurs that bumble and fumble around in crime. Everybody knows the syndicate guys are millionaires in crime. They're O.K., but out of reach. I bump into one or two now and then. The ones I know are solid. But they live in another world.

Female thieves, like male thieves, feel comfortable in the criminal role to which they are committed and in which they have received intrinsic and extrinsic gratifications. The criminal role identity of the professional thief overshadows such conventional roles as mother, girlfriend, woman. Excluding the family, they are not integrated into the wider conventional community. None are joiners, and their participation in social, religious, political, or civic clubs and organizations is negligible.

BEHAVIOR ON THE SCENE

Female thieves are regulars who form a club membership of from five to 10 of the club's population at any one time. They commonly come early (between 1:00 and 2:00 A.M.) throughout the week in female twosomes or threesomes and stay late. However, when escorted by males they come early and usually remain for only two or three hours, sitting at the bar or tables. When unescorted, they sit at the bar where they engage in social encounters among themselves, with unattached males, with call girls and party girls, and with the barmaids and cocktail waitresses. They frequently chat, drink, smoke, joke, and flirt with a wide assortment of men at the bar. When picked up, they usually move to the tables or booths. They say they come to the Rendezvous, their place, to relax and enjoy themselves among friends and acquaintances—and to do a little business now and then.

Female thieves generally converse in the language of sociability (i.e., light and gay discourse); however, they engage in shop talk about criminal activity among themselves and with male thieves when outsiders are not present. Like their male counterparts, they are open to criminal transactions with most patrons, should these would-be purchasers come highly recommended. As is the case with male thieves, club employees serve as intermediaries in these transactions. Criminal deals are primarily related to purchasing stolen property. A female fence told one of the observers at the bar:

> *We come for fun, to see a lot of our friends, listen to music, and flirt around. Sometimes we do a little business. It's hard not to. You see, we know we'll run into people at the club that might not show on the street. Sometimes you have to buy and sell when you have the opportunity. A hell of a lot of people in here are customers. Why pay three hundred dollars for a suit when I can get it for him for one and a half?*

Female thieves appear relaxed, convivial, and cheerful in the company of most male patrons in mixed company groups, including call girls, party girls, and female employees. On the other hand, they voice discomfort and avoid, if possible, social interaction with square women and female aides to businessmen. While in a table group, one female fence proclaimed:

> *We make it with all the men. Those square broads and stuck up phonies who work for the big boys* [businessmen] *are another story. They cramp our style. They act like they're too good to talk to us. You can never figure out what they're thinking. We stay away from them. You play polite when you're with them in a group of people—which happens. I just pass, and talk to the guys and the other girls.*

Female thieves in the company of male thieves assume a low profile, speak softly, and are behaviorally restrained in terms of mobility and exuberance. When unescorted or with men outside the thief fraternity, they more frequently engage in prankish and expressive behavior. Patrons from other memberships are friendlier toward female thieves than they are toward squares or male thieves—especially when the female thieves are not in the company of squares or male thieves. A check passer volunteered the following comments during her interview:

When we are with a group of girls or with men who aren't thieves, it's another story. We can cut loose more, feel free to do our thing. And we get better service too. Oh, what the hell, we have a good time anyway. It's a high-class swinging joint. So you expect a few snobs.

Female thieves get on well with all club employees, tip heavily, and receive good service. In club status hierarchy they seem to be in a niche above male thieves.

SUMMARY

Female thieves are career criminals who utilize the Rendezvous primarily as a home territory bar, a nondeviant, time-out, unserious setting. It also serves them as a cover for illegal transactions. From the standpoint of physical appearance, sociability, demeanor, and purposes at hand, they blend in well as regulars in the Rendezvous setting and round out its cast of essential actors. Female thieves are available to a larger audience of male patron types than are some other female types. This enhances their value in the setting, where they fit in with greater ease than male thieves.

Men on the Take

ASCRIBED AND ACHIEVED CHARACTERISTICS

Men on the take compose a varying age group (thirty-five to sixty) of fairly well educated (ranging from high school graduates through college graduates), skilled, and stably married individuals of lower-middle-class to middle-class origin. All are employed in one way or the other by the city as civil service employees, appointed or elected officials, or policemen. Most are policemen. On the surface, they live middle-class conventional lives and reside in middle-class suburban residential areas.

As juveniles and young adults, men on the take appear to have led uneventful, careful, conventional lives. None have official juvenile delinquency or criminal records. They were boy scouts, attended church, avoided juvenile gangs, conformed to family and school discipline, married "dear old Sally" next door and stayed married, worked regularly, kept a clean credit and reputational rating. Good old square, hometown boys, they steered clear of delinquents, criminals, hipsters, and swingers during their formative and young adult years. "Mr. Cleans," they appear to have played it safe until they found an opportunistic niche enabling them to wheel and deal as hidden deviants with impunity. Short haired and clean shaven types, they dress conservatively and speak either conventionally or in the hip vernacular, depending on the audience. They are hard social drinkers but vociferously abhor other kinds of drugs, about which they have many erroneous views.

IDENTITIES AND PERSPECTIVES

Men on the take identify ostensibly with the upperworld and its conventional institutions and participate widely in social, professional, religious, political, and civic clubs and organizations.[16] Role identities as husbands, fathers, city employees, conservators of the public welfare and interests, keepers of the peace, and Christians endear them in many ways to conservative, middle-class Americans. However, engagement in systematic criminal behavior as takers on the Rendezvous pad[17] (and probably elsewhere) renders them ambivalent in self-concept. Though passing as straights in the upperworld, they also occupy deviant positions as criminal regulators in the underworld. Living simultaneously in two worlds and possessing two sets of role identities (straight and deviant), they appear to be confused in self-concept and world view. Rigidity, narrowness, and a would-be self-righteousness prevents them from articulating the two sets of role identities— therefore ambiguity of role.

Professed law and order men down the line, they are preoccupied

---

[16] Our men on the take evinced similar identities and perspectives to those policemen on the take written about by Leonard Schecter and William Phillips in their work, *On the Pad* (New York: Berkeley Publishing, 1973), which evolved from the Knapp Commissions Reports on police corruption in New York City.

[17] "Takers on a pad" are those who receive illegal payoffs.

with street crime (e.g., retail dope peddling, shoplifting, robbery, assault, homicide, public drunkenness, and barroom brawls) and political crime (e.g., parades, sit-ins, demonstrations, public protests, and marches). They consider themselves superior to conventional criminals (robbers, burglars, and ordinary thieves) and political dissenters. As professed defenders of the "American Way of Life," they come down very hard on political dissenters (draft evaders, civil rights leaders, socialists, and liberals).

As enforcers of the law, this type helps determine what is to be regarded as legitimate in the city. Moreover, its members are in a position to violate certain laws themselves without being criminally defined, caught, convicted, and prosecuted. One city official reported to be on the take summed up this type's view on law and order in the following comments made to an observer seated at the bar:

If the courts and civil liberty boys would leave the city fathers and police alone, we could clean up crime on the streets. We could even make it safe for women and little children to come and go as they please. But these damned due process people. They don't realize that you got to play rough with the scum. So you bend a rule here and there. So you beat up a few now and then. You got to forget about legal rights sometimes. Scum have no legal rights anyway. Take these agitators and demonstrators, they're all a bunch of dirty pinko slobs. If we could shoot a few down, we wouldn't have any more trouble. Those bums get in the way and make it hard for us to run an orderly city.

Men on the take proclaim that certain aspects of the underworld and its services are necessary evils that must be regulated rather than eliminated. Viewing themselves as the necessary and realistic regulators of vice in their city, they feel entitled to certain rewards over and above those conferred by official status from both the upperworld and underworld. It is from this "realistic perspective" that they rationalize away their criminal activities and collusions. As one "perceptive" policeman who joined a table group without invitation commented during a discussion of illegal activities in the city:

Everybody knows that people want booze and broads when they want them. And everybody knows you can't stop people from gambling. As for after-hours clubs, what's the fuss? From a legal standpoint they're illegal, but that's not criminal. The way I see it, as long as people want gambling, booze, and women, and they have the money they're going to get them. If people want to drink and play all night, they're going to find a place. There's always buyers and sellers of forbidden goodies whether you like it or not. Now that's where we come in. If you left it up entirely to the buyers and sellers, you'd have a mess—cheap operators, dirty hustlers, muscling in, violence, and a hell of a lot of publicity and heat. That way it's a war and everything's messed up. Nobody can make money safely. It's better for everybody concerned including the public to have things regulated in an orderly fashion. That way everybody involved gets a piece of the cake. No city runs without some kind of financial agreement between those who give certain people what they want and are able to pay for, and those who run the city. The buyers and sellers always get theirs. We are also entitled to a piece of the action. Of course I know I'm doing things illegal—things I wouldn't want my family and friends to know about. But look at it this way. With all I do for this city, why should I let everybody else get theirs, and be left out in the cold like some dumb slob. I'll take mine, too, thank you.

Men on the take draw a clear-cut distinction between clean money (free services and goods, kickbacks, and protection money received from prestigious legitimate and illegitimate businessmen) and dirty money (gained from direct criminal activities such as theft, burglary, robbery, extortion, shakedowns).[18] One policeman reported to be on the Rendezvous pad while having a drink at the bar with one of the authors stated:

We're honest civil servants. We don't take dirty money. If we caught policemen robbing and stealing, we'd turn them in in a minute. I never stole a dime on the beat. Clean money is a different matter. I was five years an altar boy and never stole a candle.

BEHAVIOR ON THE SCENE

Men on the take, an irregular membership, come to the club unescorted in groups of three to five and usually sit at one of

[18] For further analysis of "clean money" and "dirty money" see Julian B. Roebuck and Thomas Barker, "A Typology of Police Corruption," *Social Problems*, vol. 21, no. 2 (1974): 423–37.

the tables near the entryway. When they attend solo or in the company of one other companion, they sit at the bar. They interact only among themselves and with women whom they or others inveigle to join them. Patrons belonging to this alien group know one another well, work together legitimately and illegitimately, and play together off duty. They prefer to remain anonymous (particularly to other male patrons) at the Rendezvous where their prime objectives are women and free drinks. Generally, they come in between 1:00 and 2:00 A.M. on weekends and leave within an hour if they (along with the help of the management) have not succeeded in picking up women. Even when they score pickups, they rarely stay longer than two hours. Usually, after a few rounds of drinks, they depart with or without pickups, depending on their success at sexual negotiations. They frequently expect free drinks and female companionship, and now and then free sexual favors. Arrangements for free sex are made in the club for action at some other place and time. The assistant manager detailed in an interview:

They come in for free drinks and broads. They don't want to be known around, so they put on that spy bit when they have to talk to other customers. We all know who they are. They stick out like tall weeds in a garden. Call girls will give them a play. They have to or get busted. Some party girls will, too, because they are afraid of them. Some damn John might tip them off. We have to help them pick up women, because they can't play it out in the open. Anyway, they aren't swift at the lover boy game. The thing is they know we have to deliver for them at least once in a while. They know we hate to see them coming, but we put on an act. We act like they are welcome. They try to act like they are. We try to help them with different broads. You know, we wouldn't expect the same broads to join them every time they come. The girls wouldn't stand for that. Like Joan [a call girl] told me the other night, "Hey, what's with the pig scene every goddamn time I show, lover, don't tell me I'm elected again tonight. If so, I'll see you in my dreams." Broads and booze, that's about it. As if we didn't pay them enough to stay open anyway. Most of the time they settle for some girls to talk to.

These patrons rarely venture to the booths or other tables near the dance floor. They direct their attention, heads, and bodies inward toward their own table group—with their backs turned toward outsiders. They also avoid as much physical mobility in the club as possible. They avoid the dance floor, make fewer trips to the men's room than do other males, dodge conversations and activities that might require physical and social mobility, enter and depart from the nightspot setting hurriedly without tarrying at other subsettings. Contacts with call girls and party girls are initiated through the gift drink routine with the help of the management and the cocktail waitresses. Members of other female and male memberships avoid them.

At the Rendezvous men on the take expect and demand prompt service. Their speech and actions are sexually aggressive toward cocktail waitresses who must put up with them. These employees obviously resent the propositioning, fondling, caressing, and butt smacking they must endure. One cocktail waitress commented to one of the authors seated at the bar:

What you gonna do? You got them. So you have to put up with them. I get a come-down feeling everytime they sit at one of my tables, because I know what's coming off. They paw over you like you were a slave. Like they own you. They got no class. They don't try to be friendly. Just grab you like you were a piece of meat. You have to find some girl or two who'll come over and sit with them. Creeps, man, creeps. But what can you expect from pigs on the take? If we can't find girls to join them, we're elected. What a bummer! I get real busy when I see them coming.

Even the sexual banter and other conversational forms that ensue when call girls and party girls join them sound awkward, stilted, and forced. Patrons from these two memberships must take their turn at pleasing men on the take. One call girl recounted during her interview:

Squares and other female customers don't have to sit with them. We and the party girls have to give them a tumble now and then. Would you believe we even have to screw them sometimes for nothing—and I mean nothing in more ways than one. I try to think about something else and get them off as soon as I can. But sometimes they're out to prove how good they are. That kind wants to play around and take all night. That's a bad scene. Everytime one kisses me I feel like vomiting in his face. They couldn't turn on a fire hydrant. They want all the trimmings. I tell them to take it straight or forget it. They can shove all that gymnastic shit.

Men on the take are treated in a politely formal way by the management and most employees; however, musicians and bouncers ignore them pointedly and contemptuously. They tip lightly and seldom pay for drinks or food. The management's position on this matter is: "If they pay, O.K., if not, O.K., just don't hassle them. Put up with them." All club patrons avoid them whenever conveniently possible. They see and are seen by a number of patrons with whom they are acquainted in external social contexts, e.g., criminals whom they have arrested, criminals with whom they have working arrangements, and squares they see on the street, some of whom are favorably and some of whom are unfavorably disposed toward them. In either case a two-way avoidance pattern is the rule. As one male thief explained to another thief at the bar:

Who wants to be caught talking to fuzz in a place like this? You get friendly with them and everybody thinks you are some kind of informer or something. I got nothing for them anyway. They show me nothing.

When men on the take are directly confronted in face-to-face situations with outside acquaintances, brief interchanges of nods and hellos usually occur. They look at each other and quickly look away without locking eyes. As a rule, however, these patrons are seen and not seen. In brief, they give and receive civil inattention from other memberships.

SUMMARY

The alien group of men on the take is sometimes on but never of the Rendezvous scene. Outsiders, with a status lower than that of squares, they are tolerated by the management and employees and avoided by other patrons who view them as crooked fuzz who cannot be trusted. As one patron put it, "At least most criminals are for real. They are true to their own kind. Crooked cops aren't true to anybody." Though men on the take do not find the Rendezvous a congenial setting, they have enough influence over the management, party girls, and call girls to get what they want there. One man on the take remarked to the observers seated at the bar:

*I know they hate to see us coming, but who cares. They get
theirs. We get ours. We don't move in on anybody else's action.
We know what the employees and the customers think about us.
Especially those goddamned conceited hustlers. So who cares?
We get ours, . . . booze and women.*

Despite outsider status and lack of integration on the scene,
they are necessary actors in the setting which they protect and
help maintain. Necessary but undesirable actors, they are considered dirty people who perform dirty work. Though paid for
their protection services, they demand and receive free goods and
services from the club.

Chapter 9

EMPLOYEE TYPES

Introduction

THIS CHAPTER IS A CONTINUATION of the actor typology. As explained in Chapter 4, Rendezvous actors classified themselves into two major groupings, namely, patrons and employees. This chapter presents the employee types. Unlike the patrons all employees (with the exception of the lookout men) were classified by all actors in accordance with legitimate occupational categories. That is to say, Rendezvous barmaids were classified as barmaids. Most Rendezvous employees had worked in legitimate establishments at the same kind of jobs which they held in the club. All employees in contrast to patrons utilize the Rendezvous as a serious, work time setting. Some employees are highly visible in the club's main theater of action where they not only perform functional tasks, but where they also generate and sustain an important part of the Rendezvous rhetoric. Still other employees function exclusively in backstage regions.

Owner-Manager

ASCRIBED AND ACHIEVED CHARACTERISTICS

The owner-manager is a stably married, family man of sixty who has been employed in various kinds of restaurants, bars, night clubs, and after-hours clubs one after another for over 40 years. During this period he has worked as a bus boy, dishwasher, short-order cook, waiter, bouncer, bartender, maitre d', bar and club manager, and owner. Though a product of the lower-class with only a grade school education, he generally presents a middle-class front. A versatile, witty actor, he adapts his speech pattern, gestures, and body postures to a variety of audiences. For example, he shifts facilely from a pseudo sophisticated urbanite with some actors to a hipster with others and to a hoodlum tough with still others. He claims that his work experiences with different types of people in the nightlife industry, his native intelligence, and his ability to read people have contributed to his success in the Rendezvous enterprise. During an extensive interview at his residence he specified:

You have to deal with all kinds of people in this business. You name it, I've been there. I've learned the hard way about the food and booze trade, and the way to get along with the hired help and customers. I know how to set up a club and make it look good— better than those freaky decorators. I can walk in any club and tell you in five minutes if it's got it. Of course, I got business know-how and more brains than most. The thing is you got to know how to handle people. You can't handle them if you can't read them. The higher class joint you got, the more important the service and the hosting angle gets. I never went far in school, but I learned enough to read a newspaper and add and subtract. I guess I learned more about people when I tended bar. You learn something from everybody you bump into, whether they're educated or not.

The proprietor has no official record of delinquency, though he is the son of a bookie and grew up in a delinquency area. He claimed in an interview that his respectable family background, paternal counseling, and self-motivation to get to work early in life forestalled any "juveniling around." As he put it to an observer at the bar:

We grew up in a tough area, but my parents kept us off the streets. The old man needed to be near his work [book making], but that didn't mean we had to mix with all the people on the block. All of us went to work early because we wanted to. I could have gone on to school, but that's not where the money was. My father taught me that all that juveniling around on the street and playing hard wasn't where the real action was.

He has been arrested four times for gambling (two charges for possession of gambling paraphernalia and two charges for operating gambling games), which resulted in two criminal fines and two nolprossed cases. He served only one of a three-year felony sentence for income tax evasion and was released on parole. Social drinking, gambling (primarily on the horses), and women make up his recreational pattern. Though he admits to having many underworld acquaintances, he disclaims any illegal pursuits other than operating the Rendezvous. Presently he resides in a comfortable, spacious home situated in an upper-middle-class suburb. Dressed in dark natural fabrics (wool, cotton, mohair, and silk), he drives a Lincoln Continental.

IDENTITIES AND PERSPECTIVES

The owner describes himself as a successful, respectable businessman, and legitimates the illegality of the Rendezvous in terms of providing a "respectable," safe, plush, and convenient recreational service for people employed at odd-time work hours. Though aware that some patron memberships attracted to the Rendezvous are criminals and that some patron types utilize the setting for serious purposes, he claims that he operates a clean, playtime setting for different types of patrons who like to play together. He disclaims any responsibility for any illegal activities that go on at the club. As he explained during one interview:

The Rendezvous is a business. It's not a front. It's cleaner than most legit joints I've worked in. The secret in the after-hours club business is how to put different kinds of people together in the right kinda atmosphere. The entertainers you see in here, and a lot of other people work in public places and put out for squares all night. Many don't have to go back to work till 9:00 the next night. They work in clubs, and they like to play in clubs. People like entertainers. They think they're swingers. So they come in to see them. Now, take mob guys, they're on the street eighteen hours a day. They got to have some place to go to meet people and talk. And, you know, relax or take a broad. Mob guys like entertainers. Some own clubs. Some make entertainers. So, you see, entertainers like mob people. They know mob people own the better night clubs. Something else, broads are nutty about mob people and entertainers. Watch the party girls shaking their asses around and rubbing up against those guys. Connected people draw business and broads and entertainers. This mix draws other patrons. They feed on each other. Of course, you got to give them the proper layout. The whole smear must be a come on and be safe and respectable—from the front door to the johns upstairs.

The owner commented further about his "respectability" and the legitimacy of his employees to one of the observers in his office:

I work hard and pay my taxes. I put two children through college. You don't have to be square to be respectable, do you? I don't hire hustlers either. Some of my help got busted in the past, but they're clean now. They know they gotta stay clean as long as they work for me. If they go moonlighting around and get busted, that brings heat on me. Who needs a bunch of small-time hoodlums working for you anyhow?

Viewing the conventional world and the higher echelon underworld as component parts of one gestalt, he has no difficulty in identifying with both—and he brags about having good friends in the straight and criminal worlds. He places emphasis on behavioral style, monetary success, and "class" differentials rather than on legal or illegal acts or status. Style and class obviate the label of deviance or criminality applied to monetarily successful deviants and/or criminals. Small-time criminals have no class. They are losers. According to the owner-manager, the Rendezvous caters to the cream of our capitalistic society. He volunteered the following comments during an interview:

Sure, some patrons break laws. Some are strictly legit. Some are my good friends—my kind of people. You don't see any petty criminals in here. We cater to people who show some class and style. We don't want clerks and truck drivers and no riffraff. I don't care how holy they are. It's a capitalistic society, right? So how they make their money is their business. One thing is for sure, they don't steal nickels and dimes. We don't cater to thugs and small timers. No way. The cream of the cream comes in here. Do you see any humanitarians on the street? We're all a bunch of thieves. It's just a matter of how you do it, and what you get out of it. Why don't they lock up everybody who makes good bread?

Commenting further during an interview on the serious activities
that transpire at the Rendezvous (a touchy topic with him), he
pointed out that criminal behavior takes place in all sorts of places,
but that the Rendezvous is primarily an unserious setting.

*You'll find more street criminals and small-time hoods in public
bars than you do here. If people want to work out deals, that's
their business. They can work them out in airplanes, ice cream
parlors, or restaurants, or anywhere else. If somebody wants to set
up a business deal, that's his business. I don't keep peoples' morals.
You can't walk a block without somebody offering you some kind
of deal. The thing is we don't run a pawn shop. This is a place to
have a good time, and I've been clean for years.*

Though identifying with many conventional institutions (the
capitalistic economy as a businessman, the family as a patriarchal
husband and father, the church as a philanthropic layman), his
prominent role identity seems to be a successful operator of an
after-hours club. He enjoys this role, and it gives him status, support, and gratifications in the conventional world as well as in the
underworld—a role in which he has invested a great deal of effort
throughout the years and one to which he is strongly committed.
He recounted during an interview:

*I guess the most important thing I do is run a club where all
kinds of high-class people can enjoy themselves. That's why we
have different settings—the bar, the booths, and the nightspot
area. Each setting feeds the other. That's part of putting it all together. You see, people here are from all walks of life. But when
you come up front most of them are good people. They got a lot
in common. We give them what they want—good music, good
food and drink, and good service, and the right atmosphere. They
respect me. I respect them. I'd rather run the Rendezvous than any
public bar. You think some of the high rollers we get in here
would hang out in public bars. No chance. I got a reputation for
running the highest class club in town—with no heat either.*

The owner expressed ambivalent views toward the administration of criminal justice and its employees. He reported that the
police are all right "so long as they take care of robbers, rapists,
low-class thieves, and street thugs" and "leave respectable people

like me" alone. He sees the police as performing two important functions: (1) "keeping law and order on the street" and (2) "regulating certain illegal goods and services that people are going to get anyway." He claimed that the police have the right to receive extra pay (payoffs) for the second function and reported he had a "proper working relationship" with the police.

BEHAVIOR ON THE SCENE

The owner-manager generally sits at a table near the businessmen's booths or works or entertains in his private office on the first story above the club. Intermittently, he roams throughout the club playing host and checking on various operations and performances. He helps screen patrons in the waiting room; greets and converses with affluent, esteemed patrons in the foyer, at the bar and tables, and in the northeast corner booths; observes the dispensation of drinks and services; and listens attentively to suggestions, complaints, and grievances from employees and patrons. While "on the floor" (any place outside his office) he notes mistakes or derelictions on the set and passes them on to the assistant manager or to bouncers (usually nearby) by means of whispers, eye movements, and hand signals. Since he is ostensibly the host and producer rather than the director of the setting, he rarely gives direct orders on the floor.

The owner's primary communications to the employees are concerned with customer service situations. Drink or food orders need to be hurried up, ash trays need dumping, table tops need wiping, the bar needs cleaning, patrons need fresh napkins, solo males at the bar need conversation, esteemed patrons at the bar need their cigarettes lighted. Bouncers relay messages from the owner to the assistant manager who usually waits until the owner is out of range before directing remedial measures to the personnel involved. These procedures support the owner-manager's host front and at the same time permit erring employees to save face and escape embarrassment. Moreover, employee conflict as well as work situation ambiguity is minimized, since personnel on the floor generally receive direct instructions from only one supervisor, the assistant manager. The owner detailed in the interviews:

I'm the man up front. I play host and charm the patrons. That Simon Legree stuff on the floor won't work. I'm supposed to be above all that managerial jazz. That's why I got an assistant manager. The girls don't want too many people telling them what to do in front of everybody. One boss on the floor is enough. But they got to remember they're more than a decoration. We got a chain of command. Sometimes if a barmaid is too far out of line, I'll raise my eyebrows at her on the spot. That's usually enough, but then I'll always pass on my information to my assistant manager.

General instructions and directions are directly conveyed to employees by both owner and assistant manager in the owner's office. It is here that the hiring and firing are accomplished; accounts, payrolls, purchase orders, books, and records are kept; and where the only telephone communication with the outside is maintained. A bouncer, the owner-manager, or the assistant manager is always within hearing distance of this private unlisted telephone—a phone on which messages are received but one that is rarely utilized for outgoing calls. Seldom are patrons permitted to use this phone, and most are unaware of its existence. Employees other than the owner-manager and assistant manager do not use it. Paging service by means of this telephone or otherwise is against the rule. A wall safe holds the surplus cash that is transported in from the three cash registers behind the bar by the owner-manager or the assistant manager at staggered intervals.

Serious personnel and/or patron problems are settled in this backstage region. Examples are the mediation of persistent and troublesome arguments and altercations among employees, patrons, and patrons and employees. Heated disagreements among employees about tips and work chores are settled here, as well as theft and hustling charges made against employees. Strict rules obtain against the hustling of any patron by employees. Checks over $100 are cashed here, and credit over $100 is extended. Only esteemed regulars are extended credit and permitted to write checks.

All the foregoing office transactions and tasks are conducted in a serious businesslike fashion by all concerned. The playtime atmosphere outside does not penetrate this inner sanctum unless the owner has invited a few patrons and friends in for entertainment purposes. The actors' fronts here are studied, formal, and matter-of-fact. The owner-manager assumes the serious role of director and producer of the setting. By tone of voice, speech content, and stance he lets it be known that he is the boss.

Employees who wish to talk to the owner-manager privately about work conditions, salary, days off, chores, grievances, personal problems, need for loans, legal advice, courtship or marital counseling, or housing make appointments through the assistant manager to visit with the owner-manager in the office. Employees are dealt with in a patriarchal fashion characterized by a mixture of secondary and primary group relations. The owner explained to the observers at a table:

I rub elbows with my help everyday. They look to me as the man who holds the whole thing together. Their problems have to be my problems. If I don't help them along they won't be around to do nothing for me. In this business, you deal with people, not machines. Let's say I got a good barmaid, and she gets some wild idea about leaving town with some phony who promises her the moon. Well, I have to tell her like it is. I've had a few jerks checked out for the girls. Take some bouncer who is blowing all his dough on the ponies. If you don't help him get off the kick, he might start getting into your bag. You'd think that people who know something about the life would be too wise to get in stupid jams, but sometimes they act like a bunch of squares. Anybody can be had now and then. I don't mind losing a half a cheek once in a while, but not the full moon. What I mean is, I'll help them along as long as they hold up their end. But I can't afford losers. It's bad for business. There's one thing I won't stand for. That's getting in my till. No second chance here, baby.

Assuming a dignified mien, the owner greets all patrons with whom he comes in contact, and the more worthy the actor the more hearty the salutation. He engages in brief social encounters with worthy patrons (businessmen and their female aides, night people, party girls, call girls) and interchanges grooming talk, gift drinks and jokes with them. By the uninitiated he is taken for just another worthy patron. Generally, beyond a formal greeting, he avoids squares, male thieves, females thieves, and men on the take. He stays away from the open southwest corner booths and does not participate in the happenings on the dance floor. Moreover, he remains aloof from serious, drawn-out conversations and arguments. In discussing verbal exchanges with patrons, he specified to one of us in his office:

As long as they keep it light and pleasant I go along. I move from one group to another. I really like to talk to most of my

customers. But when people get strung out on some serious matter
I just smile and move on. Who wants to hear all that heavy stuff
in a place like this? I can't get involved and take sides. I never, but
never, paw a chick on the floor.

Though acceptable in the club, squares and men on the take
are held in low esteem by the management and most patron
groups. Squares, says the owner-manager, though "good for business," are always somewhat suspect in terms of what they may pass
on to unfriendly officials and policemen. (We found this suspicion
unfounded.) The owner's avoidance of squares in the Rendezvous
probably stems from the general misgivings and antipathy that he,
along with others in the underworld, feel toward conventional
people. The following interview statements by the owner are
illustrative:

Well, squares spend money, and they don't give us any trouble.
We need them, but you can never tell about them. They talk too
damn much, and they really don't know what's going on. They
talk to the wrong people too. Hustlers talk a lot, but they know
who to talk to. Squares are just squares. They can't help it, but I
don't trust them. Come to think of it, no square ever blew the
whistle on me. Square broads also add a little class. You need them
around for the dudes on the make. In fact, you need a bunch of
good-looking broads around for decoration. Broads draw men, and
men buy drinks.

Male and female thieves, though viewed as low-class patrons, are
assets in several respects: they spend money, draw trade, and perform certain services for other patrons. The owner-manager explained the Rendezvous roles of thieves:

We go along with some thieves but most of them could use
more class. They do add a different color to the scene, and they got
money to spend. Some good people like to have them around. You
know, like lawyers and bondsmen. Maybe somebody wants some-
thing at a reasonable price. It don't make a damn whether they
are socializing or taking care of business, they're still drinking and
buying drinks back and forth. Don't get the wrong idea; they don't
bring any merchandise in here. Sure, we get a few cheap hustlers
and pretty boys [pimps], but just because we serve them don't
mean I have to associate with them. Lawyers and doctors don't
have to associate with their clients. The same thing, right? Women

thieves are about the same but they are women. Some of them look good and spend their money so they're O.K. Everybody likes to have good-looking fillies prancing around.

The owner bypasses the open southwest corner booths to avoid disturbing the amorous activities therein. On the other hand, he visits on cue the northeast corner booths where he has friends and where his company is expected now and then. As he reported to one of the observers while having a drink at the bar:

Couples sit in the booths because they don't want to be bothered. They really want to get with it. Let them have their fun. Now the other two booths are another matter. I got friends there. If I don't drop by now and then for a chat, somebody might get the idea that I'm not sociable. You know I can't afford that. I'm a very sociable person. Of course, if I see they got something going, I stay away. The right timing is necessary when you visit around. They have a way of letting you know when you're welcome. You have to keep your antennae up.

Commenting on his contacts in the club with people on the take, the owner expressed contempt for this "group of scavengers" whom he feels take undue advantage of the club and some of its patrons. However, he realizes that he must not only abide them, but provide them with certain services. As he told one observer in a table group:

What'ja gonna do? You've got them, so you make the best of it. I'm not worried about them singing to anybody about my club. They're taken care of real good. So why should they sing? And who's going to support a yellow canary's song anyhow? The problem is they're a bunch of free loaders. They want free drinks, the best service, and free ass from every good-looking broad in the joint. Would you believe, not just the hired help, but the broads who are paying customers. Too much. I'm not a whore master, and I don't run a candy factory. I try to stay away from the bastards, but I have to throw them a bone [get them a woman] once in a while. I just ask one of the girls [employees, party girls, call girls] to go screw the bastard and that I'll take care of the inconvenience [give her some money, or some other consideration, e.g., booze, night off, money] later. You couldn't keep these broads away from the entertainers and businessmen, but pigs turn them off. Most of the time they're satisfied to cop a feel at the tables.

SUMMARY

The owner-manager, the producer and director of the Rendezvous behavior setting, is an early-morning entrepreneur, a successful after-hours club proprietor. As a charming host, a manipulator of people and symbols, an impression manager, a showman, and a bon vivant, he operates successfully an illegal, but safe, playtime configuration that he himself designed. He envisions the Rendezvous, his creation, as a plush, swinging, high-class, leisure-time setting that caters to a potpourri of high-rolling, odd-time revelers from both the underworld and upperworld. The club, what it stands for, and what goes on there mirror the proprietor. Certainly he is the one most important actor in the setting.

Assistant Manager

ASCRIBED AND ACHIEVED CHARACTERISTICS

The assistant manager is younger than the owner-manager (thirty-five), better educated (high school graduate plus one year of business college), and of higher social class origin (lower-middle). In marital status (stably married with children), work background (restaurant, night club, and bar experience), recreational pattern (women, booze, gambling), and life style he is quite similar to his mentor. In reference to work experience he reported in the interviews:

Working around bars, broads, and booze is the story of my life. You got to be with it from the inside out to make it in this business. I've seen many clubs fold because the monkeys running the show didn't know shit from Shinola about the bar business. You know—good locations from bad, good lay outs from cattle pens, strobe lights from gas lights, good help from bad. This is not to mention other things like what and how to buy. And what kind of music and service you offer to what kind of people. You got to know how to keep from being stolen blind by the help. I won't go into the kind of connections you gotta have, but you know what I mean. Everybody in the bar and night club business must have connections. When you fold in this business, you fold fast. What's in today may be out tomorrow. So if you aren't careful you leave a graveyard for some other club owner to come in and build another cemetery on top of your flop. I know spots that have turned over owners and decors four or five times in a few years.

The son of a bartender and bookie, he is a witty, verbal, resilient person—an actor with many fronts who readily shifts language style and personal demeanor with changing audiences. Like the owner-manager in dress tastes, he is sharply conservative with a flair for dark, expensive, natural fabrics and flashy gold, silver, and platinum jewelry and accessories encrusted with diamonds, rubies, and sapphires—a sort of illuminated peacock. Commenting on the necessity of front in the night club business, he explained to one of the researchers over a drink at the bar:

This business is like the undertaking racket in a way. You got to have a front. By front I mean what you say and how you say it— what you wear and how you wear it. You're not a circus barker or an announcer in a strip joint. If you want the carriage trade—and we do, then you got to have the carriage house and what goes with it. You draw the cream by the way you lay out the whole joint—the floor plan, the lights, the music, the sound system, and the decorations. And how you dress the barmaids and the bar and table arrangements. All of it. Good service, of course, I'm taking for granted.

Though admitting to past criminal activity in connection with off-track horse racing, he claims no current criminal pursuits beyond his duties at the Rendezvous. He has no official juvenile record, and his developmental history, including home, school, and community life, appears devoid of adjustment problems. Presently he lives in an upper-middle-class suburban area. Though arrested twice as an adult on gambling charges for which he paid fines, he has never been incarcerated. A social drinker, he uses no other type of drug.

IDENTITIES AND PERSPECTIVES

A long-time employee and protegé of the owner, the assistant manager resembles his boss in reference to role identities and world view. He sees himself as a smooth, ambitious, sophisticated, well-connected manager of an after-hours club. He aspires eventually to own his own club. Presently his ties with conventional society are fewer and more tenuous than those of his mentor. Though a family man and sometime churchgoer, he rarely participates in social, service, or civic clubs or organizations. He views the administration of criminal justice in the same light as his boss. Though espousing respectability, he too is a product and a manipulating exponent of the underworld. In the following excerpt submitted in an interview, he designated his success and indicated his self-conception:

I was a bookie for awhile, but that life is tough. You know, twelve or eighteen hours on the street. Little home life, and you don't know when you'll leave the house or when you'll get back. You're always involved in some kind of other hustle—or trying to set something up. That's over. I got regular hours now. I can enjoy the sweet life, and spend time at home too. I don't have to be afraid somebody will lay his hand on my shoulder—roust me. I've found a good thing—and it's made-to-order. I know how to handle people, and never was an ape. You know, a gorilla with pants on and a club in his hand. I always liked to go to the finest night clubs, dress up, get a fine looking broad, and make the scene at some plush joint. The best table and the best of everything there. Most of the successful club owners I know spent a lot of time in clubs before they owned one. I'm no exception. I've gone first class, so I know how to lay it out for others who want to go that way. One of these days I'll own my own club. There's more money and less competition here than in legitimate bars. Who wants the hassle with a bunch of common drunks and the singles' trade—a bunch of snot-nosed kids trying hard to be swingers. That's what you got to do in public joints. It takes too much time the straight way. Most legit joints suck.

In discussing the attraction and the multiple nature of the Rendezvous' tableau during an interview, he confirmed the owner-manager's picture of the club and further elaborated on the self-support and group support he receives in his role identity as assistant manager of the Rendezvous:

Illegal, yes, criminal, no. We provide a place where different kinds of people can enjoy themselves. People like to play, and we furnish the play pen. It takes different strokes for different folks— and we got a variety. We couldn't stay open without people who work odd hours. It takes all kinds. Me, I make it with all kinds, but feel more at home with people who are connected and entertainers. The people you know real good are the people you like to be with —the people you can trust. And let's face it, without regulars who are good people we couldn't stay open. Good people bring in the straights like fly paper catches flies. The squares think some of the glamour of our world rubs off on them. Certainly all kinds of deals go on here, just like at other places. You can't stop that. People wheel and deal over a few drinks, and get entertained to boot. So it's beautiful for them and us. What's wrong with taking care of business, having a few drinks, scoring with a broad, and listening to good music all in the same place? Legit, illegit, who cares so long as they don't flash the money and put the merchandise on top of the table like at a public auction.

BEHAVIOR ON THE SCENE

The assistant manager is the overall supervisor of the club on the set. Unlike the owner, he mingles and converses with all patron memberships and employees. Moreover, he is more formal in speech and demeanor and briefer in all of his social and occupational club encounters than is the owner. Keeping on the move from one subsetting to another, he rarely sits down with either patrons or employees, both of whom view him as the assistant director of the scene. Actually, his work role encompasses a multitudinous diversity of duties that preclude sustained social encounters and call for great ingenuity, diplomacy, and versatility. He detailed his work roles in this way in an interview:

Everybody knows I run the show. At least the part of it that everybody can see. If the patrons aren't satisfied or need something, they usually come to me. If they want to get two tables moved together or need more chairs. Or maybe they want a certain brand of liquor that's not behind the bar. Or they want to get somebody in we screened out [of the club]. Somebody gets in a hassle with one of the girls. Maybe there is an argument about a dice game for drinks, and they ask for the house rules. Some high roller wants me to help him get a broad who's sitting at the bar two feet away. Somebody gets too drunk and wants to fight. The bouncer wants to know do I throw him out. Sometimes I say, "No you can't throw him out, he's somebody. Take him to your car and drive the clown home. And don't leave him on the front lawn or on the steps. Ring the bell and turn him over to who answers. Don't give them any explanation." Sometimes some of the lights go out or the microphones on the band stand won't work or something or other happens to the whole damned sound system. Some broad gets mad with her boyfriend and needs cab fare home. Some cocktail waitress wants to leave early when we're busy as hell. Something happens to the plumbing. You name it, I'm it. Most of the time I make them happy one way or the other. I check with the old man if I get strung out on some problem.

Though the assistant manager is more formal in his dealings with all actors than is the owner, unlike the boss he interacts with all patron memberships—including male thieves, female thieves, and squares as well as high prestige groups such as businessmen. He also serves as a buffer between the owner and the employees, as well as between the owner and certain patrons. In this capacity he conveys, mediates, and interchanges messages, information, and instructions. Referring to his buffer role, he pointed out in an interview:

The owner has to front the club. There's many things he doesn't want to be bothered with. He passes most problems and complaints to me. If I hear them first, I handle it without bothering him. I tell him about it sooner or later, but jump on it if it's not too big. There's some patrons he just don't take up any time with. Don't get me wrong, he doesn't put anybody down. He nods and speaks to everybody, but he doesn't really socialize with anybody but regulars who are somebody. Now women, that's another story. We all go for broads now and then we ought to let go by. Anyway, my position is different, I kick it around with anybody. If they're good enough to let in, they're good enough for me to mingle with. I can't play favorites. When the responsibility is on you to make everybody happy, you have to treat them all about alike—or pretend to anyway. Frankly, I never get too close to any of them. I supervise the employees. And I have to run the show for the patrons. That means I got to be kinda neutral. Business is business.

The assistant manager, like the owner, does not engage in the activities on the dance floor and stays away from the southwest corner booths unless trouble occurs there. Occasionally upon invitation he visits with the businessmen in the northeast corner booths. Though cordial and polite to all women patrons, he slides away from any physical contact with them and never openly flirts with female patrons or employees. As he put it in a private conversation with one of us in the owner's office:

> *Our set up provides a place where guys and broads can get together. Why should we cut in on their action? Certainly that's part of our action. Customers don't want to compete with the management or hired help. They think that's unfair competition. Now take the girls that work here. They're here for the customers too—at least to look at. So you see it's best for me to stay clear of all the broads. You shouldn't mix business with pleasure. If a real sharp one comes on strong and pushes it on me I might find a way.*

The assistant manager has other specific duties. He greets and helps screen incoming patrons in the foyer and checks the hors d'oeuvres in the waiting room that are brought in by a cocktail waitress. At the hatcheck room he sees to it that bouncers help patrons with the removal of their hats, coats, and wraps and with the checking in of personal belongings. Occasionally he finds a table for a very worthy party and escorts its members thereto. He checks the provisions and cash registers behind the bar, straightens out cocktail waitresses' mixed-up orders, and sees to it that all patrons are properly served. Furthermore, he chats with esteemed regular patrons and accepts and buys an occasional gift drink. In the nightspot setting he checks on drink orders, moves from table to table exchanging greetings with patrons, and now and then passes on patrons' musical requests to the band. Like the owner-manager he usually conveys corrective measures to the personnel through and by hand signals, gestures, and eye movements. When these messages are not promptly acted upon, employees are called off the floor to the owner's office for more direct instructions.

In addition to directly supervising all employees and operations on the floor, the assistant manager is also the chief security officer and trouble-shooter in and outside the club's environs. He helps the owner-manager arbitrate any work difficulties among the employees (usually in the owner's office) and when necessary resolves altercations among patrons as well as disputes between patrons and employees. In the latter case, he subscribes to the dictum, "the customer is always right." He also helps the owner-manager with the extension of credit; the payroll, bookkeeping and purchasing duties; and with the selection and firing of personnel. At staggered intervals before, during, and after work hours he examines the club's outside perimeter and environs for any evidence of heist men who might plan to rob the club or patrons en route to or from the club. From time to time he talks by telephone to the lookout men who patrol the outside environs. Finally, he is reported to be the owner's liaison officer regarding payoff matters with the police.

SUMMARY

The assistant manager in many ways is a younger replica of the owner. He meets obligations and performs duties similar to those performed by his counterparts in legal clubs and in addition some extra duties and undertakings that inhere in the illegal nature of his Rendezvous work role. He is made to order in ascribed and achieved characteristics, role identity, and world view to meet his Rendezvous managerial obligations, including the required supplementary work routines that set his work role off from that of his legal counterparts. As the assistant director of the Rendezvous, he is the man in the middle in that he mediates and negotiates matters from the top to the bottom, and from the bottom to the top, relating to employees and patrons. In this role he helps tie together and maintain the ongoing scene. In short, he is a stage manager, an expediter, a security officer, an administrator, and a diplomatic trouble-shooter. Along with the owner-manager, he helps generate and sustain activities in the setting.

Barmaids and Cocktail Waitresses

ASCRIBED AND ACHIEVED CHARACTERISTICS

Barmaids and cocktail waitresses are a group of young (ranging from twenty-one to thirty), attractive, fairly well-educated (high school graduates) women. They are either single or divorced without the encumbrances of husbands or permanent boyfriends. Residing in apartments in respectable lower-middle-class residential areas, most have been successfully employed over long periods of time (at least three years) in legitimate and respectable bars, cocktail lounges, restaurants, and night clubs as barmaids and/or cocktail waitresses.

Coming from respectable noncriminal working-class family backgrounds, these female employees report no juvenile delinquency or criminal histories. Childhood and adolescent histories indicate family and community adjustment. None note illegitimate children, drug addiction, or a history of venereal disease. All claim to use birth control pills. Sexually, they prefer one boyfriend at a time and disclaim ever working as prostitutes. They deny any criminal pursuits other than working at the Rendezvous and are probably less deviant than the general run of female bar employees because as demonstrated later on, the Rendezvous rules out certain deviant types as employees.

Currently the barmaids and cocktail waitresses represent a revolving cadre of moonlighters who work at the Rendezvous two or three mornings a week while simultaneously working full time or part time at public clubs, bars, or restaurants. A few work regularly for a few months and then move on to public establishments, returning to the Rendezvous intermittently as moonlighters. Many pick up extra money by working as barmaids and waitresses at private parties frequently hosted by patrons of the Rendezvous.

The owner-manager, assistant manager, and the female employees' accounts of Rendezvous employment procedures disclose that barmaids and cocktail waitresses are selected on the basis of several criteria outlined as follows: physical appearance and front, personal habits and "class," experience and reputation, efficiency and finesse, honesty and "rightness" (trustworthy and tuned in to the hustling world). Most prospective employees are already well known to the management in work and social context in and outside the club. Some have been patrons in the club. Others have served the management and club employees as patrons in establishments where they were working previously. Still others have had social interaction with the management and club employees at parties and social gatherings outside the club. Some are referred by Rendezvous employees and patrons and by local owners of public bars, clubs, and restaurants. As one barmaid detailed in her interview:

The management knows most of us anyway. They get around, but I'll try to fill you in on what it takes. We have to look sharp, because we're part of the decoration. We have to be sexy but not act like hustlers, and turn them on with class. They don't want girls who slop drinks all over the bar. We have to have enough brains to keep drink orders straight and talk to customers. Speed is important too, because it's a fast shuffle and you get pressure from customers who have to be served promptly. Another thing, you have to know how to handle men and keep them interested but not hanging all over you. We have to be available, but not too available. Junkies, lushes, hookers, and jailbirds are out. They got the wire on you, and they check you out. Most girls who can make it in first-rate legit places can handle the Rendezvous trade. They call up where you worked before, or they talk to somebody inside. We aren't criminals, but we have to be right. And you know, keep quiet about what goes on. If you can't live with the action they got going, you just don't fit. You have to make up your mind about that in front. It's no big thing, most of us know the score anyway. Most of us refer other girls when we need them. We know as well as the management who can make it here. It's their decision at the interview.

These female employees and the management report that high wages (more than double that paid on legitimate shifts), big tips (upward from 20 per cent), and good working conditions in a swinging, high-class club attract a limitless source of employees. Girls with "Penthouse" figures and large breasts are preferred because the management feels this come-on, lewd body type appeals to its male patrons and befits the Rendezvous cachet. "Playboy" types are out because they are considered too statuesque and wholesome with strong overtones of Miss Americas. Broody, bitchy, witchy, prototypes who prefer Shalimar get the nod over blond Chanel No. 5 types. Saucy blondes are not ruled out. Female employees must not only be sensuous but also spirited, vivacious, and "classy." A cocktail waitress explained in her interview:

You got to have the bod, but that's not enough. Who wants a marble statue? You got to move your boobs and your thighs and give them some crotch and butt shots as you move about. You swish it, and you don't bump and grind it like a stripper. Not like a whore, but like you got it, and you want to let them know in a nice way. It's not up for grabs like any free piece, but it could be available. With the high rollers you brush it up against them sometimes accidentally on purpose. If they grab you, well, enjoy it.

You have to spread a little joy—smile, talk friendly, joke. You use your eyes as well as your thighs. Put something on their mind to dream about. Follow? Always be polite. Never, never talk about boyfriends or money. Don't be commercial. I'm talking about customers without dates. You never compete with the female patrons. That's a no no. You can always tell the man at the table who's not with a date. If you're any good you learned all of this long before you worked at the Rendezvous.

Girls with official criminal records, drug addicts, lushes, and prostitutes are excluded from employment as "undesirables for this kind of club" and as "riskies" whose presence might encourage police surveillance. According to the female employees and the management, candidates must have had at least two years' work experience in first-rate establishments. They must also come recommended as "having it," exemplify deftness in serving drinks and food, and be able to take charge in the patron-service relationship in a pleasing manner. Rightness refers to loyalty, dependability, the ability to stand up under pressure, not squealing, goodness of fit among underworld characters, and a world view that is sympathetic to off-beat people and their activities. Honesty is a slippery quality related to several negative work practices: hustling patrons for money; stealing money or property from the house or customers; stealing or giving away booze; setting up customers for later hustles; giving any harmful information out (on or off the job) about patrons, employees, or the club; discussing anything about the club with the police or other law enforcement officials. As subsequently detailed, the abstract code of honesty may be stretched and is interpreted and applied in different social contexts of problematic situations.

IDENTITIES AND PERSPECTIVES

Barmaids and cocktail waitresses see themselves as hip, high-class, legitimate, attractive, and efficient service workers in the food-liquor end of the restaurant-bar-club business. Present oriented, they verbalize no occupational status problems and do not appear to be upwardly mobile. One cocktail waitress declared to one observer over a gift drink in the nightspot setting:

I know who I am. I'm a damn good cocktail waitress and I've always worked in the best spots. I never worked in a dump. I've always made more money from tips than wages. My looks help—specially in bars, and I know how to treat customers. No matter how you feel you have to give them the pleasant treatment. I don't know anything about other kinds of work. Frankly, I'm not interested. I like what I do, and get well paid. I'm young. Men like me, and I have a good time. So what else is there? I know the score, and I don't get pushed out of shape when some guy makes a pass. Wheelers, dealers, and players come from all over. Who gives a darn how they score or what they score so long as they treat me right?

These female employees view the Rendezvous as a temporary work site that provides them with "fill in" work in an exciting, pleasant, lucrative, and opportunistic milieu. They rationalize away the illegal aspects of the work situation by dissociating this so-called "temporary" illegitimate employment from their legitimate work routine and by stressing the Rendezvous' "legitimate function." A barmaid confided to one observer at the bar during a slack period just before closing time:

Sure it's illegal to work here, but then I'm only filling in for a few days. I work regular at the Golden Slipper. You've seen me there. I've always had good jobs in legal places. I don't own any part of this club. It's just a good place to pick up some extra cash. It's fun here too, and the men you meet are groovy. Let's face it, I meet more hustlers at the Golden Slipper than here. The thing is customers here show more class. People who work all night serving people like you have to have somewhere to go after hours. Legal, illegal, who gives a damn about the technicality? You are legal, aren't you? What about all the other legals in here? Sure, some people in the life and some mob people might show. They show all over—like stars in the sky. So what else is new?

These young women are acquainted with and associate with a variety of social types from both the upperworld and underworld, and the nature of their work makes it easy for them to cross between conventional and nonconventional life styles. Though not engaged in illegal criminal pursuits per se, they serve, sometimes work with or for, and associate with off-beat people and criminals. Crassly materialistic, they respect and admire all men with money and evaluate people's worth in terms of property and wealth. Social Darwinists, they think that the fittest survive and prosper in a capitalistic society where they are willing to fit in at a relatively low level. They vocalize ambivalent positions on many of the basic social institutions, express negative feelings toward the administration of criminal justice, voice fairly positive ideas about marriage and the family, and comment favorably about the capitalistic system. Quite realistic about marriage, they expect eventually to marry men on the same occupational level as themselves. One barmaid discussed her future with one researcher during a private conversation at the bar in this way:

I'm in no rush, but I'll marry. Right now, I'm having a ball. I need a husband like I need a hole in the head. You meet some dream boats here. The problem is most of them are married. I'd like to marry a man with money and education. That's hard to do in my position. I'll probably marry some bartender or waiter. But I'll never keep a man. I'll work, but you can bet he'll work too. That pimp jazz is for dingalings.

Barmaids and cocktail waitresses appear to be well adjusted and relatively happy with their present circumstances and life style. Though living in modest apartments and driving economy cars, they manage to dress well. Picturing themselves to be chic, attractive working girls, they expect their dates to take them to expensive restaurants and clubs for nightlife entertainment. For them life is divided into two parts: (1) work and fun before marriage, (2) work and no fun after marriage. Fun to them is expensive nightlife entertainment. They'll take their fun now! As one cocktail waitress remarked to one researcher in a private conversation:

It's like this, we're girls with a lot to show. And we know the entertainment business—the dumps and the good places. We work in the best and deserve to play in the best. We know how to dress, the right perfumes, how to act, and all that. The guys we go out with wouldn't dare take us to a dump. They know we aren't just ordinary broads. What's wrong with going first class? Some day I'll probably be married—then you can forget the sweet life. Right now it belongs to me.

The future role identities and perspectives of these young women are problematic, depending upon marriage and their ultimate commitment to whatever life style.

BEHAVIOR ON THE SCENE

Bar service is rendered by three barmaids who mix and serve drinks behind the bar, one on either end and one in the center. They also prepare drink orders for cocktail waitresses who serve the tables and booths. As a rule, bar, table, and booth drinks are collected for by the round when served. Some worthy patrons are permitted to run tabs at the tables and booths that are paid up at the time of departure. Cocktail waitresses keep change and pay the barmaids for their drink orders in front, usually collecting from the patrons when they serve the drinks. The same arrangement applies when tabs are run at the tables and booths; therefore the cocktail waitress rather than the barmaid must keep up with all drink orders that are not served at the bar. Using the service elevator, they pick up food orders from the kitchen located on the first story above the club proper, along with the food service check, which is itemized by the cook. The food check is paid for separately from the bar check at the time of service and delivered to the barmaid servicing the mid-bar. Each barmaid operates one of three cash registers behind the bar and rings up drink orders.

Accessible for friendly conversation to anyone who sits or stands at the bar, barmaids are expected to present a cheerful, adjustable, and seductive front to unattached males. They talk, laugh, joke, and gossip with patrons who seek encounters in a light vein and render civil inattention to those who wish to be left alone. Functioning as intermediaries, they introduce unacquainted patrons and various types of negotiators. Barmaids do not accept gift drinks or drink while behind the bar, nor do they participate in any of the club's activities beyond the realm of the bar while on duty. Occasionally, during slack periods of action, one by one (taking turns) they might move to a known table group for a brief period of time and sit down, chat, drink, or dance.

Barmaids work at creating and maintaining for male patrons the illusion of intimate sociability and possible accessibility. Several techniques are employed in this endeavor, e.g., personal attention and time devoted to the patron, verbal bantering, and body language in the form of postures and movements that indicate accessibility. Personal attention in addition to a sustained interest in what the patron says and does includes such acts as lighting cigarettes, cleaning ash trays, cleaning the bar in front of the patron, and prompt and deft service. Verbal bantering entails, encourages, and supports mild sexual flirtation. Serious direct sexual propositions are unwanted and are met by cut-offs. Body language is used to support verbal sexual flirtation and may also convey nonverbal sexual significance. For example, barmaids, none of whom wear bras or slips, may reveal their breasts by bending over the bar. They may expose their crotches and butts in several tantalizing stances by the clever use of posturing, bending, swishing and swaying (all with the aid of the back-bar mirror), touch the patron on the hand, face, or shoulder, or embrace a patron lightly and fleetingly. These sexy, come-on behaviors are in keeping with the sexy playtime features of the setting.

Professed management policy calls for barmaids to give all male patrons the same treatment; however, they actually give preferential attention to esteemed regular males. And covertly this is what is really expected. Barmaids thus perform instrumental as well as decorative and expressive functions. In a real sense they are features of the setting that symbolize a gay and sexy scene in both static (looks, attire) and dynamic (conversation, body movements, gestures) terms.

Cocktail waitresses serve table and booth drink orders from the bar and also serve steak sandwiches and nonalcoholic beverages (milk, soft drinks, coffee, and tea) from the kitchen. Like barmaids, they are expected to be decorative and seductive as well as helpful in various types of social and work encounters with patrons. They usually maintain a greater social and physical distance between themselves and patrons than do barmaids because they do not have a protective physical barrier, the bar, separating them from patrons. Though pleasant and enticing in their conversation and actions toward male patrons, they commonly parry direct propositions and physical advances in a more forceful verbal manner than do barmaids by saying such things as "cut that out," "cut it out or you might burn your fingers," "don't burn your fingers," "knock it off." On rare occasions when patrons insist on pawing them in a resolute fashion they might retreat from the floor and, if necessary, turn the problem over to a bouncer. Occasionally, to the contrary, cocktail waitresses may playfully embrace and permit themselves to be embraced by patrons. All are expected to permit limited sexual advances from certain types (typically night people and businessmen). Overall, they must combine and portray apparent sexual availability with sexual constraint in an alluring but differentiated manner. Like barmaids, they too introduce and help bring together patrons with serious as well as unserious purposes at hand.

When not serving drinks and food, cocktail waitresses might elect to sit or stand at the bar or tables and converse with patrons and other employees. Occasionally, when not busy (and space permitting) they sit with regular customers at the bar, the tables, and even in the businessmen's booths (upon invitation). During these leisure periods waitresses might accept gift drinks, talk, embrace, dance with patrons, and even take part in the impromptu acts on the dance floor. These liberties exclude noticeable intoxication, the loss of self-restraint, and serious, sustained, expressive sexual behavior. Violations in this area are met with admonition and warning from other employees and the assistant manager.

BARMAIDS' AND COCKTAIL WAITRESSES' CROSS-SEX BEHAVIOR PATTERNS AND CLUB CONDUCT

Barmaids and cocktail waitresses generally have boyfriends who are usually employed in the nightlife industry outside the Rendezvous as bartenders, waiters, musicians, entertainers, and other restaurant, night club and bar personnel. These friends, though discouraged from doing so, occasionally attend the club. They are considered undesirable patrons and in fact are prevented from attending regularly. When boyfriends do attend, they must remain anonymous and are not allowed to make any personal claims on the employee's person or time. The assistant manager reported in an interview:

We don't want their men around. They [the boyfriends] watch them and get jealous. They get possessive and want all their time. Most of them don't have enough money and come up short. They expect the girl to give them free drinks and special service. Who needs headaches? Now and then we let one in. If one gets out of line, we just tell the girl to get him out for good—you know, go now and don't come back. She has to handle the situation. Either the clown goes or they both go. Most of them feel like we do about the situation. They don't wear engagement or wedding rings at work. Rings signal they belong to someone. That's not good for business.

For the most part female employees agree with the management about the presence of boyfriends in the club. One cocktail waitress remarked to one of the observers at the bar:

There's no point in even letting them bring us to work. Most of us don't let them pick us up at closing. We try to keep our thing at the club on the q.t. Men just don't understand. It's something in their egos, I guess. Frankly, most of us don't want them around anyway, no matter how cool they play it. We aren't married, and we don't want them blocking our action.

Although these employees and the management proclaim a rule against dating relationships among club employees, and although they maintain that dating among employees and patrons is also discouraged, both occur. The latter practice happens more often and is more frequently overlooked—particularly if it is not made too obvious and does not result in jealous scenes. In fact, it is covertly encouraged or deemed admissible in special cases, e.g., in the case of a big spending high roller who happens to be on intimate terms with the owner-manager and/or the assistant manager or in the case of a girl who wishes to do a worthy third party a special favor such as going out with a patron at the request of another patron or the management.

Barmaids and cocktail waitresses who date either employees or patrons do so surreptitiously and are not expected (or allowed) to show any special feelings toward them at the club. Above all, the outside relationship must not in any way interfere with inside occupational work chores, fronts, or expectations. Flagrant and persistent violations of these rules and expectations, particularly those that lead to disruptive scenes in the club, are ultimately sanctioned by dismissal. Male and female employee transgressors are sanctioned equally regardless of the instigator. The owner says, "They both knew better than to get involved in the first place."

The management's rules, expectations, and sanctions in the sensitive area of employee-employee and employee-patron dating relationships are problematic. The assistant manager spoke about employee dating relationships during an interview:

There's no payoff in mixing business with pleasure. Let's say I started making it with one of these chicks [barmaids or cocktail waitresses]. *She'll start coming in late for work, getting headaches, and want off before closing time. If I tell her about any mistakes she makes, she'll tell me she can't help it, because she's lost too much sleep out with me. She'll expect special favors and more* money. *The other girls might find out and then you lose respect. She might get hung up on me or pretend to be. I'm a married man. Who wants to hear all that love shit? Broads are a dime a dozen. Don't get me wrong, I get mine. And not all of it at home. We don't want them dating bouncers either. They're here for the patrons to look at. Say one of the bouncers and a waitress have something going. The first thing you know he gets jealous because some customer puts his hands on her. Then you could have a scene. Who needs that?*

A cocktail waitress spoke about employee-employee dating to one of the observers in a table group:

It's no good screwing around with guys who work here. They can't do anything for you anyway. All they want is something for nothing. Friends, O.K., but when you make out with them, you take a chance on losing a friend—and respect too. It's not wise to let them know too much about your personal life. There are exceptions. Some can play it cool, but damned few. We make it with the musicians sometimes, but that's different. They move from club to club, and you don't see them every time you come to work. They don't make a big deal out of a lay anyway. With the bouncers it's different. They got the stud ego hangup thing. They're really dressed up apes. The management, that's another story. Sometimes you have no choice, but if you steer clear it's better. Once you screw them, they think they own you. You don't mind doing them once in a while, but the problem is they get demanding sometimes. Let's say you got a date, or just want to go home. What'ya do? The guy's the boss, so you got to take care of him.

In discussing patron-employee dating relationships with one observer in his office, the owner claimed that such relationships are inevitable, at times undesirable and disruptive, and at still other times desirable.

It's not good policy, but then whatcha gonna do? The high rollers are going to get to most of them one way or the other. If a big shot really has it for one of the girls, we might encourage it. We don't try to control who they date outside the club, but tell them it's not a good policy to date customers indiscriminately. They understand. Most of the customers do too. I mean they keep it cool, and don't act like they own a girl in the club just because

*they've made it with her. The girls know better than to lay claim
to a customer just because they got something going outside.
Neither party wants a long-time thing anyway. We just don't
allow them* [patron or employee] *to parade their act in the club.
We don't want them hanging all over each other here.*

The owner detailed the female employee's responsibilities regarding patron dating practices to a researcher in his office:

*The high rollers can pass them around and cut them up anyway
they want to outside, but they don't own them here. If a girl gets
so strung out on a customer that she neglects others, she's through.
If a jealous scene like bickering, or arguing, or fighting among
customers happens over her, she's through if she's been dating one
of the guys mixed up in the squabble. Of course customers when
liquored up sometimes get into it over the girls' attentions. If it's
not too bad, we smooth it down. She's got to handle the situation,
or else. We can't blame the customer unless he's way out of line.*

Barmaids and cocktail waitresses claim that they date patrons
on the sly once in a while on a discriminating basis. Furthermore,
they agree that these relationships must not interfere with their
regular work chores and fronts at the Rendezvous. One cocktail
waitress related to an observer on the dance floor:

*It's my job to shine them all on, but you can't come on too
strong. We don't go out with strangers. If a guy moves me, and
acts right, and has been around for a while, then I'll arrange to see
him somewhere else later. Most of the time we go out to dinner or
to a club. Later when we see each other at the Rendezvous—well,
it never happened.*

Barmaids, cocktail waitresses, and the management report little
fraternization among female patrons and male employees in or
out of the club, and that even when dating relationships occur
among these two groups, they are not disruptive to the club's ongoing activities. A barmaid explained to an observer at the bar:

*Women customers don't go for the men who work here. They're
tied up with the male patrons. Sometimes one of the musicians or
a bouncer will go out with one, but not often. If they've been out
with whoever works here they're as anxious to keep it under wraps
as the guy. Bartenders and waiters are always after the women
customers. That's the big reason they don't have bartenders and*

waiters here. We can handle men better without getting involved than bartenders and waiters can handle women.

In light of the foregoing, it is seen that the conformances to and the violations and sanctions of rules regarding the cross-sex behavior of female employees at the club are problematic. If transgressors generally uphold the rule they break, attempt to conceal the violation, give a good account of themselves if exposed, and manage to avoid scenes in the club, their behavior is overlooked.

Hustling Practices

Barmaids and cocktail waitresses may hustle the patrons or the house. Along with the management, they profess a set of negative hustling rules that may be outlined in the following hierarchical order:

1. barmaids may dip into the till [take money from a cash register]
2. barmaids and cocktail waitresses may pocket cash from drink or food orders, and barmaids may pocket cash from customers or cocktail waitresses and fail to ring up the total or partial part of the bill
3. cocktail waitresses may withhold from the barmaid money received from food orders
4. barmaids and cocktail waitresses may pad or underestimate drink or food bills
5. barmaids and cocktail waitresses may short-change the house or patrons
6. barmaids or cocktail waitresses may manage to give away free drinks
7. barmaids and cocktail waitresses may filch money and personal belongings from patrons (taking money, wallets, evening bags, cigarette lighters, jewelry, clothing, and the like inadvertently left at the bar, tables, booths, and hatcheck room)
8. female employees may steal property from the club
9. they may hustle patrons for drinks or sex
10. they may overtly buy, sell, barter, or dispense illegal goods and services (drugs, sex, stolen goods)
11. they may set up patrons as marks for illegal hustles at some other place and time.

Actually barmaids and cocktail waitresses engage in a wide variety of hustling activities, some of which are expected and over-looked by all actors on the scene. The situational context in which these activities occur, the finesse, skill, and timing involved, the identity of the actor hustled, the umbrella of secrecy surrounding the hustle, and the consequences following the hustle are crucial in determining the acceptability or unacceptability of such hustling behavior. One barmaid in discussing "hustling the house" confided in her interview:

In this business you're expected to take a little off the top now and then, but you never get your hand caught in the till. That's stealing. Sometimes I give my friends a free drink, and I'll take a broken bottle [partial bottle from behind the bar] *home. I might forget to ring up a drink order once in awhile, but your memory can't be too bad. It gets kinda hectic at times, and a five or a ten might just fall out of place—I just figure out where to put it. If I'm out of cigarettes, I might borrow a pack or two. I'm not greedy, and the few gifts I got coming go strictly to me. I don't work out any deal with any other girl who works here to take anything. That's stealing.*

In similar vein a cocktail waitress elaborated to a researcher at the bar:

I usually keep things straight, but I'm human. So if I mix up a drink order and find myself with some extra money, or I forget to turn in cash for an order now and then—I'm that much ahead. Or say somebody gives me too much change. The bosses in this business are the same as in legit joints. They expect you to take a little. But if you over do it, you get fired.

Reporting on hustling patrons, a barmaid submitted the following excerpt during her interview:

Sometimes customers spread their money all over the bar in two or three piles, moving all over the place. If they don't pick it up in a reasonable time, I just count it as a tip. Some don't ever bother to pick up their change. If it's not a bundle, it's a tip too. I'm a little more considerate with regulars. If a businessman leaves it, it stays there forever. Another thing, I'm not a hustler, but I go out with customers sometimes. I choose who I like. If he leaves some-thing under my pillow, maybe it came from the fairy godmother. If there's no Christmas present—so what, Santa Claus just forgot.

*There's no price tag on me. Now if the house is anxious for me to
go out with someone, it's a little different. Then I kinda expect a
little something from one end or the other. But I got some say so.
If he's a jerk—forget it.*

A cocktail waitress noted further information on this point to
an observer at the bar:

*If some good time Charlie gives me a big tip after every round,
who am I to complain? Or if he gives me a tenner to get him a
pack of cigarettes and forgets his change—it's a tip. If he's really
out of it [drunk] I don't take his money. If they want to dream
about what might happen after closing, who am I to shatter their
hopes? If the guy's a regular, I'll level with him. I go out with a
customer occasionally after closing, but that's my business. I
don't hustle him on the scene and tell him it's a hundred blocks
away. After the happenings if he leaves a present, O.K. If not, O.K.*

Another cocktail waitress disclosed to one of the researchers the
following excerpt while dancing with him in the nightspot setting:

*I'm not a hustler, but it's part of my job to help people get
together. Say some guy wants me to help him meet a chick over
a bottle of champagne. Well, I can check her out and help him
along. Say if some good people need an in with some other good
people for whatever action's up, I'll do my duty. If I get a big tip
for this, what's the fuss?*

The management tacitly accepts the female employees' preceding definitions in the hustling area where there is no rigid code
of conduct. It's a problematic matter of what they hustle, how
much they hustle, under what circumstances they hustle, how they
hustle, and who they hustle. The management is primarily interested in the amount they hustle and club disruptions that might
follow hustling practices. The assistant manager explained to one
of the observers in the owner's office:

*I don't like to talk about this subject to you or anybody else. But
these girls aren't angels. Nobody is. They're trying to make it like
everybody else. They hustle a customer occasionally for a few
bucks, and take a little change from the house. You expect a
barmaid to give her friends a free drink now and then. You expect
all the girls to take a little here and there, but you can't let them
work out a scheme to take you to the cleaners. The main thing is*

you can't let them get in the till [cash register] *or take too much. And you don't want a scene with a customer who thinks he's been had. Nobody wants a girl to play a number on him. If a girl quietly arranges a date with a patron after closing, beautiful. We don't want any guy who has got to one of the girls coming back here and making any claims on her. And we don't want a number played on a good customer either. She's got to know who to hustle as well as how to hustle.*

SUMMARY

Barmaids and cocktail waitresses make up a group of swinging, present oriented, working girls who come to the Rendezvous work situation well prepared physically and mentally for the role performances required of them. Well-trained and experienced in the service end of the restaurant-bar-night club food and beverage business, they stand ready to provide in a deft and efficient manner for the patrons' needs—food, drink, and personal services. Stacked, alluring, vivacious, and suitably costumed to display their natural charms, they are sexy symbols on a risqué scene. Sensual, supple, beguiling, and equipped with a wide repertoire of body language, they serve as "come on's" to male patrons who purchase drinks. Hip, materialistic, pseudo-sophisticated, other directed, and tuned in with nightlife swingers and actors, they are facile manipulators and negotiators in the customer-service relationships. They engage in and foster social encounters that make for club sociability and thereby viability. In front and behavior they contribute to, as well as reflect, the kind of scene that all the actors wish to present to one another. The way they look and the way they behave functionally as well as expressively symbolizes the Rendezvous scene. Without them there could be no Rendezvous setting.

Jazz Musicians

ASCRIBED AND ACHIEVED CHARACTERISTICS

Musicians vary in age (twenty-one to sixty), educational attainment (grade school to college), class origin (lower-class to upper-middle-class), and marital status. Most of them are neither stably married nor anchored to any one woman. Occupational status among them varies from local knowns to nationally knowns. Most are white, under forty, and well integrated into the local jazz community.[1] Occasionally a black American is included, though the leaders are invariably white. Moonlighters at the Rendezvous, they play in one or more combo groups (3 to 6) that service legitimate night clubs, bars, taverns, and restaurants throughout the city that feature jazz dance music. Most have played at one time or another at jazz concerts but prefer to work in night clubs where they perceive their greatest occupational opportunities and feel more comfortable.[2] All are professional musicians with union cards in the American Federation of Musicians, and most are established musicians who have achieved some degree of success in their chosen field.[3] Though claiming no other form of employment, some reported in the interviews that they had worked at part time jobs between gigs. In Nat Hentoff's terms, these day jobs are a part of "paying dues"—the hardest dues of all. None express interest in ever pursuing nonmusical careers.

Rendezvous musicians' formative years up to late adolescence, as they tell it, appear conforming and problem free. None reported adjudication as juvenile delinquents or noted juvenile delinquent gang activity. Though none have served felony time, a few have been "busted" for the possession of soft drugs and have served misdemeanor time. Most use alcohol, marijuana, hashish, and some amphetamines. All have experimented with various kinds of drugs, and many use cocaine from time to time when they can get it. Despite drug use and a knowledge of the drug world, none appear to be addicted to heroin.

All began playing and studying jazz music seriously by their late 'teens, at which time they were resocialized into the jazzman's isolated and nonconforming subculture that is characterized by the hang-loose ethic, disregard for nonmusician groups' norms, freedom

[1] Similar in these and other respects to the musicians researched by Robert A. Stebbins. See Robert A. Stebbins, "The Jazz Community: The Sociology of a Musical Sub-Culture" (unpub. Ph.D. dissertation, University of Minnesota, 1964).

[2] On this point see Nat Hentoff, Chapter 1, "The Changes," in his book, *The Jazz Life* (New York: Dial Press, 1961).

[3] For a definition of the "established musician," see Charles Nanry, "Jazz and All That Sociology," in *American Music: From Storyville to Woodstock*, ed. Charles Nanry (New Brunswick, N.J.: Transaction Books, Rutgers University, 1972), pp. 168–98.

from established restrictions generally applied to other working groups, youthful and progressive occupational seriousness and dedication to jazz (an outsider's esoteric art form), independence gained from earning and spending their own money very early in life, sophistication beyond their years in terms of street and hipster knowledge, and early entree into a promiscuous sexual environment and a permissive drug scene.[4]

As jazz musicians, they sleep while others work, work while others play, and play while others sleep. Mobile, they perform in small working groups in establishments unknown to and unfrequented by many, and they practice an esoteric art so closely bound to performance that nonperformers know little of its meaning. Therefore they are (and have been) segregated from many conventional persons and groups in the larger society. An exclusive group even when not performing, they spend most off-work time practicing, jamming, or cabareting in the company of musicians, aficionados of jazz, people in the musical world, and other nightlife types—all of this regularly interspersed with sexual trysts. One musician commented about women to an observer at the bar:

So many you forget their names. And faces. Sometimes you don't even remember them the second time around unless they were real special. Sometimes I don't even bother to kiss them first. And that's a crime. Of course there are exceptions—and that's what makes it worth the game.

Their adult lives have been marked by the frustrations of many ups and downs including periods of unemployment, flushed success, economic and professional insecurity, health problems linked to overwork, lack of proper food, loss of sleep and dissipation, and, for many, periodic bouts with booze or drugs. For most of them, work mobility and the ever-present number of sexually available women admirers have precluded meaningful and lasting relationships with family members, wives, or girlfriends. Overall they have led hectic and frenzied lives. Most are nervous among strangers off the bandstand to the point of appearing jittery. They manage

[4] For an excellent account of the jazzman's isolation and subcultural experiences, see William Bruce Cameron, "Sociological Notes on the Jam Session," *Social Forces*, vol. 33, no. 2 (Dec. 1954): 177–82. For a later account of the same phenomenon see Robert A. Stebbins, "A Theory of the Jazz Community," *The Sociological Quarterly*, vol. 9, no. 3 (Summer 1968): 318–31.

in some unknown way (that is, to these observers) to camouflage this edginess behind a hip mask. As one musician remarked to one of the observers at the bar, "I'm always nervous in public, especially when I'm not playing. You know, 'on,' but you learn to control it."

IDENTITIES AND PERSPECTIVES

Musicians at the Rendezvous are similar in many respects to Howard Becker's dance musicians of a few years ago.[5] Viewing themselves and other esteemed musicians as people with a special talent that makes them different from and superior to nonmusicians, they do not feel subject to nonmusicians' control either in musical performances or in ordinary social behaviors. To them, squares are the "natural" opposites of musicians. That is, they are ignorant, strange, unpredictable, intolerant, inferior people who are feared because they might bring pressures to bear on the musician's artistry (playing style) and life style (freedom of conduct). They fear the former may be accomplished by not supporting or paying for the kind of music played and the latter by reporting "misconduct" to any number of moral entrepreneurs.

Though differentiated in terms of playing skills, style, technique, repertoire, and musical reputation (among other musicians and nonmusicians), they share the label "jazz musician" and concomitant self-conception and life style. They define themselves as musicians and verbalize aspirations to become creative artists, i.e., a desire to transcend money-making commercial dance or listening music. Picturing themselves as belonging to an exclusive aesthetic cult, they demonstrate little interest in the outside world. Jazz as an art form offers them ample opportunity for creativity and also reflects, generates, and complements an undisciplined, off-beat unrestricted, and exotic way of life. In talking about themselves and their conduct in different social situations, Rendezvous musicians say in many different ways: "We are cool, superior, smooth, nonviolent, tolerant people who engage in an art form extended into a way of life incomprehensible and inaccessible to nonmusicians."

Hedonistic existentialists, jazz musicians consider themselves to be characters highly differentiated from others. They live for kicks

[5] See Howard S. Becker, *Outsiders: Studies in the Sociology of Deviance* (Glencoe, Ill.: Free Press, 1963), pp. 101–19.

and play what they feel spontaneously, never playing the same number exactly the same way twice. Their time is spent in improvising new musical styles and forms, jamming, seeking out exotic experiences with drugs, experiencing a connoisseur's sex life in variety and technique, and pursuing various and unusual experiences. They live in the here-and-now and claim little concern for what they refer to as "the moral hang-ups of yesterday, today, or tomorrow." Verbalizing what is defined as tolerant and liberal views on politics, race, religion, social class, and economics, they really have no basic interests in or knowledge of the issues related to these concepts. Actually, indifference rather than altruism or analysis fathers these so-called "liberal" perspectives. Serious concerns outside the area of jazz simply make no difference. From their perspective, different people have different bags, and whatever they do to get their kicks is fine so long as they don't "bring other people down." The "we" feeling is so strong among them that all is forgiven, tolerated, or overlooked where other jazzmen are concerned, no matter how deviant or criminal they might be. Though jazzmen are suspicious of all people outside the fraternity, they are more favorably inclined toward interaction with nonconformists of whatever type than with straights.[6]

The prominent identity of the Rendezvous musicians is that of jazz musician, an identity that is buttressed by a great deal of self-support and group (other jazz musicians) support. Members of a status group—jazz musicians—their everyday round of activities occurs within core institutional arrangements: jazz jobs, jam sessions, after-hours social life, and clique memberships. The role identity of jazzman is inseparable from the man. Other identities such as brother, father, husband, boyfriend, lover are either subsidiary to or immersed in the prominent identity of musician. All appear to enjoy their work, the proceeds of which have enabled them to live sporadically (materialistically) at or above a middle-class level. Intrinsic and extrinsic gratifications, then, are in evidence. All are committed to a career in jazz and have invested large amounts of time and energy over long periods in this endeavor. Nonetheless, many verbalize anxiety over and over again about their highly competitive occupation. One musician commented to one of the observers at the bar:

[6] It could be that our respondents in their reports to us were attempting to contribute to what Charles Nanry refers to as the "Jazz Myth": Charles Nanry, "Jazz and All That Sociology." However, from our observations, the respondents actually lived the myth.

I am happy with what I'm doing, and I wouldn't do anything else. The eight-to-five shit you can forget—and the square life that goes with it. I've been playing these ivories [piano] for years. I know I'm good, damn good. But that don't cut it. You have to create and get above that commercial junk. Playing on the job is not where it's at. You can be away or asleep and still do that. And what do squares know about jazz anyway? Man, jamming is the real test, and you got to prove yourself over and over again. Like, this makes you wonder if you really got it sometimes. Too many fuckups and you blow your rep. And you can get outdated real fast. Your audiences are fickle, especially the youngsters. They're always looking for something new—some new fad they can define as "in."

Confined to a narrow society, jazz musicians are confused and unknowledgeable about the outside world and their place in it. The larger world is viewed as unstructured, disorganized, problematic, and threatening. As one musician proclaimed to one observer at the bar:

Those squares out there want to control my life—the way I live and what I play. They want musicians to be as clean as toothpaste ads. Ninety per cent of them have no notion of what I'm trying to get over. As long as they hear a melody and the beat of the drum, that's it. With show people and entertainers and a few other people who are into jazz, it's different. But most of the squares should be on the Lawrence Welk Show—I mean as performing clowns.

Jazzmen speak in the hip vernacular and associate with other jazz musicians, promoters and agents of jazz, an entourage of hangers-on, show people, and successful criminals. They verbalize nonconforming or indifferent positions toward conventional social institutions. Openly and blatantly cynical and apolitical, they express little interest in anything besides music and getting their kicks. The following commentary by one musician to another at the bar was overheard by one of the authors:

Squares mess up their heads with booze, religion, politics, and all that morality stuff, but I say, let it be. Life's too much of a drag anyhow to string it out. We juice, too, but we're not hogs. Too much booze is a down trip. If you know what you're doing, the right kind of shit [drugs] for the right time will get you some distance. Say you got a real foxy lady, and you want to do her real good. And you got the time. Go ahead and snort a little coke [cocaine] *and blow a few numbers* [joints] *before you ball her. She'll come on strong, and she'll be back for more. But you see dumb squares don't know nothing. They just pile a broad for a minute or two and roll off and watch T.V. They don't know her clit from her big toe. If they had the right stuff, they wouldn't know how to use it. That's why so many get strung out. We're* [musicians] *different.*

BEHAVIOR ON THE SCENE

Our musician interviewee stated that musicians enjoy working at the Rendezvous for one or more of several reasons that may be delineated as follows:

1. they receive much higher pay than the union scale
2. comparatively speaking, they play to an appreciative, selective, knowledgeable (about jazz), congenial audience
3. they derive recognition by working for an "in" establishment known for providing excellent jazz music
4. they are permitted to play what they want to play by the management
5. they are expected to be musicians rather than showmen
6. they perform under pleasant and facilitating, comfortable conditions that include: a physically adequate bandstand separated from the audience; a good piano; an excellent sound system; good acoustics, lighting, heating and air conditioning; a lively and permissive atmosphere; and availability of good food and drink
7. they have the opportunity to participate in jam sessions
8. they make connections and learn about job openings and what's going on in the musical world
9. they meet and socialize with friends and musical acquaintances
10. they have the opportunity to pick up attractive women.

Various combos ranging from four to six male musicians are selected by the owner and assistant manager to play one-week stands. Generally these groups comprise a moonlighting, mixed membership obtained from several bands that play legitimate shifts from 9:00 P.M. to 2:00 A.M. In the event of absences or openings, musicians known to the group are recommended to the management. The repertoire varies from classical jazz to modern jazz. Swing numbers and an occasional blues piece enable those who so wish to dance. The selection of jazz numbers depends in large part on the musicians who happen to be performing at a particular time and their type of music. Dance numbers are usually included because many patrons at the Rendezvous, especially males, either like to dance or watch other people dance. Moreover, some patrons visualize nightspots in terms of dancing couples. Hard rock is out because it does not reflect the age or the tastes of most patrons, particularly males.

Musicians view the bandstand as their territory and prefer that all other nonmusician actors stay clear. Musical requests are not solicited, and when actors (employees or patrons) enter the musician's domain asking for special numbers, they are expected to speak briefly and exit quickly. Musicians do not like to be told what to play or how to play it. Many times intruders are ignored. The musicians avert eye contact with the intruders and pretend that they neither see nor hear them. Other subterfuges are employed to minimize contacts with and control by the audience. For example, musicians may pretend not to know the requested number or extend an undelivered promise to play it later. Musical requests, however, are less likely to be dismissed should they be accompanied by largesse. One musician reported on his interactions with the audience to one of the observers at the bar:

People here know more about music and dig what we're into better than most. They understand that we're going to do our thing. We don't mind a request if it fits in. If it don't—"we don't know it." A little grease [tip] helps it fit in better. One of us takes all the tips and we cut it up later. The problem is some of the broads want you to play too many free numbers. They think all they got to do is smile and shake their ass at you—that won't get it. If they don't lay some dust, we just smile back and tell them later—and it's much later. We like it better when the cocktail waitress brings in the request from the customer. That way we're sure of a tip because some bread comes with it. And that's the way it usually goes. One good thing, we don't have to worry about a bunch of wild youngsters who don't know anything about jazz.

Communication with the audience is primarily nonverbal and unidimensional by means of a musical medium played for themselves and for other actors who can participate in it vicariously.

While performing, communication among themselves is achieved by gestures, nonliterate utterances, posturing, and through previous arrangements, key, tempo, and free improvisations. When on stage, musicians effect a serious mien and talk and socialize at a minimum. Far from being mannequins, they desire and expect the audience's approval, without which most say they could not go on. As one musician says, "If they can't dig it, I can't play it." Despite the fact that the Rendezvous audience is rather stingy with applause, which usually occurs in a restrained way after featured solos or at the end of sets, musicians say they can tell when the audience is with them. One musician explained to an observer at the bar:

> We don't want a lot of hollering, shouting, amening—and loud clapping and cat calling. We're not performing in Chicago on the south side. We don't play gut bucket and misery music. It's all right but we don't play it. We can tell if they're hip to us by the way they look, move their bodies, and wiggle their feet. The best clue is when they dance. If they're with it, their body movements and rhythm tell the story—even when they're half drunk. A little applause when you get on or off the bandstand between sets helps along. A dancing audience is easier to read than a listening audience. A dance number now and then keeps you going too. You play better if you know the audience is with you. It's not a one-way street in this business.

Between sets, musicians hang together in a cluster at the far northeast end of the bar. Off as well as on stage they constitute the club's most serious and remote membership affecting a self-contained front such as a quiet demeanor, soft speech, and a faceless expression. They drink, eat, smoke, chat, and exchange information among themselves and with barmaids, cocktail waitresses, party girls, and call girls. From time to time they join other musicians and entertainers known to them at the bar. Conversational topics range from unserious matters to shop talk about what's happening in the musical and entertainment world: who's playing what, where, and when; who's cutting what albums; what clubs are opening and closing; the changing policies of record companies and music unions; changes in club ownership, management, and personnel; modification in production formats in night life establishments; innovations and innovators in jazz music; and the fortunes and misfortunes of fellow musicians.

Musicians at the bar make up a self-sustaining group that frequently utilizes avoidance practices to screen out conversations with outsiders. This is accomplished by civil inattention, verbal cutoffs and put downs, and deliberate and pointed preoccupation with the "we" group. Sometimes they exchange gift drinks with acquaintances along the bar and, as individuals, temporarily join some other bar cliques for brief conversations and exchanges about the passing scene. They hustle and are hustled by women at the bar. Working musicians rarely become emotionally or physically involved with activities beyond the bandstand and the bar. Rarely do they sit at tables in the nightspot setting or visit the booths. They seldom dance on the dance floor, nor do they physically engage in the pantomimes, comical skits, and exhibitions occuring thereon. However, they occasionally provide musical background accompaniment for these shenanigans such as strip tease scores. When off duty and attending the club as patrons, which most do, musicians are more carefree and act in much the same way as other night people at the club.

The chief recreational activity of musicians at the club is the jam session, a traditional once-a-week (no set day) happening at the Rendezvous. A self-selected group of elite jazz musicians throughout the city (locals and out-of-towners) congregate at the club after hours to play music they feel like playing—i.e., music according to their personal esthetic standards without regard for outsiders (squares, the buying public, music critics). Jamming musicians customarily invite the house musicians (those employed by the club at the time) to sit in. One musician stated to a researcher at the bar:

The Rendezvous for years has been the place for jam sessions. Jazzmen who want to get together and play for fun and for each other know where to go. The noise doesn't bother anybody. Playing after hours and the legal shit don't bind you. You're off limits to the fuzz, square clowns, and the union. You eat and drink all you want. You don't have to care about an audience that only digs commercial stuff. And you can play long sessions. You are playing with a group of friends who you've known for years. The broads are all over you, what else you need?

Jam sessions serve commercial and vocational as well as recreational needs for actors. Rendezvous patrons are an appreciative audience, and many come to listen to good music. The owner and assistant manager are jazz buffs and have enjoyed good working relationships with musicians in several nightlife settings over a number of years. Additionally, many club employees and patrons (some of whom have direct or indirect vocational tie-ins with jazz) are jazz aficionados. The management encourages jazz musicians in and outside the city to jam at the club where free drink and food are provided for them during jam sessions. Musicians' accounts to us indicate that the jam session provides a learning experience for new arrangements, for the communication of musical ideas and expressions with fellow jazzmen and a nonplaying, sophisticated audience, experimentation with new musical idioms and for ensemble improvisation, and a testing ground for their musical proficiency.

Summary

Jazz musicians are a group of professionals who look upon playing engagements at the Rendezvous much in the same way as they do performances in legitimate clubs. Despite an awareness of the illegal aspects of their work roles at the Rendezvous, work is work wherever it might be—and as such, fits into a jazzman's career. The Rendezvous offers them diverse career opportunities as well as recreational outlets, including an arena for sociability. Many patronize the club when they're not working. On the other hand, as important, necessary employees and as musical personalities in their own right, they draw patrons. Therefore, in a double barrelled fashion musicians help create the scene that all actors want it to be. In ascribed and achieved statuses, role identity and perspectives, and behavior in the setting, they mesh well with the mise en scène. Without these integral actors on the scene there could be no Rendezvous. Moreover, Rendezvous actors are off-beat and probably need a further-out group than themselves (that is, musicians) to identify with, a group that can lead the way and at the same time mark boundaries beyond which most patrons would not wish to go. As one musician remarked to an observer at the bar: "These people in here who think they are players need us to tell them where it's all at, if you know what I mean—music, dress, front, the game. I mean the whole thing."

We did not observe the tension reported to exist elsewhere between an audience that desires to drink and dance and musicians who desire to create good music.[7] We found the Rendezvous audience appreciative of modern jazz. This lack of tension may be attributed to several factors:

1. the Rendezvous audience digs modern jazz more so than do many traditional night club audiences
2. the life style of the musicians and patrons at the Rendezvous is more similar than the life style of musicians and their audiences in public night clubs
3. there is a more relaxed and congenial atmosphere in the after-hours setting at the Rendezvous than that found in public nightspots
4. the unstructured situation and the diversity of settings at the Rendezvous vs. public nightspots permit more freedom of action and self-expression and therefore less tension.

In any event, jazz musicians are well integrated into the Rendezvous setting.

Bouncers

ASCRIBED AND ACHIEVED CHARACTERISTICS

Bouncers, young (twenty-five to thirty-five), unskilled products of the lower-class, are educationally limited (grade school), though their simulated hip language style conveys to some people a pseudo-sophisticated front. Aging jocks, they are athletic in appearance and movement. Most have fought at one time or another as amateur or professional boxers, and all lift weights, work out in the gym, and follow closely the sporting scene. Small-time gamblers, they play poker and wager frequently on the horses, numbers, and sporting events. Their work histories at unskilled jobs are varied and sketchy. Single or divorced, none have established permanent relationships with women. For the most part they have lived a disorderly, purposeless life marked by careless and variegated criminal activity. Currently they live in lower-middle-class residential areas.

[7] Richard A. Peterson, "A Process Model of the Folk, Pop and Fine Art Phases of Jazz," in *American Music: From Storyville to Woodstock,* ed. Charles Nanry, pp. 140–47.

Gang juvenile delinquents grown up, all have long juvenile and adult criminal arrest records for assault and occasional property crimes. Self-defined ex-criminals, they are currently "small time" criminals and have served brief bits of reform school, jail, and prison time. Adult offenses have been of the heavy variety (assault, robbery, burglary) committed at low *modi operandi* levels. Bouncers claim no current criminal pursuits; however, our observations and interview materials indicated that they deal currently in stolen property with fences, thieves, and boosters. They acknowledge acquaintances among former rap partners and brothers in crime but claim to have put down most of their past since coming up in the world. One bouncer interviewee reported:

Since I've been working at the Rendezvous, I've cut out a lot of my past. I'm working with better people now. Sure, I see many of my friends around, but I don't fool around like I used to. I don't want to get busted again.

All drink heavily but disclaim the use of narcotics. None have been arrested on drug charges.

IDENTITIES AND PERSPECTIVES

Though bouncers come from an ever-available labor pool of unsuccessful, semiprofessional property offenders with a record of crimes lacking sophistication, planning, or pattern, they pawn themselves off to some unknowledgeable patrons as highly successful ex-offenders—bragging about Cadillacs, big scores, classy broads, and high living. Far from being money men, most have experienced financial difficulty in paying off personal debts, attorneys' fees, criminal fines, and bail bondsmen. Their unguarded remarks to the researchers at the Rendezvous denote role confusion about who they are and what the real world is all about. Committed to "doing wrong," "getting into trouble," and "fucking up" early in life, these lower-class, unorganized criminals aspire to the successful thief's world but for several reasons have fallen short: lack of finesse and criminal skill, inclination to violence, frequent incarcerations, and the lack of acceptance into successful, professional criminals' working groups. One bouncer noted to an observer at the bar:

I was always ready to go on most any job. I had the heart and the guts, but somehow the guys that made the big scores passed me up. They used to tell me I fucked up too much—was too rough and got into too many fights over women and gambling. They told me I'd been busted too many times—that I would bring heat. They told me to forget the life—and get a see-through lunch pail and go to work. Maybe they're right. Small scores and too many busts was the story of my life. I just couldn't stay outa trouble. One of those things if you know what I mean, but I had a hell of a lot of fun. And man, I busted up a few pretty good [worked a few over].

Bouncers see themselves as ex-losers in flux, who are now regularly employed under the aegis of a strong boss in a safe work situation where opportunity beckons. As another bouncer remarked to an observer while consuming a gift drink at the bar:

This is the best job I ever had. The boss has done a lot for me. Before, I was in trouble all the time. He holds me down and keeps me outa trouble. From him I can take orders. I'm straightened out. You don't have to steal for a living. I mean the kind of stealing I used to do. I woke up. Who wants to go to jail? Of course this is technically a illegit joint, but it pays off. So anybody working here is safe from the frigging pigs. It's really a respectable place. I'm up in the world. All I needed was a chance.

Aware of past failures, bouncers look forward to a more successful underworld life at the Rendezvous. Like the thief and hustler, they view society as corrupt and subscribe to a dog-eat-dog philosophy of life. Unlike the thief or hustler, they do not share a cohesive world view, and they are still "hung up" on some problematic lower-class focal concerns, e.g., machismo, fate, and being tough. Still another bouncer explained to an observer at the bar:

I finally got my shot. Just luck, man. I'm going to try not to mess it up. If I do—there's nothing up the road for me. Here you learn to handle people the easy way. You have to or get fired. You don't get rough, and you can't hurt anybody. You gotta talk real quiet and shoot the patrons a lotta crap. Most of them are kinda soft anyway. What really gets to me is having to be so nice to the women customers. They're so damned uppity. I feel like knocking them on their cheating asses and dicking them right out in front of everybody. But you gotta be polite—pat them on the ass and smile. You just grin and bear it.

Bouncers, then, are aware of their marginal status in the underworld and vaguely aspire to bigger and better things, though they are not clear about any criminal or noncriminal course of action. Would-be hustlers, they express negative positions toward the basic social institutions, particularly the police, correctional personnel, and administrators of criminal justice with whom they have had negative contacts. They acclaim successful criminals of whatever type but vituperatively denigrate the rich and the powerful people out there in Squaresville. A bouncer's overheard remarks to a musician at the bar are illustrative:

Man, I've never had nothing before. These big squares tell you to get a job and go straight. For what, a hundred a week and a bunch of debts. Why work my butt off for those rich bastards and still have nothing? The straight world has got you by the balls. Them that get education and a good start that's different. The only way for a proud dude like me to make it is some kinda hustle.

Behavior on the Scene

Two husky, sharply dressed bouncers constantly wander throughout the club checking the action and mingling with various patrons with whom they are acquainted. A third bouncer wearing a tuxedo is usually stationed at the speakeasy-type entrance door to the club and helps with the screening procedures. Since they are expected to be low-profile rule enforcers (particularly in cases involving arguments and violence) in a fictive, status leveled milieu, they are required to present an affable, equalitarian front. At the same time they must protect the patrons and the house. Along these lines one bouncer outlined the nature of his work to an observer in the waiting room:

We try to treat all the customers alike 'cause we have to call some of them down once in a while. Sometimes you get a pushy big mouth. But the tough guys leave when you have to tell them the sad story. Like, "go home now" I tell them when they really get out of line. Like fighting or pushing around, or turning over a table or throwing a drink at somebody. I tell them to leave now and come back later when they've slept it off. We gotta protect the house. You gotta step between two roosters sometimes. And you gotta pull some bastard off a cocktail waitress once in while. But you gotta use the soft touch. I never had to put one to sleep yet. They're a bunch of pussy cats anyhow.

In the general course of events the bouncers appear to behave in much the same way as the patrons, though they hold drinking to a minimum and avoid open flirtation and body contact with female patrons and employees. In a polite and courteous manner they help settle disruptive disputes and arguments among patrons and between patrons and employees, usually as backups to the assistant manager. Verbal manipulation and the show of force are the rule; actual physical force is utilized only when absolutely necessary, such as, restraining drunks who get too physical with one another or the female employees. Bouncers' work roles include additional duties: They assist with the screening procedures; listen to and report customers' grievances to the management; check on, report, and help stop any open, flagrant criminal activities observed in the club; and check out activities on the first floor above the club. Furthermore, they constantly observe and read unknown patrons for any signs of undercover or untoward actions. When necessary they protect, support, and clean up helpless male drunks and at times make arrangements for cab drivers, themselves, or others to drive heavily intoxicated patrons home. Occasionally they "lay out" (place in reclining position on floor or sofa) worthy drunk patrons in the male employees' lounge.

Bouncers exchange pleasantries with all patron groups and are frequently indistinguishable from male patrons to neophytes in the bar subsetting. In the nightspot subsetting, however, where the scene is more constrained and heterosexual, their social encounters are generally restricted to male and female thieves. Bouncers, like other employees, tend to avoid the booths unless disturbances therein interfere with ongoing activities in or outside this area.

The form and content of bouncers' conversations with most actors represent small talk and reflect bar sociability. When acting as go-betweens for illegal dealers, their verbal encounters become more formal and goal directed. When at the tables with male and female thieves, talk shifts between unserious and serious topics.

Bouncers separate their sex lives from the Rendezvous. Girlfriends and pickups are found elsewhere and kept elsewhere. Moreover, they generally refrain from expressive sexual behavior at the club and neither flirt seriously with female patrons nor come on physically with them. Though enjoying good working relations with female employees, they rarely make it with them sexually. Patrons are strictly off limits to them by management rules, but under certain circumstances these rules may be circumvented. Bouncers agree with the management's sexual rules about female employees and patrons and the rationale behind them. They see no percentage for themselves in hustling females at the club. One bouncer summed up this sensitive situation as it applies to bouncers in the following terms:

It's better to keep your broads away from here. The boss and other people you work with ain't got no respect for a guy who plays stud at work. I don't bring my women here—for what? For some other guy to cut in on me? It costs too much money. Why spoil them? The girls working here are O.K., but they're looking for bigger game. Why bother? Now the she customers. You gotta be careful. Most think they're too good for you. And they're looking for richer dudes. Even the thieves and whores got big ideas. I tell you, if one pushes it on me, I'll find a way to cut her. After it's over, forget it.

Bouncers claim that they avoid criminal pursuits and contraband within as well as outside the Rendezvous and make a big point of "being clean"—and of "not holding." Such references apply to the possession of and transaction in drugs, numbers receipts, counterfeit money, weapons, fake credit cards, false identifications, and stolen property. On the other hand, they admit to introducing and bringing together all sorts of patrons who wish "to do business." Acting as messengers and agents at the club, they receive and pass on information about who desires to negotiate what, when and where, with whom. Moreover, they communicate information to certain patrons about what's up in the nightlife world and underworld, and they receive, hold, exchange, and deliver messages, money, packages, and personal property for some patrons.

Bouncers on a rather dubious base do not define any of the foregoing behaviors as criminal. As one bouncer argued in a table group, including an observer:

Now if I introduce a couple of studs who want to deal, what's wrong with that? I didn't steal nothing. When I pass on messages for people, that don't get me involved. If some guy gives me some money to give to somebody else. What do I know? Maybe it's house rent. Maybe I see to it that a package gets to the right person. It could be a box of candy. Who gives a shit? It's none of my business. I don't hold any stolen property in here and sell it to anybody. You're not a criminal til you get caught and convicted. If I do a few things for customers once in a while, you know, pave the way, what's wrong if they lay a little on me? It's like a tip.

SUMMARY

Bouncers are mediocre, conventional criminals who have finally found or stumbled onto a safe, opportunistic niche in the underworld. In the Rendezvous setting they act as agents for those with unserious as well as serious interests at hand. At times they act as intermediaries in criminal activities, but they function primarily as necessary security personnel for all actors. In short, they deal with problematic behavior and support and protect the patrons, the employees, and the ongoing activities within the club. They also do the club's necessary dirty work. Adequately equipped to play their Rendezvous roles, they are more adept in dealing with certain types of patrons than with others. Although low-status actors in the eyes of most patrons and employees, they mesh fairly well into the overall scene. As is the case with other security personnel (e.g., the police) elsewhere, they are considered by some to be necessary evils. Still others (e.g., thieves) accept them wholeheartedly. Through and by a combination of roles, bouncers help make the Rendezvous setting what it is and aid in its maintenance, preservation, and unity.

Lookout Men

ASCRIBED AND ACHIEVED CHARACTERISTICS

Lookout men are middle-aged, unskilled, semiliterate members of the urban lower-class who have eked out an existence in the slums. Though at one time married, they prefer common law sexual relationships. They grew up in multi-problem families without supervision or direction and have spent most of their lives on the streets stealing, drinking, panhandling, wenching, selling booze, running numbers and messages for bookies, and bumbling and fumbling around with all sorts of petty criminal activity. Disorganized criminals and losers, they have never settled down in any pattern of crime or legitimate activity.

Similar in social background to bouncers, they do not possess the bouncers' "stand up" qualities of toughness, loyalty, and commitment to the criminal world. Delinquent and adult arrest histories are lengthy and marked by frequent incarcerations for unspecialized, unsophisticated, planless offenses (theft, gambling, intoxication, assault). Frequent incarcerations have been interspersed with brief legitimate, unskilled work stints—and then back to crime and subsequent incarceration. In brief, the major life themes of lookout men, petty, habitual offenders, have been getting into trouble, self-defeatism, and a readiness or availability for almost any low level criminal pursuit. As our lookout interviewee reported in an interview at his home:

Man, getting into trouble is the story of my life. I never set up a good score. I always was around listening to that big talk and trying to make it. I've just been unlucky. Too many busts for small change. Guess I just took too many chances. I never was connected. I worked legit, too, but never could hack that grind. Things are looking up though. Otherwise you'd be talking to me in jail.

IDENTITIES AND PERSPECTIVES

Lookout men appear to be confused in self-identity and world view. Slipping and sliding through life, they have gravitated from one legal or illegal pursuit to another with little hope or interest of settling down in any one type of job. Relationships with peers, women, children, straights, and criminals have been brief, tenuous, and for the most part unrewarding. Gratifications from childhood have been of the action-seeking, short-lived, physical variety, and they tend to see themselves as action oriented, put-upon, powerless members of an under class. To lookout men both the outside world and their own confused world teem with unpredictable dangers. Outsiders are viewed as powerful, would-be controllers of their episodic lives and pleasures—self-righteous kill-joys. These losers view their confused world as a hostile jungle. Social participation in conventional or even nonconventional institutions is practically nonexistent.

Lookout men are pleased to find regular work at the Rendezvous and claim that they are going straight as long as they hold their current jobs. The lookout man interviewed stipulated:

I got it made for a change. I ain't rich but I get steady bread. The boss is good to me. He's solid. This way I don't have to hustle, and fool around with a bunch of bums. The cops don't hassle me any more, I can't believe that. Must be a dream. The pigs can go shit on somebody else.

BEHAVIOR ON THE SCENE

Two regular lookout men patrol on foot the outside premises of the club on both sides of the street of the Rendezvous site. They observe outside pedestrian and vehicular traffic throughout the club's operating hours. Should they suspect the presence of undercover agents, police activity, or heist men (robbers who might plan to hold up customers outside the club or who might plan to rob the club itself), they report these misgivings by means of a pay station telephone to the management inside the club. They also call in reports on noisy patrons or groups of patrons who approach the club in a rowdy fashion. Patrons are expected to come upon the scene in a quiet, orderly manner; otherwise, they might not be permitted entrance. Lookout men also have access to two alarm bells at the front and rear entrances of the club proper which ring in the owner-manager's office and behind the bar. In addition to lookout duties they perform the club's janitorial services after operating hours. Lookout men have no contacts with patrons or with club employees with the exception of the owner-manager and assistant manager. They are selected by the management on the basis of loyalty, sobriety, and physical fitness.

SUMMARY

Lookout men, ex-habitual petty offenders, are marginal but necessary actors for the protection and maintenance of the Rendezvous setting. A paternalistic-subordinate relationship with the management buttressed by financial reward ensures their loyalty to the club. Actually they have very little to report, but they do function as boundary insurance agents as well as janitorial personnel.

Other Employees

Cook

A middle-aged male cook has been regularly employed at the Rendezvous for 10 years. A stably married, conventional black American without a criminal record, he worked several years as a salad boy and cook prior to his present employment. He sees himself as a legitimate cook and disassociates himself from what he calls "the illegal carryings-on at the club." As he reported in the interview:

Man, a cook is a cook. I do the same thing as any cook would be doing anywhere. I don't own any part of the club. I don't bother myself about what goes on downstairs. I got a regular job, and mind my own business. That's the way it is. I've been a cook for a long time. And I've done a good job too.

He cooks steak sandwiches and baked potatoes and prepares salads in the first-story kitchen. Contacts are made only with the management, a kitchen helper and dishwasher, the cocktail waitresses, and the women patron's lounge maid. The kitchen helper and dishwasher (selected by him with the approval of the management from a large pool of unskilled workers) helps prepare food orders and passes them on to cocktail waitresses through a locked kitchen dutch door directly across the hall from the service elevator. This helper also receives dirty dishes from the cocktail waitresses, who have access to the kitchen by a service elevator that operates between the basement and the first floor. Occasionally this helper is called downstairs to clean up food and drink spillovers in the various subsettings.

Hatcheck Girl

Cocktail waitresses divvy up the hatcheck chores throughout each shift, taking one-hour turns. They receive and hang up or lay away (on shelves or in drawers) patrons' wearing apparel and personal belongings. No house charge for this service is incurred; however, the girls expect (and usually receive) a minimum tip of two dollars per checked item. The girls put on a sexy front by way of seductive chitchat, musky perfumes, come-on smiles, and sexy and revealing postures: bending over to expose breasts and derrieres, sensual undulations, crotch shots, provocative clothing and foundation adjustments—all in order to conduce bigger tips. Belongings are returned at departure by check stubs.

WOMEN PATRONS' LOUNGE ATTENDANT

One female ladies-room attendant, a middle-aged, stably married, conventional black American, has worked at the Rendezvous for the past five years. A "straight" without a criminal or juvenile delinquent record, she has had past legitimate employment as a housemaid and as a practical nurse. She uses neither drugs nor alcohol. Like the cook, she dissociates what she terms her legitimate work tasks at the club from the illegal aspects of the Rendezvous. She stated in her interview:

Mister, I'm only the maid here. I been a maid and a nurse for a long time. I've always had good jobs where people trust me and treat me right. What goes on downstairs is none of my business. I take care of my duties up here. I got a good, steady, paying job. What I do is strictly legal from my way of thinking. What's wrong with jumping around or working after hours? People can't work or play when they want to all the time.

Stationed in the women patrons' lounge on the first floor across the hall from the men patrons' lounge, she does not interact with male patrons or employees with the exception of the management, cook, and kitchen helper (from whom she receives food and with whom she chats occasionally). Patrons' access to bathroom facilities is by the patrons' elevator only. Acting in the capacity of a handmaid, she dispenses toiletries, linens, and tissues, mends and cleans wearing apparel, nurses occasional female drunks and distraught women patrons, and cleans and tidies up the vanity and toilet fixtures. She effects a pleasing, courteous, helpful front, chitchats and engages in small talk with patrons disposed to talk, acts as a sounding board for those inclined to sound off, and aids patrons in their personal grooming tasks.

The attendant views the Rendezvous as a pleasant unserious setting for the patrons. For her it is a serious work situation. She explained:

The Rendezvous is a place where people come to have a good time. I know about nothing else. All I know is the young ladies who I see up here are a bunch of nice people. Most of the time they be laughing and talking. And carrying on a bunch of nonsense. They flit around and talk about how they look and clothes. They laugh about their boyfriends. Now and then I get a drunk girl—or a girl on a crying spell. They be all right though mostly. They just want to frolic about and have some fun. I was young once. I understand. I try to help them along. It's my job. You got to remember they tip me good. And you know that helps. The Rendezvous is a good place to work.

Club Secretary

A young (twenty-five) female aide to a businessman regularly employed as a secretary in a real estate office comes in two afternoons a week. She types, audits receipts and expenditures, and helps with inventory, filing, bookkeeping and payroll procedures. She has work contacts only with the management. Occasionally she is a patron at the club.

Chapter 10

SUMMARY AND CONCLUSION

Introduction

ACCORDING TO SIMMEL, metropolitan man faces pressures that promote his continual attempts to break out of interactional routines.[1] Urbanites in any event regularly schedule time-out periods (periods that are not consequentially connected with work or family pursuits and biographies) for the pursuit of unserious activity in all sorts of informal settings, such as trips to the beach and the bar, where the predictable features of everyday life do not apply. In such playful settings one can drop daily routine cares, relax, engage in new experiences with new objects, try out new selves, and take part in a variety of sociability play forms.[2] The Rendezvous and other after-hours clubs offer one such time-out, unserious setting for some urban men and women in the rounds of everyday life. Yet play acting in the club as in other time-out settings inevitably reflects and symbolizes in part the actor's more serious life situations. In this case study of the Rendezvous, we addressed a series of sociological questions utilizing a behavior setting-symbolic interactionism framework: What is an after-hours club? (In this case, the Rendezvous.) How is such a place possible?

[1] Georg Simmel, *The Sociology of Georg Simmel*, ed. and trans. Kurt H. Wolff (New York: Free Press, 1965), pp. 409–24.

[2] Norman K. Denzin, "Self and Society," in Jack D. Douglas, *Introduction to Sociology: Situations and Structures* (New York: Free Press, 1973), pp. 224–25.

What goes on in such a setting? What are the consequences of these goings-on? Who goes there? When? To do what with whom? Where in the setting?

What Is the Rendezvous?

The Rendezvous was found to be a popular, time-out, unserious, heterosexual behavior setting for odd-time revelers of varying degrees of respectability—*a regular place for irregular people* to relax, socialize, and play in while most regular people are asleep. A deviant setting where the straight and criminal worlds intersect, it supports not only deviant behavior but provides a place for deviants to act "normally" and for straights to act "deviantly." More specifically, this club is an illegal (unlicensed), plush, semisecret, exclusive drinking establishment where alcoholic beverages are sold and dispensed by the drink during illegal closing hours. Like some public bars and nightspots, it also furnishes other goods and services including food, cigars and cigarettes, and live music, along with the necessary physical accommodations and service personnel. It's the "in" place to go in the city if you are somebody in the nightlife world.

How Is Such a Place Possible?

The Rendezvous is made possible by a combination of factors. The city it services affords a substantial population base including a sizable number of people employed at odd-time hours: nightlife entertainers and musicians; bar, restaurant, theater, and night club employees; criminals; call girls; and the like. Some of these are swingers who prefer to spend their odd-time, recreational hours in a convenient, plush, exclusive, sexy, exciting, safe bar-nightspot setting. The Rendezvous is the only club in the city open after hours that meets these needs and expectations. In addition to being a hideaway or haven away from the public eye, the Rendezvous offers the best drinks, jazz music, food, and supporting services that are available in the city after hours. Moreover, these goods and services are available within a "respectable," dynamic, and sexually exciting space-time configuration that provides several subsettings for a variety of actors with varying interests at hand. For both unserious and serious reasons, several types of patrons have vested interests in ensuring the club's survival.

The city also supports a large pool of trained workers in the nightlife industry, many of whom are eager to earn extra money by moonlighting at the club. Finally, the club's low visibility, ready accessibility, security features, internal front and layout, and special arrangements with the police make the Rendezvous possible.

What Goes on in Such a Setting?

Actors at the Rendezvous turn night into day and create their own social world where they engage in two major concurring standing behavior patterns that are sometimes intertwined. The primary overt pattern is heterosexual sociability and play. These activities are characterized by freedom, equality, novelty, stepping out of reality, space-time circumscriptions, order, permanency, and secrecy, which vary in degree from subsetting to subsetting. (See Chapter 2, pp. 48–49.) For example, social encounters are more secret in the two booth subsettings than at the bar or tables. The secondary covert pattern is dealing in illegal goods and services. Subsumed within this pattern is any serious discussion of criminal activities. When actors engage in the covert pattern, their behavior must be masked within a sociability and play context or physically hidden from other actors. For example, a group of male patrons may be engaging in round drinking at the bar while surreptitiously negotiating criminal deals. The coexistence of these two patterns is made possible by the physical milieu, the type of actors on the scene, and the club rhetoric. For example, a female thief and a male patron may go from the bar to a booth (ostensibly a part of the pickup routine) and negotiate the sale or exchange of stolen property.

Because the major overt behavior pattern is sociability and play, Rendezvous actors have a great deal of freedom in initiating and terminating social encounters. They also enjoy wide latitudes of behavior such as sex play, intoxication, clowning activities, loud talking, staggering, singing, and the like. Though behavior at the Rendezvous is more spontaneous and problematic than is behavior in more serious settings (e.g., work settings), certain ground rules of an enabling and restricting kind obtain. For example, in the bar subsetting, anyone may start a social encounter with anyone else at any time. On the other hand, the visible physical exchange of stolen property or the direct soliciting for prostitution is prohibited. Latitudes of behavior vary by subsetting; a couple may engage in sexual intercouse in the open booths but not in the nightspot setting. Behavior is also more constrained in some settings than others. For example, in the nightspot setting the physical milieu and the actors' expectations compel one to sit at a table where interaction is usually confined to one's table group. Patrons move from subsetting to subsetting depending on their interests at hand and occasionally modify one of the subsettings to suit their interests. For example, in the case of a crowded bar, a group of male actors may obtain box dice from the bar and roll for drinks at a table. In general, we found that the patterns of interaction in the club reflect behavioral rituals similar to those utilized by middle-class "straights."

The owner-manager's private party seems to be a unique feature of the Rendezvous. We did not encounter similar parties in either our visits to a number of other after-hours clubs or in the bar literature. These exclusive, private, secret, sex parties where middle-aged men pass around young women for heterosexual sex play are restricted to an esoteric membership. Male membership includes only those actors enjoying the highest club status: the owner-manager, businessmen, and a few prestigious night people. Female membership is made up of very attractive, trustworthy party girls, call girls, and night people. Though there is variation among individuals invited to these parties, the guest list is always restricted to the same actor types. Based on reports, certain special patrons leave the main theater of action (the club proper) for sociability and play and go to the owner-manager's office (a more seclusive behavior setting) *to engage in sex as play*.[3] When taking this extra step from reality these actors are approaching what Simmel terms "playing around with empty forms"—i.e., their behavior

[3] Nelson N. Foote, "Sex as Play," *Social Problems*, vol. 1, no. 4 (April 1954), pp. 159–63.

in the owner's office is of less future consequence in the real world than are their playtime activities in the club proper.[4]

What Are the Consequences of These Goings-on?

In great part the behavior that takes place in the Rendezvous, a time-out setting, matters only for the present—and only for the actors in the Rendezvous. That is what is said and done in the here-and-now is of no consequence in the there-and-then. Said another way, the sociability and play activities that go on in the club do not count in the real world beyond the Rendezvous scene. For example, whomever a patron picks up at the Rendezvous and whatever sexual activities occur between the two makes no difference to either party at some other place at some other time. Many married men take their girlfriends to the club without fear of the outside world finding out about it. Patrons talk and joke with a number of people at the club with whom they never associate outside the club. They find them there and they leave them there. Furthermore, in this setting actors take part in all sorts of permissible activities that are never discussed outside the club. A woman may lift her skirt to show off her sexy panties, undress in a mock strip act on the dance floor, dance on the bar or on a table; or a man may play with his girlfriend's breasts, hold her head in his lap, place his head in her lap, or have sexual intercourse with her in the booths.

On the other hand, some covert behaviors count within as well as beyond the club. Some things that are said and done in the setting have serious consequences in the actors' workaday life. For example, some actors deal in illegal goods and services. Some criminals discuss past, present, and future capers and keep one another abreast of what's going on in the underworld. Call girls and party girls meet potential customers in the Rendezvous and sometimes trick from the setting. Additionally, night people keep attuned to what's happening in the nightlife world by frequenting the Rendezvous. Some hear about and negotiate nightlife industry deals and jobs at the club. These serious activity patterns typically occur within the context of sociability and play.

[4] Simmel, *Sociology*, pp. 55–57.

Who Goes There? When? To Do What with Whom? Where in the Setting?

PATRONS

The Rendezvous attracts a wide assortment of early morning players because it is a special kind of space-time configuration in terms of operating hours, rhetoric, divergent subsettings, type of behavior expected to take place, and goods and services provided. Patron types range from hip squares to organized criminals who differ in social background characteristics, role identities, and world views. All types of patrons however engage in similar free-time activity in the club. Though they differ somewhat in their reasons for attending, most go to socialize and play in a semisecret setting beyond the closing time of legal establishments. There is some variation in club activities as well as in types of patrons present overtime. Patrons' choice of subsetting and activities therein depend upon their club status and interest at hand. A status hierarchy determines in large part who engages in what behavior with whom.

Some actors who are anchored in the straight world, such as hip squares, go to the Rendezvous to deviate occasionally in a deviant but safe place. They gawk at what they consider to be a wild scene, and frolic with a number of career deviants. Many arrange to purchase illegal goods and services there. However, the club and its long-term activities are not a part of the rest of their way of life. Other actors, for example night people and party girls, attend regularly for the purpose of socializing among themselves without fear of having to interact with squares and rule makers— and being publicly processed as deviants. Segmental deviants, their deviant behavior makes up an important part of their lives (long-run situational involvements of great significance to them at the time), but deviance does not constitute a basic identity, rather a style of deviance. Though night people and party girls interact occasionally on an intimate level with hustlers, organized criminals, call girls and thieves; and, though some participate in criminal activity from time to time, most are not committed to career oriented underworld pursuits. In short, they alternate between two life styles.

The conventional, regular workaday world takes a definite moral exception to the character (or worthiness) of the criminal patron types who frequent the Rendezvous. Therefore, they do not have access to respectable, middle-class sociability and play settings in the conventional world. Actors among these criminal types appropriate the club setting for behaving "normally." The Rendezvous to them is a microcosmic reflection of the "straight world" —a play world in which to remark upon their workaday world (criminal) accomplishments. The Rendezvous affords these life organization deviants a "respectable" place to show off their monetary and occupational success—a place to display their success symbols such as verbal repertoire, flashy jewelry, expensive clothing, rolls of money, and attractive, well-dressed sex partners. By heavy tipping, the liberal purchasing of gift drinks, and gift giving, they call attention to the sound and importance of their money.

The Rendezvous furnishes the businessmen, organized criminals, more so than other patron types, a place to validate a status denied them by the respectable social world. The club supplies these high ranking, wealthy, systematic deviants with an audience that pays homage to their money and success. This membership that "plays society" has a truncated view of middle-class respectability evidenced by the setting it helps create at the Rendezvous—to it a high-class place. Of all patron types, businessmen enjoy the highest status.

In focusing on the matrix of patron types in the Rendezvous, we found that each contributed to the setting in different but complementary ways by what they looked like, what they symbolized, and what they said and did. We discovered a high degree of synomorphy between the actors' behavior and physical milieu. All types either meshed with or were well articulated to the behavior setting. Night people, a gregarious, playful group more so than any other patron type, generate, maintain, and reflect the Rendezvous milieu.

EMPLOYEES

The Rendezvous is a serious work setting for all employees; they work hard to make it a gay, playtime setting for the patrons. Most say they enjoy their work. Several types of Rendezvous employees share long-time career interests in the setting: owner-manager, assistant manager, bouncers, cook, and ladies' room attendant. Kitchen helpers and lookout men are the most transient workers. Barmaids, cocktail waitresses, and musicians, intermittent moonlighters, are replaced from time to time by younger counterparts. Bouncers, security personnel, protect the setting and do the dirty work, such as chaperoning drunks and helping sellers and buyers negotiate illegal deals.[5] The owner-manager and the assistant manager produce, direct, and orchestrate the scene, and therefore the setting mirrors their definition of a plush, respectable setting. This is made possible by the cooperation of the patrons and employees who share a similar definition of the situation.

In addition to their functional duties, the musicians, barmaids, and cocktail waitresses in appearance, dress, and behavior aid in generating and sustaining the setting's jazzy, exciting, and sexy atmosphere (rhetoric). Barmaids and cocktail waitresses socialize with and serve as "come on's" to male patrons who purchase drinks. As intermediaries they facilitate the pickup routine and also engage in and foster social encounters that make for club sociability. Employees as well as patrons utilize the Rendezvous as a clearing house for information about what is going on in the city's nightlife world. In personal characteristics, role identities, and world views all employees seem well suited for their work roles at the Rendezvous—to serve the tribe at play.

Contrasts between the Rendezvous and Public Drinking Establishments

Throughout this work we have pointed out similarities and differences between the Rendezvous and kindred settings. Here we recapitulate some of the more significant differences between these two sociability and playtime behavior settings. Past bar studies have attempted to classify public drinking places on the basis of one or more of the following variables: ecological location, characteristics of patrons, space-time properties, goods and services, use, and behavior patterns. This case study represents the first attempt to analyze one particular kind of drinking place along all of these

---

[5] For a discussion of dirty workers as agents for "good people" see Everett C. Hughes, *The Sociological Eye, Selected Papers* (Chicago: Aldine-Atherton, 1971), pp. 87–98.

variables. Additionally we include the setting's history, rhetoric, the synomorphy between the physical milieu and the standing behavior patterns, and a patron typology. Furthermore, within our theoretical frame of reference we reconstruct the setting insofar as possible from the viewpoints of the actors.

Unlike many public bars the Rendezvous is a multiple use setting housing several subsettings. Each subsetting provides the actors with a variety of goods and services and affords them several activity patterns over time. At any given time the club is used by one or more patron types for one or more purposes as a: convenience bar, nightspot setting, marketplace bar, home territory bar. The Rendezvous, therefore, is a much more complicated setting to analyze than are most public bars.

Differing from public bars and nightspots, the Rendezvous is an illegal, semisecret, exclusive setting that attracts certain discriminating types of patrons with similar recreational interests. This closure enables actors to step further out of reality here than in public bars. The exclusiveness of the Rendezvous reinforced by screening procedures makes for a more open and equalitarian situation among actors than does the public bar setting. This is not to say that status leveling is complete; however, playing the equality game is easier than in public drinking establishments. Furthermore, women at the Rendezvous are treated on a more equalitarian basis with men than they are in most public drinking places. Latitudes of behavior are wider in this secluded sociability setting than in public bars—the exceptions being violence and open dealing in illegal goods and services. In this permissive, multiple action, problematic setting novel behavior is expected, and found more often than in legal bars. The expectancy that something unusal or out of the ordinary will happen is ever present. Examples here are the spontaneous acts that take place on the dance floor and the jam sessions. Unlike many public bar patrons most Rendezvous patrons are regular, permanent customers. In contrasting the nature of sociability and play in the Rendezvous with that found in public bars, we noted variations in secrecy, space-time circumscriptions, stepping out of reality, freedom, equality, order, novelty, and permanency. Finally, our studies in a number of legal and illegal bar and clubs throughout the United States suggest that the behavior patterns found in after-hours clubs more closely resemble those found in singles bars than those obtaining in more traditional bar settings.

Suggestions for Further Research

The paramount reason for additional research in after-hours settings is that such places offer the investigator an opportunity to study the behavior of a variety of marginal, deviant, and criminal types in natural settings where there is an intersection and confluence of the straight and deviant worlds. The findings in this case study and our knowledge about other after-hours clubs indicate that many features of the Rendezvous obtain in all after-hours clubs. Therefore we suggest comparative studies on a number of after-hours clubs throughout the United States. Results of such studies could enhance our knowledge about such places in general, specify divergencies from club to club, aid in the development of an after-hours club typology, and provide more data on the conjunction of the straight and deviant worlds.

In retrospect, we suggest that nonmember researchers collaborate with member participant observers in future studies of after-hours clubs and related unserious settings, because native researchers, whatever their stance, may overlook taken-for-granted features that need, but sometimes escape, description and analysis. As an additional triangulation source to facilitate a more complete understanding of heterosexual settings such as the after-hours club, we suggest that female researchers would prove invaluable in front stage regions where women interact with men as well as with each other. Women posing as patrons or acting as employees would also have easier access to certain backstage regions and social encounters than men. Women's interests and world views often vary somewhat from those of men. Therefore a combination of male and female researchers would provide multiple perspectives on after-hours clubs and behaviors taking place therein.

BIBLIOGRAPHY

ADAMS, RICHARD, and JACK J. PREISS, eds. *Human Organization Research*. Homewood, Ill.: Richard Irwin, Inc., 1960.

BALL, DONALD W. "An Abortion Clinic Ethnography." *Social Problems* 14, (1967): 293–301.

———. "The Problematics of Respectability." In Jack D. Douglas, ed., *Deviance and Respectability: The Social Construction of Moral Meanings*. New York: Basic Books, Inc., 1970.

———. "Self and Identity in the Context of Deviance: The Case of Criminal Abortion." In Robert A. Scott and Jack D. Douglas, eds. *Theoretical Perspectives on Deviance*. New York: Basic Books, Inc., 1972.

———. *Microecology: Social Situations and Intimate Space*. New York: The Bobbs-Merrill Company, Inc., 1973.

BARKER, ROGER G. *Ecological Psychology: Concepts and Methods in Studying the Environment of Human Behavior*. Stanford, Cal.: Stanford University Press, 1968.

BATESON, GREGORY. "A Theory of Play and Fantasy." *Psychiatric Research Reports* 2. American Psychiatric Association, 1955.

———, and GEORGE HERBERT MEAD. *Balinese Character*. New York: New York Academy of Sciences, 1942.

BECKER, HOWARD S. *Outsiders: Studies in the Sociology of Deviance*. Glencoe, Ill.: The Free Press, 1963.

———, and BLANCHE GREER. "Participant Observation and Interviewing: A Comparison." *Human Organization* 16 (1957): 28–32.

———. "Participant Observation: The Analysis of Quantitative Field Data." In Richard Adams and Jack J. Preiss, eds., *Human Organization Research*. Homewood, Ill.: Richard Irwin, Inc., 1960.

BENCHLEY, PETER. "Five In Spots for the Midnight Chic." *The New York Times Magazine* (November 8, 1970), pp. 25–26, 117–22.

BERDIE, R. F. B. "Playing the Dozens." *Journal of Abnormal and Social Psychology* 42 (1947): 120–21.

BLUMBERG, ABRAHAM S., ed. *Current Perspectives on Criminal Behavior*. New York: Alfred A. Knopf, 1974.

BLUMER, HERBERT. *Symbolic Interactionism: Perspective and Method*. Englewood Cliffs, N.J.: Prentice-Hall, Inc., 1969.

BRUYN, SEVERYN T. *The Human Perspective in Sociology: The Methodology of Participant Observation*. Englewood Cliffs, N.J.: Prentice-Hall, Inc., 1966.

BRYAN, JAMES H. "Occupational Ideologies and Individual Attitudes of Call Girls." In Earl Rubington and Martin S. Weinburg, eds., *Deviance, The Interactionist Perspective*. New York: The Macmillan Company, 1968.

BUCKNER, H. TAYLOR. *Deviance, Reality, and Change*. New York: Random House, 1971.

CAMERON, WILLIAM BRUCE. "Sociological Notes on the Jam Session." *Social Forces* 33 (1954): 177–82.

CAVAN, SHERRI. *Liquor License: An Ethnography of Bar Behavior*. Chicago: Aldine Publishing Company, 1966.

CLARK, WALTER. "Demographic Characteristics of Tavern Patrons in San Francisco." *Quarterly Journal of Studies on Alcohol* 27 (1966): 316–27.

CLINARD, MARSHALL B. "The Public Drinking House and Society." In David J. Pittman and Charles R. Snyder, eds., *Society, Culture and Drinking Patterns*. New York: John Wiley and Sons, Inc., 1962.

——— and RICHARD QUINNEY. *Criminal Behavior Systems*, 2nd ed. New York: Holt, Rinehart and Winston, Inc., 1973.

COOK, FRED J. *The Secret Rulers: Criminal Syndicates and How They Control the U. S. Underworld*. New York: Duell, Sloan and Pearce, 1966.

COWIE, JAMES B., and JULIAN B. ROEBUCK. *An Ethnography of a Chiropractic Clinic: Definitions of a Deviant Situation*. New York: The Free Press, 1975.

CRAIK, K. H. "Environmental Psychology." In Craik *et al.*, eds., *New Directions in Psychology*, vol. 4. New York: Holt, Rinehart and Winston, 1970.

CRESSEY, DONALD, and DAVID H. WARD, eds. *Delinquency, Crime, and Social Process*. New York: Harper and Row, Publishers, 1969.

DENZIN, NORMAN K. *The Research Act: A Theoretical Introduction to Sociological Methods*. Chicago: Aldine Publishing Company, 1970.

————. "The Logic of Naturalistic Inquiry." *Social Forces* 50 (1971): 166–82.

————. "Self and Society." In Jack D. Douglas, ed., *Introduction to Sociology: Situations and Structures.* New York: The Free Press, 1973.

Dollard, John. "The Dozens: Dialect of Insult." *American Imago* 1 (1939): 3–25.

Douglas, Jack D., ed. *Observations of Deviance.* New York: Random House, Inc., 1970.

————, ed. *Deviance and Respectability: The Social Construction of Moral Meaning.* New York: Basic Books, Inc., 1970.

————. *American Social Order: Social Rules in a Pluralistic Society.* New York: The Free Press, 1971.

————, ed. *Research on Deviance.* New York: Random House, 1972.

————. *Introduction to Sociology: Situations and Structures.* New York: The Free Press, 1973.

Fast, Julius. *Body Language.* New York: Pocket Books, 1970.

Filstead, William J., ed. *Qualitative Methodology: Firsthand Involvement with the Social World.* Chicago: Markham Publishing Company, 1970.

Finestone, Harold. "Cats, Kicks and Color." *Social Problems* 5 (1957): 3–13.

Firey, Walter. "Symbols and Sentiments as Ecological Variables." *American Sociological Review* 10 (1954): 140–48.

Foote, Nelson N. "Sex as Play." *Social Problems* 1 (1954): 159–63.

Garfinkel, Harold. *Studies in Ethnomethodology.* Englewood Cliffs, N.J.: Prentice-Hall, Inc., 1967.

Goffman, Erving. *The Presentation of Self in Everyday Life.* Garden City, New York: Doubleday Anchor, 1959.

————. *Encounters: Two Studies in the Sociology of Interaction.* New York: The Bobbs-Merrill Company, Inc., 1961.

————. *Behavior in Public Places.* New York: The Free Press, 1963.

————. *Relations in Public: Microstudies of the Public Order.* New York: Basic Books, Inc., 1971.

Gordon, Raymond L. *Interviewing: Strategy, Techniques and Tactics.* Homewood, Ill.: The Dorsey Press, 1969.

Gottlieb, David. "The Neighborhood Tavern and the Cocktail Lounge: A Study of Class Differences." *American Journal of Sociology* 62 (1957): 559–62.

Graves, Robert. *The Future of Swearing.* London: Kegan Paul, 1936.

GREENWALD, HAROLD. *The Call Girl: A Social and Psychoanalytic Study.* New York: Ballantine Books, Inc., 1958.

GUMP, PAUL V. "The Behavior Setting: A Promising Unit for Environmental Designers." In Rudolf H. Moos and Paul M. Insel, eds., *Issues in Social Ecology: Human Milieus.* Palo Alto, Cal.: National Press Books, 1974.

HASSLER, ALFRED. *Diary of a Self-Made Convict.* Chicago: Regnery, 1954.

HENSLIN, JAMES M. "Studying Deviance in Four Settings: Research Experiences with Cabbies, Suicides, Drug Users, and Abortioners." In Jack D. Douglas, ed., *Research on Deviance.* New York: Random House, 1972.

————. "Sociology of Everyday Life." In Jack D. Douglas, ed., *Introduction to Sociology: Situations and Structures.* New York: The Free Press, 1973.

HENTOFF, NAT. *The Jazz Life.* New York: The Dial Press, 1961.

HUGHES, EVERETT C., ed. *The Sociological Eye: Selected Papers.* Chicago: Aldine-Atherton, Inc., 1971.

HUIZINGA, JOHAN. *Homo Ludens: A Study of the Play-Element in Culture.* Boston: Beacon Press, 1950.

HUMPHREYS, LAUD. *Tearoom Trade: Impersonal Sex in Public Places.* Chicago: Aldine Publishing Company, 1970.

IRWIN, JOHN. *The Felon.* Englewood Cliffs, N.J.: Prentice-Hall, Inc., 1970.

KLOCKARS, CARL B. *The Professional Fence.* New York: The Free Press, 1974.

KOBLER, JOHN. *Capone: The Life and World of Al Capone.* New York: G. P. Putnam's, 1971.

KOCHMAN, THOMAS. " 'Rapping' in the Black Ghetto." *Trans-action* (February, 1969), pp. 26–34.

KRAUSE, ELLIOT A. *The Sociology of Occupations.* Boston: Little, Brown and Company, 1974.

LARGEY, GALE PETER, and DAVID RODNEY WATSON. "Sociology of Odors." *American Journal of Sociology* 77 (1972): 1021–34.

LEFTON, MARK, JAMES K. SKIPPER, JR., and CHARLES H. McCAGHY, eds. *Approaches to Deviance: Theories, Concepts, and Research Findings.* New York: Appleton-Century- Crofts, 1968.

LEMERT, EDWIN M. *Human Deviance, Social Problems, and Social Control,* rev. ed. Englewood Cliffs, N.J.: Prentice-Hall, Inc., 1972.

LIEBOW, ELLIOT. *Tally's Corner.* Boston: Little, Brown and Company, 1967.

LOFLAND, JOHN, and LYN H. LOFLAND. *Deviance and Identity*. Englewood Cliffs, N.J.: Prentice-Hall, Inc., 1969.

LYMAN, STANFORD M., and MARVIN B. SCOTT. *A Sociology of the Absurd*. New York: Appleton-Century-Crofts, 1970.

LYND, ROBERT S., and HELEN M. LYND. *Middletown in Transition*. New York: Harcourt, Brace and Company, 1937.

MAAS, PETER. *The Valachi Papers*. New York: G. P. Putnam's, 1968.

MACRORY, BOYD E. "The Tavern and the Community." *Quarterly Journal of Studies on Alcohol* 13 (1952): 609–37.

McCALL, GEORGE J., and J. L. SIMMONS. *Identities and Interactions*. New York: The Free Press, 1966.

McCANNELL, DEAN. "Staged Authenticity: Arrangements of Social Space in Tourist Settings." *American Journal of Sociology* 79 (1973): 589–603.

MEAD, GEORGE HERBERT. *Mind, Self and Society*. Charles W. Morris, ed. Chicago: University of Chicago Press, 1934.

MESSINGER, SHELDON L., HAROLD SAMPSON, and ROBERT D. TOWNE. "Life as Theater: Some Notes on the Dramaturgic Approach to Social Reality." *Sociometry* 25 (1962): 98–110.

MOORE, E. C. "The Social Value of the Saloon." *The American Journal of Sociology* 3 (1897): 4–12.

MOOS, RUDOLF H., and PAUL M. INSEL, eds. *Issues in Social Ecology: Human Milieus*. Palo Alto, Cal.: National Press Books, 1974.

NANRY, CHARLES. *American Music: From Storyville to Woodstock*. New Brunswick, N.J.: Transaction Books, Rutgers University, 1972.

PETERSON, RICHARD A. "A Process Model of the Folk, Pop and Fine Art Phases of Jazz." In Charles Nanry, ed., *American Music: From Storyville to Woodstock*. New Brunswick, N.J.: Transaction Books, Rutgers University, 1972.

PITTMAN, DAVID J., and CHARLES R. SYNDER, eds. *Society, Culture, and Drinking Patterns*. New York: John Wiley and Sons, Inc., 1962.

PSATHAS, GEORGE. "Ethnomethods and Phenomenology." *Social Research* 35 (1968): 500–20.

REISS, ALBERT J. "The Study of Deviant Behavior: Where the Action Is." In Mark Lefton, James K. Skipper, Jr., and Charles H. McCaghy, eds., *Approaches to Deviance: Theories, Concepts, and Research Findings*. New York: Appleton-Century-Crofts, 1968.

RIESMAN, DAVID, ROBERT J. POTTER, and JEANNE WATSON. "The Vanishing Host." *Human Organization* 19 (1960): 17–27.

———. "Sociability, Permissiveness, and Equality: A Preliminary Formulation." *Psychiatry* 23 (1966): 323–40.

RIEZLER, KURT. "Play and Seriousness." *The Journal of Philosophy* 38 (1941): 505–17.

ROEBUCK, JULIAN B., and S. LEE SPRAY. "The Cocktail Lounge: A Study of Heterosexual Relations in a Public Organization." *American Journal of Sociology* 72 (1967): 386–96.

ROEBUCK, JULIAN B., and THOMAS BARKER. "A Typology of Police Corruption." *Social Problems* 21 (1974): 423–37.

RUBINGTON, EARL, and MARTIN S. WEINBURG, eds. *Deviance, The Interactionist Perspective*. New York: The Macmillan Company, 1968.

SCHECTER, LEONARD, and WILLIAM PHILLIPS. *On the Pad*. New York: Berkeley Publishing Corporation, 1973.

SCHUTZ, ALFRED. *On Phenomenology and Social Relations*. Helmut R. Wagner, ed. Chicago: University of Chicago Press, 1970.

SCOTT, ROBERT A., and JACK D. DOUGLAS, eds. *Theoretical Perspectives on Deviance*. New York: Basic Books, Inc., 1972.

SIMMEL, GEORG. *The Sociology of Georg Simmel*. Kurt H. Wolff, ed. and trans. New York: The Free Press, 1965.

SIMMONS, J. L., and BARRY WINOGRAD. "The Hang-Loose Ethic." In H. Taylor Buckner, *Deviance, Reality, and Change*. New York: Random House, 1971.

STEBBINS, ROBERT A. "The Jazz Community: The Sociology of a Musical Sub-Culture." Unpublished Ph.D. dissertation, University of Minnesota, 1964.

———. "A Theory of the Jazz Community." *The Sociological Quarterly* 9 (1968): 318–31.

SUTTER, ALAN G. "Worlds of Drug Use on the Street Scene." In Donald Cressey and David H. Ward, eds., *Delinquency, Crime, and Social Process*. New York: Harper and Row, Publishers, 1969.

TERESA, VINCENT, with THOMAS C. RENNER. *My Life in the Mafia*. New York: Doubleday and Company, 1973.

THOMAS, WILLIAM I. *The Unadjusted Girl*. Boston: Little, Brown and Company, 1923.

TYLER, GUS. *Organized Crime in America*. Ann Arbor: The University of Michigan Press, 1962.

———. "Roots of Organized Crime." In Abraham S. Blumberg, ed., *Current Perspectives on Criminal Behavior*. New York: Alfred A. Knopf, 1974.

VAILLARDS, ROGER. *The Law*. Peter Wiles, trans. New York: Bantam Books, 1969.

VEBLEN, THORSTEIN B. *The Theory of the Leisure Class: An Economic Study of Institutions*. New York: The Modern Library, 1899.

WALKER, ANDREW W. "Sociology and Professional Crime." In Abraham S. Blumberg, ed., *Current Perspectives in Criminal Behavior*. New York: Alfred A. Knopf, 1974.

WALSHOK, MARY LINDSTEIN. "The Emergence of Middle-Class Deviant Subcultures: The Case of Swingers." *Social Problems* 18 (1971): 488–95.

WATSON, JEANNE. "A Formal Analysis of Sociable Interaction." *Sociometry* 21 (1958): 269–80.

WHYTE, WILLIAM F. *Street Corner Society*. Chicago: University of Chicago Press, 1955.

WICKER, ALLAN W. "Processes Which Mediate Behavior-Environment Congruence." In Rudolf Moos and Paul M. Insel, eds., *Issues in Social Ecology: Human Milieus*. Palo Alto, Cal.: National Press Books, 1974.

YABLONSKY, LEWIS. *Hippie Trip*. New York: Western Publishing Company, 1968.

INDEX

Achieved characteristics: *see* Ascribed and achieved characteristics
Activity, criminal: *see* Behavior, criminal
Activity patterns: *see* Behavior patterns
Actor typology, 54, 58, 67–68, 72–75, 134
After-hours club, 4–8, 15
  definition, 1, 7
Ascribed and achieved characteristics, 67, 74, 135–136, 143–144, 151–154, 160–161, 167–168, 175–176, 181–183, 189–190, 194–195, 202–204, 212–213, 218–221, 233–236, 244–245, 250–251
Assistant manager, 62, 64, 65, 69, 75, 212–215
  ascribed and achieved characteristics, 212–213
  behavior on the scene, 215–218
  identities and perspectives, 213–215
Avoidance pattern, 171, 176, 200
Avoidance procedures, 242

Backstage regions, 92–96, 208
Ball, D., 51n, 54–55, 60–61, 76n, 79n, 103n
Bar, 100–115, 257, 264
  convenience, 85–86, 264
  encounters, 38, 103–115
  home territory, 19–20, 86, 151, 194, 264
  marketplace, 18–19, 264
  nightspot, 17, 87–90, 257, 264
  rituals, 39, 41
  setting, 81–86
  sociability, 38–39, 248
  talk, 108–110
  use, 85–86
Barker, R., 51n, 53
Barmaids, 75, 85, 87, 104, 218–233
  ascribed and achieved characteristics, 218–221

Barmaids (*cont.*)
  behavior on the scene, 224–233
  identities and perspectives, 221–223
Bateson, G., 43n, 44
Becker, H., 61n, 63, 88n, 134n, 236
Behavior; *see also* Behavior patterns
  covert, 50, 72, 258, 260
  criminal, 130, 167, 250
  cross-sex, 226–230
  expressive, 48, 124, 127–128, 132, 149–150, 159–160, 193
  improper: *see* Fights; Improprieties; Violence
  latitudes of, 41–42, 57, 72, 123–132, 139, 157, 164, 173–174, 258–259, 264
  marginal, 149
  on the scene, 74, 137–142, 147–151, 156–159, 163–166, 170, 179–181, 185–189, 192–194, 197–200, 207–211, 215–218, 224–233, 239–243, 247–250, 252
  overt, 50, 54, 72, 97, 258
  permissive, 123
  proper, 125–126
  sexual, 42n, 127–128, 132, 149, 158–160, 225
  unserious, 42, 80
Behavior patterns, 2n, 53, 100, 120, 264
  covert, 56, 120, 122
  overt, 55–56, 99, 120, 122
  standing, 2n, 39, 48, 52, 57, 70–71, 99, 120, 122, 258, 264
Behavior setting, 50, 57, 67–68, 96, 257
  analysis, 52
  approach, 52–54
  conventional, 2, 3n
  definition, 2
  natural, 60, 76
  time-out, unserious, 1, 24, 25, 80–82, 121, 142, 167, 181, 260
Behavioral expectations, 24

278 INDEX

Sexual (*cont.*)
    marketplace, 86, 155, 188
Shop talk, 109
Simmel, G., 26–28, 30*n*, 37, 39, 82*n*,
    99*n*, 101*n*, 109*n*, 112, 114,
    126*n*, 174, 256, 259, 260*n*
Simmons, J., 51, 74*n*, 135*n*
Situational variables, 53
"Situationally deviant," 80, 142
Skid row taverns, 16
Skipper, J., 142*n*
Sociability, 88, 101, 113, 117, 150–
    151, 187, 193, 224
    changes in style, 30, 32–35
    classical, 26–28
    contemporary, 28–32
    cross-sex bar, 113
    erotic, 112
    settings, 32–33
    theory, 26–41
Sociability and play, 25–48, 71, 97,
    99–122, 258, 260, 263
    characteristics: *see* Equality; Free-
    dom; Novelty; Order in play;
    Permanency in play; Reality;
    Secrecy; Space-time circumscrip-
    tions
Social institutions, basic (conven-
    tional), 136, 146, 155, 169,
    185, 191–192, 206, 238, 247,
    251
Social meaning, 50, 55–56
Social order, 124–125, 133
Social visibility, 8, 11, 12, 15, 47
Solidarity, 34, 36–37
Space-time
    circumscriptions, 43–45, 48, 109,
    121, 264
    configuration, 95, 97, 258, 261
    properties, 57, 69, 76–98
Spatial change, 117
Speakeasy, 1, 46–47, 77
Spontaneity, 33–34
Spray, S., 22, 23, 71*n*
Square couples, 137
Square men, 139, 141
Square women, 140–141
Standing behavior patterns, 39, 57,
    70–71, 99, 120, 122, 258, 264
Status leveling: *see* Equality
Stebbins, R., 234*n*, 235*n*
Supportive exchanges, reciprocal,
    106–107
Sutter, A., 46*n*
Symbolic interactionism, 2, 3, 50, 51,
    54–57, 61, 256

Synomorphy ("goodness of fit"), 3*n*,
    52–54, 71, 74, 262, 264

Talk
    bar, 108–109
    booth, 119–120
    shop, 109
    table, 117–118
Tavern
    keeper, 24
    neighborhood, 16–17
    patron, 20–22, 24
    skid row, 16
Theoretic stance, 60, 62
Theoretical orientation, 3, 61, 96*n*
Thieves, 69, 73, 210; *see also* Female
    thieves; Male thieves
Thomas, W., 51*n*
Towne, W., 96*n*
Transsituational, 20, 24, 49–50, 119
Triangulation, 63–64, 73, 125
Tricking, 155, 159, 161–162, 166
Tyler, G., 5*n*, 167*n*
Typology, 54, 58, 67–68, 72–75,
    103*n*, 134

Underworld, 10, 122, 135, 144, 154,
    161, 168, 176–179, 183–184,
    188, 191, 195–196, 205–206,
    210, 212, 214, 221–222, 246–
    247, 260–261
Undesirables: *see* Patron types
Unserious behavior, 42, 80
Unserious behavior settings, 4, 8, 25,
    47–48, 50, 97–98, 115, 180,
    194, 206, 255–257
Unserious sexual play, 111

Vaillards, R., 43*n*
Veblen, T., 30*n*
Vincent, T., 5*n*
Violations, serious, 130–132
Violence, 124, 130

Walker, A., 181*n*
Walshok, M., 136*n*
Watson, D., 83*n*
Watson, J., 28*n*, 29–39, 40*n*, 41,
    43*n*, 44, 51*n*
Whyte, W., 62*n*, 134*n*
Wicker, A., 51*n*
Winograd, B., 135*n*
Women employees' room, 94
Women patrons' lounge, 93–94
    attendant, 254–255

Yablonsky, L., 134*n*